PRAISE FOR *COMPOSE YOURSELF!*™

"Andy Barnett celebrates his deep devotion to exploring how music-making can be interwoven into the lives of many—from beginners to professionals."

—PAUL WINTER, SAXOPHONIST, RECORDING ARTIST

"All vibration is the life breath of a conscious universe, singing creation into manifestation. Our own breath is the leading edge of this universal process, unfolding its creative potential as our life. Andy Barnett reflects this truth in the poetry of *Compose Yourself!*™ and shares the music of his heart in every loving paragraph."

—BRUCE BURGER, MA. RPP., FOUNDER, HEARTWOOD INSTITUTE,
AUTHOR OF *ESOTERIC ANATOMY: THE BODY AS CONSCIOUSNESS*

"Here is a wonderful offering of the many interlocking treasures that make up the rich world of music, set as a metaphor for the equally complex and beautiful world about us and our life in it. Open it at random, read a few words, and you will be unable to put it down."

—ALEXANDER T. SHULGIN, AUTHOR OF *PIHKAL,* CHEMIST AND MUSICIAN

"Barnett eloquently and passionately presents music as a master teacher, a guru, leading us to balance with our body-mind experiences, thereby helping us sustain vibrant, enriching, and spiritually fulfilling lives."

—LINDA SIEVERS, CHAIR, DEPARTMENT OF THEATRE, FILM, AND DANCE,
HUMBOLDT STATE UNIVERSITY

"Contrasting the search for molecular "magic bullets" pursued by medical science, Barnett presents music as a rich source of healing. I think he is right! When he writes, 'Music is in perfect balance at every level, resonating every aspect of our being,' he sounds a theme of holistic healing central to exciting new directions in medicine."

—ROBERT DOZOR, MD., FOUNDER,
CALIFORNIA INSTITUTE OF INTEGRATIVE MEDICINE

"Clear explanations and compelling examples from every musical tradition provide extraordinary insight into living in harmony with our self, our loved ones, and our world. Read this wonderful book. It will make your heart sing."

—WILLIAM M. LOWMAN, HEADMASTER, IDYLLWILD ARTS ACADEMY

ABOUT THE AUTHOR

Andy Barnett is a musician, producer, radio personality, and educator. He has taught music, instrument building, and performance technique at every level, and presents Resonance Training at teaching hospitals, schools, and nonprofit groups. For several years he has served as a consultant to organizations promoting community development and the performing arts. Andy is also a top-ten children's recording artist.

TO WRITE TO THE AUTHOR

If you wish to contact the author or would like more information about this book, please write to the author in care of Llewellyn Worldwide and we will forward your request. Both the author and publisher appreciate hearing from you and learning of your enjoyment of this book and how it has helped you. Llewellyn Worldwide cannot guarantee that every letter written to the author can be answered, but all will be forwarded. Please write to:

Andy Barnett
℅ Llewellyn Worldwide
P.O. Box 64383, Dept. 0-7387-0418-0
St. Paul, MN 55164-0383, U.S.A.
Please enclose a self-addressed stamped envelope for reply,
or $1.00 to cover costs. If outside U.S.A., enclose
international postal reply coupon.

Many of Llewellyn's authors have websites with additional information and resources. For more information, please visit our website at
http://www.llewellyn.com.

COMPOSE YOURSELF! ™

AWAKENING TO THE RHYTHMS OF LIFE

ANDY BARNETT

2003
Llewellyn Publications
St. Paul, Minnesota 55164-0383, U.S.A.

First Edition
First Printing, 2003

Book design by Karin Simoneau
Cover design by Kevin R. Brown
Cover imagery © DigitalVision, Digital Stock, and PhotoDisc
Interior art by Llewellyn art department

Library of Congress Cataloging-in-Publication Data
Barnett, Andy, 1952–
    Compose yourself!: awakening to the rhythms of life / Andy Barnett.
       p. cm.
    Includes bibliographical references and index.
    ISBN 0-7387-0418-0
    1. Music therapy. 2. Chakras. 3. Music—Psychological aspects. 4. Music—Philosophy and aesthetics. I. Title.

ML3920.B24 2003
615.8'5154—dc22   2003054664

Llewellyn Worldwide does not participate in, endorse, or have any authority or responsibility concerning private business transactions between our authors and the public.

All mail addressed to the author is forwarded but the publisher cannot, unless specifically instructed by the author, give out an address or phone number.

Any Internet references contained in this work are current at publication time, but the publisher cannot guarantee that a specific location will continue to be maintained. Please refer to the publisher's website for links to authors' websites and other sources.

Llewellyn Publications
A Division of Llewellyn Worldwide, Ltd.
P.O. Box 64383, Dept. 0-7387-0418-0
St. Paul, MN 55164-0383, U.S.A.
www.llewellyn.com

Printed in the United States of America

"Music touches our innermost being, and in that way gives us new life."

—Sufi Inayat Khan

CONTENTS

INTRODUCTION

The clear tone of a trumpet, a child bouncing a ball, and the pulse of the human heart all exhibit resonance. A physicist would define resonance as the enhancement of response occurring within any system when the frequency of a periodic force driving the system is equal to the inherent frequency of the system itself. For example, when a piano string is struck, the sound of the string, by itself, is quite soft and bland. It is enhanced in volume and richness of tone through the resonant relationship between the string and the inherent vibratory qualities of the sounding board. The piano, as a system, displays resonant response.

On some level, everything exhibits resonance. Resonance between subatomic particles determines the forms and qualities of the elements. The forces of gravity and angular momentum establish resonant relationships that sustain the solar system and every galaxy in the heavens. We resonate emotionally, sharing moods and reactions with other people. When a system falls out of resonance, the form of that system must alter, and many times the system disintegrates. When the lip falters, the clear trumpet note cracks. When the child missteps, the ball is dribbled away. The heart ceases to beat and silence envelopes a life. Kindness wanes and love withers.

Music touches us on physical, mental, and spiritual levels through the same resonant principle that shapes the galaxies and weaves the web of life on earth. Music is a highly refined expression of the resonant core of nature. Music sings not only of the human mind and spirit, but also of the power humming at the center of every atom.

In fact, for centuries Western thinkers believed—in a very mystical and magical way—that music was the highest evidence of the divine. The planets themselves were envisioned to be moving on cosmic crystal spheres, making music as they progressed through the heavens. To the Renaissance man, humankind and the stars danced to the same strains of God's perfection. Johannes Kepler, using Tycho Brahe's meticulous observations of the planets, applied brain-crunching mathematics and discovered that their paths were elliptical rather than circular. Kepler was first of all a cleric, and so his reasoning had to, in the end, express aspects of the dominant paradigm of God's beauty. So naturally, the final reduction of his theories, the essential outcome of his labors, and the required expression of his age were the actual melodies, scales, and musical modes of each planet's part in God's perfect counterpoint, the notated expression of the fabled Harmony of the Spheres (figure 1).

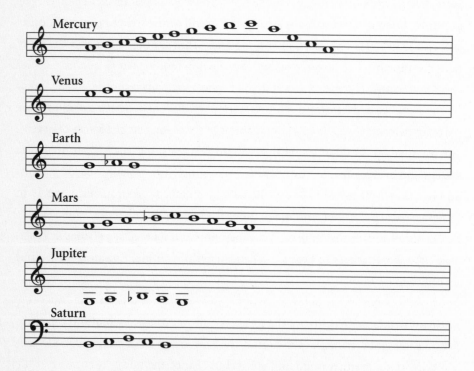

Figure 1: Kepler's Notation of Planetary Sounds.

Our innate love of music can be a key to discovering our individual resonant nature, and how we can best harmonize in all our relationships. The musical art is a model for composing an intentional approach to life. The ideas and exercises in this book will inspire a new appreciation for the inherent musicality we all express in the rhythm of every step, the melody of every voice, and the feelings coursing through every heart.

The resonant system of life on earth displays enhanced response each spring as new life unfolds in harmony with the cycles of the seasons. Living within these cycles is key to physical survival. We can progress through life more successfully if we tune our awareness to the resonant aspects of nature. There are deep chords of resonance binding all of humanity. Empathy, compassion, inspiration, fear, and love are some of the themes we all share in our common human nature.

Music touches us so profoundly because, more than any other human activity, it directly articulates our basic temporal experience into forms laden with emotional overtones. Sound vibrations *composed with intent* create what I call temporal artifacts, sonic sculptures or stories if you will, capable of imparting specific emotional experiences. Noise just happens. But through our intentions every action creates a certain type of music.

Music resonates feelings within us through the composition and arrangement of rhythmic patterns, harmonic sonorities, and melodies. These so-called "elements of music" are similar to the physical elements of nature in that they have specific qualities and tendencies determined through resonance. By articulating these musical elements the composer literally alters our experience of time. A lullaby echoes tender memories of childhood. The opening bars of Beethoven's Fifth Symphony conjure a restless, passionate insistence.

Qualities of experience, like musical compositions, result from resonant relationships occurring over time. Some relationships may articulate harmonious results, while others may intone chaos. In this view, the times of our lives—the good, fun, fast, boring, challenging, pointless, ecstatic times of our lives—are musical in nature. The composer intentionally shapes sound vibrations into profound musical expressions. Similarly, our physical, mental, emotional, and spiritual intentions are directly composed into our experience.

Our physical habitat is created through resonance in the realms of matter and energy. And through the resonant power of emotions and intent our personal tone contributes to a communal temporal habitat of feelings and "vibes." Using music as our guide we can intentionally compose ourselves in any situation, bringing a voice of harmony and inspiration to play anywhere, anytime. By acting with musical intent we can enhance the response of any system, be it one's body, family, household, or community.

The universe is dancing. Developing and practicing personal resonance brings the essential musicality of nature into our lives and helps project harmony into the world. With musical intent you can change a walk to the newsstand into a *jaunt.* Your presentation at work becomes a *theme and variations.* Personal interactions become *duets.* A love affair can reach symphonic proportions. It has always been this way. A flute found in a cavern in France was made from a cave bear bone tens of thousands of years ago. Like speech, music is part of our human nature.

The strength of the beat, the expressiveness of the melody, and the transcendence of harmony can all be applied to our everyday experiences. By recognizing the resonance at play around us everyone can learn and apply the discipline and joy demonstrated by musical performance. Gregory Bateson, the great mathematician, calls resonance "the pattern that connects."

Even though we are flesh and bone, rooted in the dirt and muck of a very three-dimensional world, humans are primarily concerned with forms of the fourth dimension of time. We can no more exist out of time than a fish can live out of the water. As air is to birds, time is to humanity. Perhaps more than any other attribute, our awareness of time makes us human. Music is the clearest articulation of this basic human perception, and can teach us how to move flawlessly through our primary element of time with the ease and grace of a dolphin in a clear sea.

Our sense of time has two attributes. First, we have an awareness of elapsed time. We can sense how long things take, perhaps seconds, a moment or two, hours or weeks. We record longer expanses of time in our stories and histories. Second, we perceive qualities of time as it passes. I call this aspect of our temporal experience *musical time.* The infinite variety of musical styles and forms mirrors our multifaceted experience of time. A march rouses us. A sweet melody soothes us. A ritual drum transports us. Music demonstrates that the intentional articulation of temporal qualities is an integral part of human nature.

The composer intentionally juxtaposes resonant patterns of beat, rhythm, tone, and so on, and changes the quality of time for the duration of his or her composition. Each element of music has its own range of effect on the quality of the music and the quality of experience for the player or listener. The composer articulates the musical elements to create an intentional experience. As we strive to live in harmony with our surroundings, it is our job to emulate the composer and articulate our lives with inspired intention.

As the composer changes tempo, we can alter the pace of our day. A harp carries a different message than a fuzz-tone electric guitar. And so can we change our tone of voice to blend with, or stand out from, the crowd. Every aspect of musical performance, from playing in tune to symphonic composition, illuminates attributes of the time-field of everyday experience.

The Vedic system of the chakras is central to the structure of this work. The key to many spiritual traditions and healing practices, the chakras represent seven levels of consciousness that are clearly in resonance in the human body, mind, and spirit. Forces and attributes of the physical and metaphysical worlds resonate the chakras. Through rhythm, tone, and form, music stimulates the chakras, resonating enhanced response within the physical body, the perceptions of the mind, and the longings of the spirit. Music has always been a primary tool for physical, emotional, and spiritual atonement. This book provides readily acquired techniques along this path.

Music has accompanied the human experience throughout history. From the tone of that bone flute echoing in the cave to the highly refined orchestrations of classical composition, music reveals resonance as the balance point for all of nature. Music somehow communicates that we are imbued with spirit. We are stardust and the star, the instrument and the player.

Every new era brings new empires, new architecture, new insights and challenges. But like the turning of the planets, the elements of music remain constant. This book will show how music can be a guide to a more resonant and expressive life. Performing our daily tasks with an awareness of musical time makes great art out of every moment. We can learn to harmonize our intentions and actions with the musical time at play all around us. From this awareness we can orchestrate the ever-changing flow of time much as a composer arranges timbres, beats, keys, and dynamics. Music shows us how to manipulate time, giving us tools to articulate our most inspired intentions.

We start by looking at resonance in the natural world. Next we examine how the pulse, patterns, tones, and forms of music clearly mirror the resonant relationships in nature, and our human nature. Finally, we will learn how to express our newly revealed natural musicality throughout all the times of our lives. We will build a progressive practice method for intentional action in our personal lives. These activities are tuned to the keynotes of consciousness resonating in the seven chakras of the human body-mind. We will gain a new awareness of the musicality of the natural world and learn how to creatively articulate our intentions, acting in counterpoint to the forces around us.

The beaming child in first-grade rhythm band and the triumphant opera diva celebrate the same musical relationships. They articulate intentions through resonant activity. Following their example, we can all be divas, virtuosos of the moment, composing ourselves for the time of our life.

Part One

RESONANCE IN NATURE AND MUSIC

1 THE COMPOSITION OF NATURE

To compose a life rich in musicality we need to understand that resonance is a universal attribute common to all that exists. An understanding of the dynamics of resonance in the natural world is the first lesson in the discipline of living a musical life.

Simple numerical ratio is the underlying principle of all resonant phenomenon. Integral relationships between forces and materials manifest all around us, creating an inherently resonant universe. Resonant qualities are displayed in the rainbow, the hardness of a stone, and the phases of the moon. The ancient Pythagorean school of natural philosophy saw the rhythm of the cosmos in the simple vibrations of a string.

A constant stress or load is put on the string by means of a weight (figure 1, page 4). Internal resilience generated by molecular bonds within the string pull against the stress, keeping the string from flying apart. The balance of load and resilience is called the rest state of a resonant system. This balance is crucial in sustaining any resonant system. Too much stress and the system falls apart; too much inner resilience and the system stiffens, becoming brittle and unresponsive. Similar relationships between forces and materials sustain everything in the universe.

Striking the string lengthens the string ever so slightly, disturbing the rest state. Set in motion by the impact, the inner resilience of the system instantly begins to return it to the balanced condition of the rest state. Waves of energy travel back and forth along the string until all the energy of the initiating blow has been dissipated into the surrounding environment. In the case of the string, we experience

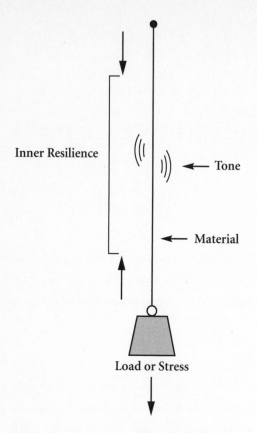

Inner Resilience

Tone

Material

Load or Stress

Figure 1: The Four Elements of Resonance.

this dissipation of energy as sound. Inner resilience, load, impact, and dissipation are common elements to all resonant systems, including stars, church bells, atomic quantum fields, and a love-struck heart.

The Pythagoreans observed the oscillations of the string and saw that they described whole numbers and their ratios (figure 2, page 5). These ratios are called "the harmonic series of vibration." To the Pythagoreans these harmonic ratios were sacred symbols representing aspects of nature, especially the movements of the heavenly bodies, as well as aspects of human nature long associated with the planets.

These ancient thinkers perceived a critical truth. They saw that physical phenomena could be expressed truthfully with numbers. This was the first elucidation of the Western scientific paradigm in which natural events and processes are

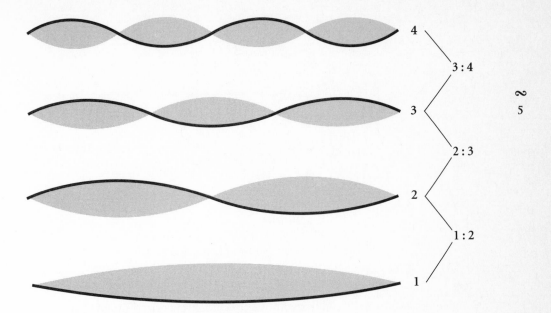

Figure 2: Harmonic Series of Overtones.

seen as a physical manifestation of numeric principles. The tone of a musical instrument is a clear example of this truth, but all systems in resonance generate the same harmonic ratios. Ever since Pythagoras, the evolution of science has shown us the depth of this insight. Resonant principles are at the heart of existence itself. Quantum mechanics pictures the nucleus of the atom as surrounded by electron clouds, harmonic levels of energy where particles exist as frequency patterns and waves of energy are measured in discreet units (figure 3, page 6).

All matter consists of a just few types of subatomic particles—principally protons, neutrons, and electrons. The vast array of atomic qualities—hardness, lightness, radioactivity, and so forth—are the products of resonant relationships *between* the subatomic particles, especially the resonance binding the positively charged nucleus with the negatively charged electrons resonating around it. The material world, and our experience of it, is composed from the massless harmony generated within the atoms, not the physical particles themselves.

A good example of this elemental harmony is the two forms of oxygen. Commonly, two atoms of oxygen join together and create molecular oxygen (O_2), the

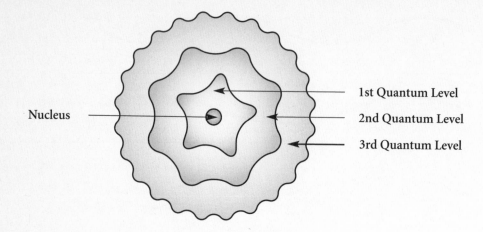

Nucleus

1st Quantum Level

2nd Quantum Level

3rd Quantum Level

Figure 3: Resonant Model of Quantum Levels.

life-giving gas no animal can live without. In a highly energized situation such as a lightning storm, oxygen atoms form ozone (O_3). In the lower atmosphere, ozone can be highly poisonous. In the upper atmosphere, however, it blocks ultraviolet rays, a form of electromagnetic radiation destructive to life. Although the atoms making up the two forms of oxygen are the same, the resonant forces binding O_2 and O_3 take different forms, and these patterns of energy create vastly different effects. Every element shows us how relationships between matter and energy within atoms define identity and behavior more than the atomic material itself.

Imagine a hydrogen (one proton and one electron) twice the size of a football field. At this scale the proton would be the size of a tiny pebble. The single electron would be resonating in a probability cloud around the proton. Step away from the proton-pebble. The mass of the electron would not be evident for a hundred yards. Invisible forces of charge and angular momentum bind the system over the distance. Atomic fission and fusion break these subatomic patterns. The amazing power of the sun and thermonuclear bombs show us that incredible energy is held in the "empty space" between subatomic particles.

In similar fashion, celestial resonance operates over the light years of outer space, and deep feelings are sustained between people separated by great distances. Every aspect of matter, the cosmos, and living relationships exists *between* the bits of physical matter. Proportionately, the solid matter of any atom (or galaxy) is incredibly small when compared to the expanse of the resonant field holding the matter together. We experience not the solid stuff of creation, but a harmony of binding resonant relationships.

The miraculous beauty of the stars in the night sky comes primarily from the forces that continually keep them in motion century after century. We do not experience the material of the material world. We live and love in a multitude of interpenetrating fields of resonance, from the quantum fields of atoms to the whirling of the star fields. Weather, the abundant earth, political power, art, and all the rest are essentially complex harmonic wave patterns, a great repertoire of natural musicality.

Take a look around and imagine the electrons singing in their clouds around the nuclei. Our nervous system is "tuned" to perceive these leaping quantum energies. We literally feel specific resonant qualities operating at the atomic level in the hardness of iron, the invigorating breath of fresh air, the silkiness of polished silver, and the richness of the azure twilight. The mellow sound of the cello and the skirl of the bagpipe results from qualities of atomic relationships deep within the instruments themselves. In the softness of a kiss, the coldness of the stone, or the blast of the trumpet, forces singing at the core of the elements touch us.

Everything that really matters in our lives—stability, self-expression, empathy, and inspiration—follows the same scheme. Dynamic relationships and interactions *over time* create the variety of life on earth. Resonant principles define atomic and human relationship alike. Resonance plays between atomic particles, and the elements spin before our eyes. The forces of empathy and desire dance between hearts, and loving relationships grow. An active, swirling, dynamic harmony of forces moves through time and space, binding star to star and heart to heart.

All matter is composed of a few elemental particles. Music is composed from discreet elements as well: simple pulses of time and a limited number of tones. The building blocks of matter and the elements of music are held together by similar principles, resulting in more complex expressions. Our eyes, hands, and ears inform us of the harmony singing throughout the material world. Our feelings, fears, emotions, and inspirations inform us of the resonance at play between people. The forms of resonance in the natural world are as varied and diverse as the range of human thought, and yet from the simplest to the most complex, the musicality of creation presents itself as clear as a bell.

MOLECULES AND GENETICS

Every molecule is a unique harmony of atoms, a harmony of harmonies. We cannot say that molecular forms have intentions similar to our own, but elements do tend to act in certain ways. These "intentions" are a product of the internal resonant forces. Due to the configurations of quantum energy in the outer electron clouds, the inert gasses are very set on autonomy. They strongly resist combining with any other element. In contrast, oxygen is a molecular floozy, readily bonding with any number of various elements. Crystals exhibit a repetitive geometry that is similar to the sonic geometry of a round such as "Row, Row, Row Your Boat." In both forms exact copies of resonant forms are linked one after the other.

Certain complex organic molecules can actually grow under the right conditions even though they are not alive per se. The biochemistry of proteins and DNA suggests that the geometry of molecules determines their function. These qualities are the products of the dynamic forces whirling in resonance within all these various molecules.

Your genetic material is a stern conductor, leading a many-voiced ensemble of cells ruled by laws of organic harmony. Cell by cell, your unique genetic harmony rings out consistently true and clear. In your blood, your marrow, and your gut, a unique genetic harmony sings *your song* over and over again. Through molecular replication, every note in the genetic composition is rendered generation after generation.

Every cell has all the information needed to make another identical organism. Genes are the blueprint for the synthesis of enzymes and proteins that knit together to form the different tissues in your body. Every cell is tuned to the specific genetic resonance of the parent organism, and foreign material is diligently shunned like an out-of-tune musician is shunned from the orchestra.

Like a dissonant instrument, an organ transplanted from a foreign body just does not fit in. It is out of harmony with your finely tuned instrument. Highly responsive to dissonant conditions, the body begins to intently reject the interloper. To keep it, all sorts of serious chemical agents must be employed to create an alternative resonance, dampening your body's natural tendency to kick the offender out of the band.

Atoms, molecules, and life forms are articulations of resonant forces that set relatively small chunks of material into relationship over vast relative distances. These forms become more and more complex as resonant patterns blend and interpenetrate within wider and wider harmonies. As systems become more complex, they are more easily impacted by outside forces. Living matter is more responsive than rock. I call this tendency *responsibility*. Our highly developed senses, including our sense of musical time, reveal that we demonstrate a natural ability to respond to our surroundings. We feel this responsiveness as we run to a crying child, crave the sumptuous meal, long for the perfect love, and strive to manifest our highest intentions.

RESPONSIVENESS AND MUSICALITY

The human condition shows us how sensitive we are to every form of influence. One virus, one blow to the head, one stock market fluctuation, one sharp word, and the sweet melody of our day turns to a jumble of despair, a mire of illness, a storm of confusion. But we have our musical nature as a constant presence in our evolution. Music demonstrates that we are able to perceive and manipulate the forces swirling through time. To the extent that we respond musically to our surroundings, the more we make a composition of our lives.

A proton is highly stable and basically nonresponsive, changing its form only under the bombardment of billions of electron volts of energy. A molecular bond can be broken by an exchange of a few hundred electron volts. An organic bond and the heartbeat respond to even smaller amounts of energy. Our ears are our most responsive sense organ, requiring only a tiny amount of energy to fire off a neural message to the brain, even less energy than it takes to trigger the visual perception of a pinprick of light.

This is why music is our primary expression of resonance and perhaps the subtlest example of our responsibility as humans. The art of making music shows the rewards of being receptive and responsive *at the same time.* In my view, musical responsibility is expressed when we intentionally relate to waves of energy, be they the tones of a saxophone, the swirl of the surf, or the intimate warmth of a shared heartbeat. In this way music can illuminate the responsive, attentive nature of all that we recognize as being alive.

The good musician never goes off willy-nilly. The musician's ear is always tuned to the keynotes, and his or her eye fixed on the score, listening and articulating at the same time. In the same way an adult must listen carefully to the child in order to respond authentically to the young one's needs. To the extent any system demonstrates responsiveness, it demonstrates a primary characteristic of life that can be seen as a pervasive *musicality of intent*. Rocks respond to weather. Shorelines respond to the tides. Animals respond to threats. Humans respond to the qualities of time articulated through musical tones and patterns. The quality of tone is inherent in the structure of a musical instrument, even if it is silent. Musical sound is the expression of resonance inherent in the internal tensions of the string. And so life expresses the intentions within the silent atomic, molecular, and cellular configurations. From this perspective the atoms, molecules, and stars can all be seen as being musically expressive. Atoms and living beings are playing from the same score. The diamond is the crystallized expression of the internal resonance of a single carbon atom. The most refined expressions of human nature result when the pure essence of our inner resonance (our soul?) is revealed through inspired actions.

The silent string waits for the music to be released. A lump of coal waits for the right spark to set it aflame. Our silent intentions are akin to the dynamic tension in every atom and molecule. Fired by the spark of inspiration we articulate our intentions into our environment. The insistent pulse, powerful tones, and evocative forms of music remind us that as a species we have always been capable of flawless articulations of universal forces.

The evolution of the human mind has brought us to a place where the realms of spirit, science, and art now blend in wonderful harmony. Listening carefully for the essential music of our nature, we can bring resonance to our lives as clearly as a bird brings a song to the dawn.

Cultural attitudes and intellectual tools have evolved to give us a deeper awareness of both the harmony of the natural world and disharmonies of our own making. Ecological dissonance abounds. Our ability to perceive and respond to sour notes of our own creation may determine the fate of all life, not just our own.

Our personal peace of mind and the life of the planet as a whole depend on a sense of intonation, an ability to sense the delicate balance between things. We are learning to act in accordance with the music of life. Responsiveness is the basic sign of life. As we respond, so do we evolve. Is it our intention to respond to televised sports and talk shows or to the insistent zaps and shocks of ecological arrhythmia?

We have created a tumultuous cacophony of information. The media screams in our ears with a nonstop fanfare of flash and glitter. How does the ingenious and seductive *virtual* reality we have created harmonize with the *actual* reality of food supply, water cycles, atmospheric conditions, and the music of the heart? As our oldest and best articulation of resonance, music can teach us how to listen through all the noise to the eternal themes running through every aspect of life. Appreciating the songs of the atoms and the rhythms of nature opens our perceptions to what our part might be in the greater composition of life.

THE TEMPORAL HABITAT

A long-standing Western myth says we are separate from nature, building our own world on top of the natural one. Yet all forms of life scurry around together under a microthin atmospheric membrane. Algae and attorneys alike are protected from ultraviolet rays by the same delicate layer of ozone hovering miles above the earth.

Just as every cell beneath our skin exists in amazingly close communication, every slime mold and TV talk-show host is integrally related through the subtle web of life under the ozone membrane. Rocks, rivers, bugs, animals, and humans seem to exist in discreet niches in the physical habitat. But by the virtue of the rhythms of sun, tide, birth, and death, we exist in a resonant *temporal habitat,* a multileveled composition of cycles, patterns, and evolving forms where every rock and empire has a voice.

Humans respond to a deep animal nature as readily as the next mammal on the evolutionary charts. We are just as susceptible to natural rhythms as the next critter. The weather, the bugs, the seasons, and the waves of invading microbes all work us over. We get grumpy in winter, wacky at the full moon, giddy in the spring, and aroused at the whiff of the right pheromones.

Every animal population influences their environment in turn. Migrations transform landscapes. Insect invasions pollinate and decimate. Our human activities—agriculture, technology, literature, the Internet—bump against all the other dancers in the temporal habitat and new patterns emerge. As more of us crowd together the patterns get very complex, filled with the melodies, harmonies, and raw noise of our interactions.

Why does Cleveland feel different from Austin? What creates the allure of Paris, the magic of Rome, and the spiritual power of Jerusalem? Certain places just feel different. We catch a whisper of the musical time, the cumulative pattern of all the songs resonating within that temporal habitat. The life cycles of pigeons, politicians, empires, sports dynasties, epidemics, and local food products produce the temporal quality of a place.

A tiny sapling becomes a great tree in a public park. A family grows into a clan and then a dynasty under the shade of this tree. A growing population organizes itself into a city or nation. The city-state sings an evolving, dynamic harmony of architecture, geography, and culture. All these things are compositions within the temporal habitat, taking decades and centuries to perform. Some compositions in the temporal habitat carry mixed blessings. Money, for example, seems to be like a great tune that sticks in your head and then proceeds to drive you nuts.

It is obvious that our survival is linked to the continued resonance of life in general. We appropriately protect ourselves from dissonant forces like disease and danger. We should also strive to recognize when our own creations are dangerously disrupting the harmony of the temporal habitat. It is becoming more and more apparent that we carry a dominant voice in the music of the earth. We need to learn how to listen and stay in tune.

The patterns of harmony in nature are sternly determined on one hand and fragile on the other, often in strangely ironic ways. The African wildebeest lives within the gyres of an eternal migratory cycle that moves the vast herds thousands of miles year after year. At one point in the cycle, shortly after the calving season, the herd crosses a lake. Many of the newborn die in the water.

The lake crossing has always been a critical point in the life cycle of the species. The weak and old perish, and the stronger animals survive. The lake has actually dried up and shrunk over the millennia and the herd could easily go around. In fact, many do. But this phrase of the wildebeest melody will not be silenced. The watery scene of death fits with the harmony of the land, the turning earth, and the storms of vultures circling overhead. It has remained part of the song out of harmonic necessity.

What do we actually know of our place in all of this? Are we blundering into lakes on our journey through the temporal habitat? Perhaps we cast ourselves into pits without a care. Over the long run it's hard to judge whether religions, the scientific method, or Wal-Mart have helped or hindered our atonement with our world. And what of our poets and the musicians with their rhythms, words, and branching melodies? Is art just diversion, a fancy way to stare into the campfire? Does a triple-platinum album really mean anything? Are we giving all our attention to pretense and image while the lasting masterpieces of our temporal habitat are decaying and blowing away under our noses?

There is a lot of fluff on the surface of our temporal habitat. But underneath all the fashion, hype, and public opinion the primary forces are constantly at work shaping the longer cycles, the deeper waves. It's always a good idea to be ready for the Big One: the 9.1 earthquake, the sea change, and the next megatrend.

When great resonant patterns of nature collide we get a display. The energy of both systems is released in great bursts. The glacier falls into the bay. The volcano erupts into the sea. The thirst for freedom violently confronts greed. Many casualties occur in the crosscurrents. If we are too concerned with the fluff and foam on the wave, the deeper tides might roll right over us. There are warning signs. Serious undertones inevitably make their presence known.

You are accelerating onto the freeway. You feel a deeply ominous, very low, ka-thumping sort of shudder moving through the entire frame of your car. Be responsible. Pull over.

UNDERTONES

If two flutes play exactly the same pitch, we hear one sound (figure 4, page 14). If the tones are slightly out of tune, we hear *three* tones. Trying to occupy the same air space, the two dissimilar sound waves beat against one another creating an "undertone" (figure 5, page 14). We hear the undertone as a dissonant grinding or

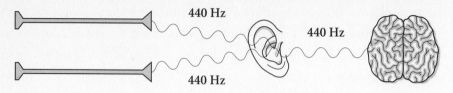

Figure 4: Two Tones in Tune. The Unison.

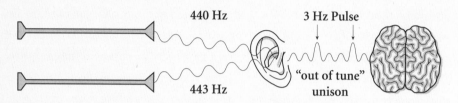

Figure 5: Two Tones Creating an "Undertone" Pulse.

a howl in our ears. The frequency of this third tone is the numerical difference in cycles per second between the two original tones. A very slight interval between two tones creates a very low vibration, which is perceived as an unpleasant pulsing or growling quality to the sound. Two tones vibrating in this way create a dissonant, *nonharmonic* relationship. We will see in later chapters how two tones in *harmonic relationship* actually create undertones that are pleasing to our ears.

Cycles play upon cycles across the face of the planet the way the tones of the flutes play in the air. The sun rises and falls. The moon resonates tides and the nocturnal activity of animals. The rhythm of the seasons generates color and new life. In many instances the year is the *shortest* unit of vibration in earth cycles. Myriad tones of the music of the earth interact and create undertones that oscillate over very long cycles of time. Many very deep undertones are noticeable only over very long cycles. Ice ages move over the planet in cycles tens of thousands of years long.

The cycles of culture—population growth, fashion fads, politics, economic growth, urban sprawl, and the spread of religions—are all undertones, the result of many resonant forces bumping up against one another. Acknowledging our personal role in creating and sustaining undertones creates mindful and loving action in the music of the earth.

Our personal choices and actions reverberate throughout our temporal habitat like sound echoes into every corner of a great cathedral. Buying habits, community action, employment, voting, religious practice, and Wednesday night bowling leagues all exert their influence to create the powerful undertones of culture. Every group, every family, neighborhood, church choir, school, or punk rock band has the ability to influence its surrounding environment in some way through the resonant principle of *entrainment.* Entrainment is the natural process underway when things "fall into step." Through entrainment a resonant force activates elements of the environment that are "tuned in" to the frequency of the force. We have all seen how the powerful rhythms of a great dance band bring a crowd into resonance on the dance floor, the music grabbing hearts and bodies primed to move and celebrate together. Entrainment can be observed in a pond full of frogs. Sooner or later many of the frogs will croak in time together.

A dramatic natural example of an undertone is the phenomenon of the *soliton.* This is a single wave that can rise up out of the ocean and capsize a ship or destroy a stretch of coastline. This is not a *tsunami,* the huge wave created by an earthquake. The soliton is a rarely observed and highly unpredictable resonant occurrence.

Vast tidal energy travels through the depths of the sea with very little action on the surface. A surge off the coast of Japan, for example, could send a giant shock wave eastward into the Pacific. El Niño conditions in the Eastern Pacific might just then shrug off a monster pulse headed west. When these travelers meet, the two converging impulses compete for the same water, just as two flute tones compete for air space. The massive forces pile up against each other, and a huge soliton rises up, a single wave that could swallow a tanker or kill a pod of whales. Hundred-year floods, earthquake clusters, ice ages, and the shifting of the magnetic poles are other examples of long-term undertones generated from the melodies of the living earth.

How can we know the long-term effects of our presence in the temporal habitat? Undertones of our own making are certainly lurking in the depths. Keep watch. When catastrophe strikes, remember: the energy for the Big One comes over a long distance and over a long time. Live as close to the earth as you can, aligned with the purest of cycles. Having just enough is a feast. Avoid situations and systems that seem to rip the life out of things. Ride bikes. Practice forgiveness. Take a day of rest. Listen for the dissonance grinding away under your feet. To get what you want, whom are you stepping on? Empathy, that deep understanding of the heart, can be easily drowned out by the louder and more demanding voices of ambition, fear, frustration, ego, and worry.

Listen for the keynotes of resonance heard in the free-flowing river, the scream of the hawk, the easy laughter at the dinner table, and the luscious fall into silent slumber and meditation. If you have a hard time hearing these songs, turn to your innate musicality for inspiration. Take a walk and sing in time to your steps. Play catch. Turn the music up.

CULTURAL RESONANCE AND THE IMPULSE MOMENT

History teaches us that virtually every attribute of culture manifests in cycles. Just as atoms, molecules, life forms, and planetary systems are composed of resonant patterns, human cultures express a deep musicality as well. If culture is resonant by nature, how do historical cycles resemble the musical model of resonance?

The stress or load placed on a string is counterbalanced with the inner resilience of the string's material. These two forces create a dynamic equilibrium within the string. An impulse sets the balanced system into motion and harmonic resonance is displayed in sound. What aspects of culture correspond to this process?

What are the most resilient forms of culture? The family. The community. The farm. Music. Religions. Language. The sense of place. Ethnicity. The bonds of love. These are some of the strings on the harp of culture. The loads placed on these strings are many, and are themselves resonant in nature just as the bow drawn over the taught string is a bundle of taut filaments itself.

What forces impact the cultural instruments? Everything from wars to the weather to the evening news constantly bangs on the strings of the cultural harp. *Impulse moments* continually play over the dynamic equilibrium of societies. Remember the soliton. The right impulse, the perfect stroke of luck, the violent attack, one person's fate, or the action of another could set off a crushing wave of change.

The atomic bomb explodes. China invades Tibet. Rosa Parks stays on the bus. The guns fire at Kent State. The Berlin Wall falls. A fringe element lashes out. Small events have deep effect as well. In fact, by nature of its incredible responsiveness, culture often registers the effects of isolated, singular events. Whole nations can be resonated by a gunshot in a schoolroom, the ax falling in a boardroom, or a bullet on the Billboard Charts.

We all carry common intentions for survival, pleasure, and atonement close to our heart. Lurking in our gut and the darker recesses of our being is greed, anger, fear, and self-doubt. History is composed from all these social impulses and currents. The institutions and artifacts we create are the articulations of these intentions, culture-wide compositions of musical proportions.

The joy of music encourages us to choose our instrument. The jazz musician calls his instrument his ax. How and when do you wish to strike? We have both freedom and responsibility when it comes to our participation in the ensembles of culture. A heavy metal guitarist smashes his guitar. A politician usurps power. Any instrument can be abused. In expressing our intentions we must guard against overplaying, hogging the stage, or simply being unprepared and blundering. But practice makes perfect. The more we stay tuned to our highest intentions, diligently articulating our instruments with attention to our fellow players, the closer we come to musical responsibility and atonement with the forces of nature.

Everyone loves music because rhythm, melody, and harmony so clearly express the universal ideals of unity, honesty, and love. We physically register all this in our feet, gut, and heart. As we become more practiced at appreciating and articulating the harmony of nature we amplify the respect and cooperation central to survival. Never forget that musical resonance *is* our nature.

Language is a major artifact of a culture, the evolution of a grand improvisation. Over the centuries a choir of voices experiments with sounds, creating a song everyone in that particular choir recognizes. Language defines culture because it gives birth to names everyone agrees upon. When something has a name, it becomes real, and a sound becomes its identity. But identities evolve and themes modulate into variations. Listen to this.

The ancient word *ar,* meaning "shoulder,"* came to describe the quality of "fitting together," as in the way the parts of the arm fit and work together. This Indo-European root sound gave birth to articulate, art, arm, part, harmony, and army. And so our name for the simultaneous resonance of tones (harmony) is an echo of how our body fits together (arm). Within the elementary particles (hear the *ar* in there?) as well as the labyrinth of the human mind, the forces of resonance articulate matter and everything fits together in perfect harmony. The musical evolution of *ar* reveals a common intention of meaning stretching back in time from our present variations to the original themes from ages past.

Here's another theme and variations. The words "intention," "tone," "attention," "tune," "tendency," and "tension" spring from the Latin *tendere,* meaning "to stretch," as a tendon is stretched. These words echo the underlying resonant patterns we have seen in the forces of nature. All that we see, touch, know, and feel is an amazing dance of intentional forces stretching out to bind everything together. And all the dancers are on the beat. The taut string, the ringing drum, the beaming radio waves, and the loving arms outstretched for a hug all have internal dynamics, patterns of resonance waiting to be engaged.

Music is the standard by which we can measure our level of performance in this dance. Our perceptions, feelings, and actions do much to create harmony (and dissonance) for our inner life and for the life of the planet. Music teaches us to listen and play at the same time. Is there dissonance in the home or workplace? Do we feel peace in our heart? Are we losing muscle tone through idleness or abuse? Do we speak in a clear and sonorous voice? Are we expressing ourselves clearly? Tuning in to the deep resonance of nature is the first step in composing ourselves. Tune in and take a place in the choir. As we begin to appreciate the harmony of the

---

* English is a member of the Indo-European family of languages, a group of related tongues that includes Danish, Italian, Russian, and Sanskrit, among many others. They are related through sonic similarities of words and their associated meaning. This relation occurs by means of the way sounds within words evolve over time. Linguists, studying extinct and modern languages with ancient written records, have determined that certain sounds will predictably evolve into certain other sounds. In this way, common sonic ancestors to many words within the Indo-European family can be confidently inferred. These ancestors are the "root" of English, and a score of other tongues. The root words I cite in this book come from *The American Heritage Dictionary of the English Language.*

myriad spheres singing all around us, we gain the ability to act accordingly, sending our unique articulations into the resonant cathedral of life on earth.

THE MUSIC LESSONS FROM OUTER SPACE

When I was about ten years old I was struck by a stark revelation. I had just learned about the orbital model of atomic structure. All at once I saw the universe as a set of nested Chinese boxes. From atoms to the stars all natural forms seemed to be held inside progressively larger forms. Atoms are tiny solar systems of protons and orbiting electrons. Planets and stars hold the atoms. Planets orbit around stars. Stars swirl in galaxies, which rotate in clusters. In my young mind there just *had* to be another magic box that held the clusters of galaxies. And another one after that.

Perhaps I wasn't far off. The forces of resonance displayed in the atom are identical to the forces binding planets to stars, stars to galaxies, galaxies to clusters of galaxies, and clusters of . . .

Thankfully the Ultimate Causative Agent remains hidden from view. Gravity lies beyond explanation. Scientists imagine *gravitons, gravity waves,* and *string theory.* Dream on, Einstein!

With the Hubbell Space Telescope probing the limits of space, and electron microscopes diving into the nuclei, we diligently attempt to describe how things work. But remember the root, the *ar* of it all. Fitting it together, elucidating the inspiration behind it all, is still left to the *ar*tists and the *har*monists.

As children we doodle, hum, dance, and play. As our innate artistic nature matures we write poetry, compose music, create visual artifacts, all in a sweetly innocent pursuit to describe that next magic box in the nested series of mysteries we perceive all around us. As we ponder the mysteries of time and space through the ages, all eyes seem to turn toward the sky: wheels within wheels, the divine clockwork, levels of reality, gods and demigods, the harmony of the spheres, Sputnik, close encounters.

In my opinion the most important result of our adventures in outer space are the startling portraits of planet earth. The biosphere—the thin layer of life—is touchingly delicate and vulnerable. Life seems to be but a silken shawl draped on the shoulders of Mother Earth. A fragile fabric in a vast ocean of black space. The images expose something starkly obvious. There is no way we can continue to conceive of ourselves as separate from the planet in any way.

New discoveries indicate that life on earth is inseparable from outer space as well. Biomolecular experiments replicating conditions in space have generated molecules with a distinctly cellular structure. Microscopic analysis of ancient rocks reveal that similar structures were present *billions* of years ago on this planet. Lifelike forms may have arrived on earth relatively quickly after the birth of the universe. The shock waves of the Big Bang might be carrying the seeds of life to every corner of the cosmos. From this point of view the notion of an evolving universe gains scientific credibility.

The cyclic yet eternal nature of time displayed in the stars has always been a point of reference in our temporal habitat. The celestial rhythms seem to remind us of something deeply important. We look to the sky for inspiration, guidance, and prophesy. It's like a tune is stuck in our head but we can't quite recall the entire melody. Preoccupation with the patterns of the heavenly clockworks—like our love of music—is a clear sign of our primary concern with the dynamics of time. As a species we have always stretched our curiosity into the heavens and into the future. Many cultures, including the Druids, Aztecs, Chinese, Hindus, Greeks, Jews, and Christians, used the stars as their oracle, pantheon, and prophet. The stars reveal the eternal. In their movement—as in the patterns of dance and music—the nature of time itself is magically illuminated.

When you look up into the sky tonight, try to sense the timeless resonance of the starlight as it sparkles on the back of your eye. Imagine the tones of atomic resonance stretching out to you over the light years. Each element sings with its own unique quantum harmony. Radio-physicists make recordings of this music, and these recordings are called spectrographs. At the same time, imagine the seeds of life falling from space, filtering through the thin, watery veil. Listen with your heart for the slow and sensual hum of the turning earth, the rock and roll of birth and death, and the improvisations of evolution. Intention, impulse, and dissipation play all around you. Take a breath. And another. Hum a favorite tune. It all fits, doesn't it?

The pace of the modern world handicaps our appreciation of the resonance of nature. The fields of activity all around us affect our slow, animal rhythms sympathetically. Much of our time is spent in a digitized, mechanized, and mediated virtual reality of our own creation. Our health and spirit need daily contact with the actual reality of the natural world. Here is a technique for appreciating the rhythms of the actual world we live in.

Note: Most of the exercises (including this one) can be done alone, but will be more fun and more easily mastered if done with a partner or in a group setting.

Exercise 1: A Walking Tour of the Universe

This will take about fifteen minutes. The best time for this is sunset. Pick a clear day. Find a spot outside where you can see as close to the horizon as you can. If possible, take off your shoes.

When the sun just goes down, begin to walk *very slowly.* Hold your body gently erect, with your hands relaxed at your sides or clasped behind your back. As you walk feel your toes lift off, the balance point when you are on one foot, your heel touching the earth, the transfer of weight, and the toes lifting off once more.

Notice the force of gravity moving through your body. Notice your will power playing upon the resilient muscle fibers up and down your legs and back. Breathe.

At sunset the colors are saturated and rich, slightly muted and yet luminous. Begin to notice the colors and objects around you. Do not change your pace. Slowly turn your head this way and that. As you notice things around you, gently but clearly speak their names *out loud.* Notice and name a new object every two or three steps. Allow the image and sound to connect in your mind before giving your attention to the next one. *Get a feeling for each thing.*

Notice the air moving over your skin. Remember the hum of the quanta, the resonance of the molecular bonds, the palpitations of the chromosomes. Try to sense the space between everything where immense power resonates, even in the petal of the tiniest flower. Intentionally articulate in sound the essence of this power for each thing you name: scrap of paper; tree; vehicle; pavement; hand; child; sky.

If you have timed this right the sky should be a deep indigo blue by now. The birds are singing goodbye to the sun. The shadow of the world passes over your head. The evening star or perhaps Jupiter is blinking at you. Remember that *everything* exists in resonant relationship in the temporal habitat. Sense the musical time generated between you and the sky, between you and the edge of space only a few short miles above. Dance on step by step.

There is a pervasive harmony in the natural world. The qualities of materials, and the actions of living and nonliving systems are articulations of this harmony on different physical scales, and within different cycles of time. The blinding light of the sun and the advance and recession of the ice ages are different tones in the temporal habitat generated by the same resonant principles. With our perceptions sharpened to notice this universal harmony, we will now examine music itself, the best example of how humans *intentionally articulate* these principles. We will see how the elements of music correspond to specific areas of the human body-mind represented in the chakras.

2 THE ELEMENTS OF MUSIC

All music is made from seven basic elements. These are (1) pulse, (2) rhythmic pattern, (3) sustained tone, (4) harmony, (5) melody, (6) compositional form, and (7) inspiration. Each element resonates more prevalently in respective areas of our body, stimulating behaviors and emotions associated with these bodily regions.

Our framework for examining how the musical elements resonate in our body-mind is the ancient Vedic system of the chakras. This system describes seven whorls of physical and spiritual energy spinning at points along the spine from the coccyx to the crown of the head (figure 1, page 24). The chakras offer a concise and logical system for actually experiencing the many relationships between our physical and spiritual natures. By turning our attention to the resonant power flowing through the chakras we begin to master the skills needed to articulate our highest intentions. Focusing on the chakras, we will examine the seven elements of the musical art, noticing how they affect us on physical, emotional, and spiritual levels.

Musicians and athletes are always encouraged to warm up before they play. To compose a life in resonance, we need to do our warm-ups, too. In the first chapter we tuned in to the resonant principles revealed in the atomic, molecular, biological, and cosmic realms. Now we will open our ears and stretch our innate musicality as we explore the resonance at play in the seven musical elements. Appreciating the direct correspondence between musical resonance and our body-mind is the first lesson in orchestrating a musical life.

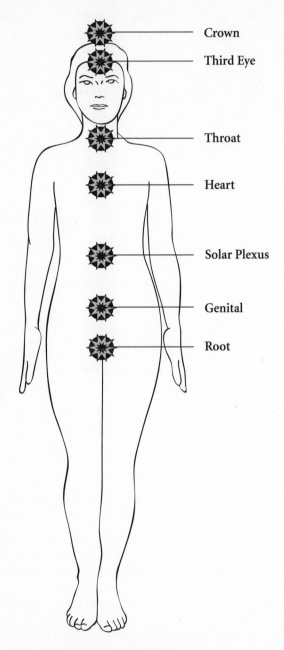

Figure 1: The Seven Chakras.

ELEMENT 1: THE PULSE

A pulse is simply an equal division of time. As the basic building block of all resonant phenomenons, pulse is the most essential musical element. If hydrogen is the stuff of the universe, making up the bulk of every star, then pulse is the stuff of music. The pulse of the drum is easily perceived. A much faster equal division of time creates the phenomenon of tone as well. (See "Tone," page 35.)

Every musical tradition rides squarely on a pulse. Tribal ceremony and chant, classical forms around the world, popular music, and every other style and genre tap into the pulse. Pulse, at its roots, means "to push," and that is what the beat of the drum does. It moves us along, reflecting the basic physiological forces surging through the veins, throbbing in the chest, and thumping on the ground as we run for our lives. The pulse is the life-blood of music.

The vibrations of an atom or a string, the rotations of the galaxy, and the thump of the sneaker in the dryer all describe a pulse (or frequency) of some sort. In the form of a musical beat, pulse provides the temporal structure over which the other elements of music are played. The concept of "push" at the root of the word "pulse" infers a pushing *against* something.

Step by step we push ourselves around through time. Feel it as your heels click on the pavement. Hear the pulse in the fist pounding on the door. Feel it as you chomp on the carrot, and in the drub of the tires. The beat always reminds us that there is some pushing going on.

A sustained resonance requires a push-and-rebound cycle occurring at equal intervals. When this happens the system achieves resonance and everything becomes easier. When an initial impulse is balanced against the internal resilience of the system, we are in the flow of a musical experience. Bounce up and down on the bed. Dribble the basketball. Swing the ax. Play the drum. Jog to the mailbox. Ride the beat.

Imagine a bouncing ball. The rhythmic thump-thump of the ball reveals an essential aspect of pulse, and why we respond so deeply to it. The ball goes up and down in direct relationship with gravity. The resilience of the air pressure in the ball works in resonance with the pull of the earth. Activated by the impulse of our hand, the structure of the ball and the constant force of gravity establish a resonant relationship.

The first sign of response-ability in the human embryo is to orient itself to gravity. Our heart rate, our step, our posture, everything we do, is grounded in variations on this primary gravitational relationship. Every biological rhythm, every dividing cell, every mating dance, migration, and sock hop rides on waves of gravity. In the basic pulse of the dance, in the beat of music, our musical intelligence senses this deep intonation between the earth and the body.

Musical pulse pushes us onto the dance floor. It gets us marching, swinging, and floating. Through the feet, legs, and buttocks the beat articulates our direct connection with the earth. There is a primal quality present when pulse is the predominant element in a style of music, as in jump-style jazz or African drumming. The source of this primal nature is the resonance established between the pulse of the music and the forces of gravity.

Gravity reaches up through the earth. We push away. It pulls us down. Like a bouncing ball, our internal resilience sends us flying upward again and again. Music praises the power of gravity every time it brings people together in dance.

Gravity appears to pull everything downward in parallel lines of force. This is not true. Gravity operates in *radial symmetry* and is *convergent* in nature, not parallel. Everyone stands aligned along rays of gravitational force emanating from the center of the earth.

Born out of our relationship with gravity, it follows that the pulse of music is a convergent, unifying force. As gravity unites us around the center of the earth, the rhythmic pulse of a strong musical beat unites us at common points in time. This point in time is *the now moment,* that place in the temporal habitat where generations stand united and a culture is rooted in ritual.

TEMPO

The frequency of the musical beat is called the *tempo.* Changing the tempo changes the contour of the time field created by the pulses of energy. In this way changing tempo modulates the emotional response of the listener.

In classical terminology, the easy walking rhythm is called *moderato,* the jogging tempo is *allegro,* the sprint tempo is *vivace.* Since the rhythm of our step is so intimate to us, the different paces in music naturally resonate our memory, reminding us of the different tempos of life. Forty to fifty beats-per-minute is a very slow pace for the heart. This is also a very relaxed and elegant tempo in music. If your heart gets going around 180 beats per minute, you better take a break because the old ticker may be on overdrive. Music at that tempo drives us, prods us with an equally breakneck, insistent pace.

The basic beat communicates unity, connection, coherence, and survival. Tempo articulates more specific qualities of musical time. Changing the tempo of a piece can significantly alter its effect in musical time. Our personal pace shapes our temporal experience as surely as tempo influences music and architecture shapes our physical experience.

Tempo is the most important aspect of the pulse. It significantly shapes the meaning of any piece of music. Too fast a pace resonates fears of friction, burnout, and cardiac infarction. Too slow a pace and we topple over, overcome with excess weight. We just can't get ourselves to put one foot in front of the other.

THE FIRST CHAKRA: SURVIVAL

The first chakra is located in the lower pelvic region. Here we are hard-wired into our crucial relationship with gravity. The first chakra carries the message of survival and unity into our consciousness. Through the essential lessons of gravity we realize in body and mind that we must keep moving or we will stagnate and perish. Our legs and hips join us to the planet. The first chakra resonates in sympathy to the insistent force of gravity, and we dance . . . or fall to our death.

The message of the pulse resonating in the first chakra calls out as sure as a drumbeat: each individual is a discreet example of the wisdom and beauty of the universal creative force. This call demands that we master two lessons. First, we must accept our unique and separate selfhood. Every being exists as an independent and autonomous example of the powers that be. Second, we are called by the power of the pulse to notice the effects of our actions on the whole. If we fail in this task the pulse of our surroundings may *beat* us down.

Imbalance in the first chakra manifests as a blockage of basic energy, a constipation of the soul, and crippling inertia, an inability to change even under the threat of stagnation. What are the life lessons within this essential aspect of musical resonance?

Like a pungent fragrance, the beat has circled the globe in the last fifty years. The beat is the anchor for rhythm and blues, rock and roll, reggae, the rich African tradition, world beat, and jazz. When we bounce to the beat of these ubiquitous styles we are dancing with everyone all the way to the other side of the world. The message of unity comes up through our feet and legs and grinds away in our pelvis. The relationship between gravity and the beat assures us that when we dance we make love to the whole world.

Exercise 2: Pacing Yourself

Take a well-known tune. Go for a walk with the tune in your head. Slowly saunter with a steady step and hum the tune in time with your footfall. Let the quality of that tune at that tempo sink in. Now pick up the pace. Try jogging, singing the tune at that new tempo. Repeat the tune several times until the feeling of the tune at the faster tempo sinks in. Try various tunes at various tempos. Sing tunes that are normally slow while you jog; hum a fast tune at a slow tempo as you plod along at a snail's pace. You will find that even though the song remains the same, changing the tempo changes your experience.

Awareness of pacing is a basic first chakra music lesson. At the right pace we can play the tune forever. At the wrong tempo sooner or later everyone throws down his or her instruments in disgust. The relationship between object and force determines the optimum pace in any situation—try riding a bike on the beach. Now we will move into areas of musical resonance where we can see our intentions articulating more and more complex relationships.

ELEMENT 2: RHYTHMIC PATTERN

A pulse has no contour or temporal shape. It simply measures a movement through time at a certain pace. When the pulse is grouped or subdivided by means of selected accents, a repetitive *pattern* results and rhythm is born. In this way the endless pulse of time is modulated into recognizable forms. Repeated patterns are the hallmark of unique identity. Out of the one emerge the many.

Rhythmic pattern is the first order of musical organization. There are two building blocks in the world of rhythmic pattern. One results from accenting every other beat. The other comes from accenting every third beat (figure 2). From these two building blocks (along with a single pulse) all other rhythmic patterns can be constructed as simply as one, two, three.

Carved out of the anonymous flow of a simple pulse, a rhythmic pattern ushers musical time into the world of identity and personality. Even the simplest rhythms impart personality to a composition. Musicians use words like "feel," "groove," "riff," "figure," and "shape" to describe rhythmic patterns. Rhythms alter the feel of the time at hand. Specific patterns have taken root in certain musical styles. The signature rhythms of a musical style can be as consistent and recognizable as genetic traits in living beings. Styles can blend and create hybrids, but the original patterns of the rhythmic time fields remain clear and vital. The driving sound of Carlos Santana derives its rhythmic identity form the ancient Afro-Cuban patterns at the heart of salsa.

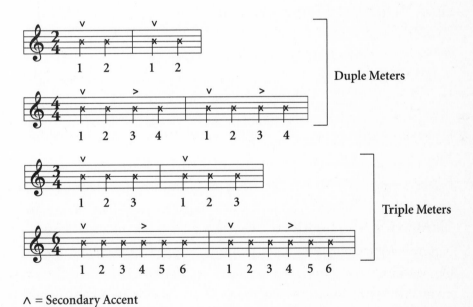

∧ = Secondary Accent

∨ = Primary Accent

Figure 2: Notation of Duple and Triple Meters.

Exercise 3: The Building Blocks

While walking at a strong, quick pace, articulate the two simple patterns that were previously described. First, accent every second step by saying "ONE two, ONE two," then every third step with "ONE two three, ONE two three." Accent your step in the same pattern. Throw yourself into the ground a bit on the "ONE." Surprise! You are dancing. In the first case you are measuring out the essential feel of a march. In the second case you have created the primordial waltz. These basic units of musical rhythm are called *meters*.

THE SECOND CHAKRA: THE DANCE OF LIFE

Throughout human history, rhythmic time fields have appeared most clearly in the dance. Ritual movement and social forms literally embody cultural identity. Polka, tango, waltz, jig, tarantella, calypso, salsa, and the twist declare ethnic and national identity in a clear and explicit manner. All this is centered around the second chakra, the whorl of muscle, hormones, and genetic material that demands to be known, felt, and appreciated as unique in all the world.

In our physical body the second chakra is located between the pubic bone and the navel. In the consciousness the second chakra sings of our basic personality, sexuality, body image, and our sense of personal integrity. Here we find a swirl of currents where our ideas of identity dance in the arms of desire and the biological imperative to procreate.

Our identity is a complex composition of biological patterns (genetics), behavior, and environment. When these currents meet in the second chakra they resonate ego and all the associated aspects of self-determination. Imbalance here can manifest as a lack of focus, sexual issues, stress-related illness, and an "identity crisis."

Rhythms grind out identity straight from the hip, or maybe a little below the hip. As the simple clarity of dance rhythms swirl through our second chakra we are stimulated to grab a partner and swing! Our second chakra asks us to commit to a step, a partner, or a culture. The repetitive patterns and habits in our lives become the signature riffs composing our identity, our dance, and our music. Dance along. Learn a new step. The idea of "making sweet music together" probably was conceived on a dance floor.

Some cultures have gravitated toward *compound* meters, where many different groups of twos and threes are strung together. Music from the Balkan region and the Indian subcontinent is often based in cycles of seven, nine, thirteen, thirty-one, or more! By breaking these compound meters into subunits of twos and threes, very complex compound meters can be learned and mastered (figure 3).

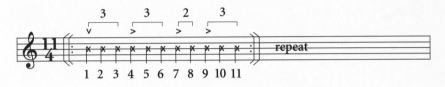

Figure 3: Balkan Compound Meter.

The beat can be *subdivided* as well. The *clave* [clah-vay] rhythms of African and Latin American music accent specific subdivisions of the beat (figure 4a, page 32). The complex flavor of these forms results from regular accents in the time field riding on rapid subdivisions of the basic pulse. This musical technique is called *syncopation.*

Rhythmic pattern is the basic genetic material of music. Permutations of rhythm generate offspring. These variations evolve into distinct forms while remaining true to the basic lineage. The blues, for example, has a signature pattern drawn from its African clave heritage (figure 4b, page 32). Over the generations this figure has been incorporated into jazz, swing, rock, hip-hop, and many other forms. When this riff appears, the tune grooves to African roots, no matter if it's B.B. King, k.d. lang, or Bob Marley.

Exercise 4: The Power of Patterns

Here are two ways to experience the message within rhythms. Write down two short phrases that have different rhythms. For example, "Blowing my own horn," and "Waaaay over there." Now use these two phrases to accompany the same repetitive motion such as jogging, digging, or throwing a small child into the air (and

Figure 4a: Mambo Clave.

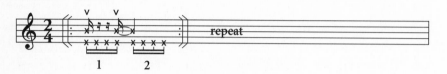

Figure 4b: Basic Blues Rhythm.

catching the child, of course!). Repeat the first phrase several times. Say the words out loud with a full tone as you proceed. Move accurately to the pattern of the phrase. Devise an articulation that flows easily in your body. Get the identity of the pattern into your bones. Stay connected with gravity. Keep your motions constant as you fit the second vocal pattern into the flow of the movement. You will discover that the different phrases literally make the same motion feel different.

Next, try the above exercise using a single phrase articulated in two distinct ways. For example: "Ohhhhhhh! What can the matter be?" and "Oh, what caaaaaaan the matter be?" You will see that even when the words are the same the rhythmic pattern of each phrase has an identity all its own.

The rhythms in your own habitual vocal patterns influence the dynamics of your ego. So do the rhythms of your movements. This is your "body language." In further chapters we will learn techniques for literally moving through life in creative new ways. Vocal patterns, movement styles, and habitual behaviors are just some of the tunes that mix in the ego. Many times the tones of other egos fill your time field, bringing their own influence into play.

ELEMENT 3: SUSTAINED TONE

In our discussion of tone, we need to make a distinction between raw sound and musical tone. Bursts of pressure waves in the air of sufficient strength and audible frequency will create perceivable sounds. Both musical tone and the jumble of noise are created this way. In the oscilloscope, musical tones are configured in what physicists call *standing wave patterns,* and are integrated and harmonic in nature (figure 5a). Noise—such as traffic, rain, or the clanging of dishes—is complex, random, dissonant, and *nonharmonic* in nature (figure 5b, page 34). Our hearing apparatus perceives standing waves vibrating from about 20 to approximately 30,000 vibrations (Hertz or Hz) per second.

Below 20 Hz our aural apparatus goes out of resonance and we perceive sound patterns as atonal rattles, thumps, and clicks. In other words, noise. Above 40,000 Hz most of us are out of luck again; the equipment just doesn't respond to the tiny vibrations at that upper frequency. Those upper vibrations are reserved for dogs, owls, bats, and other creatures.

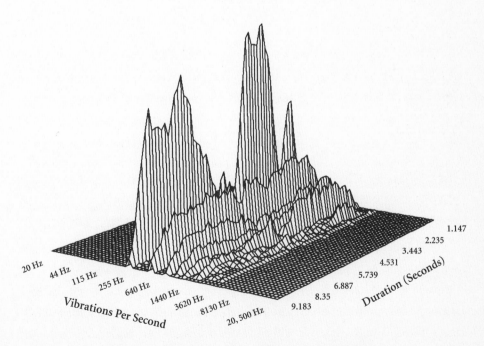

Figure 5a: Sonogram of the Viola; a Resonant Tone.

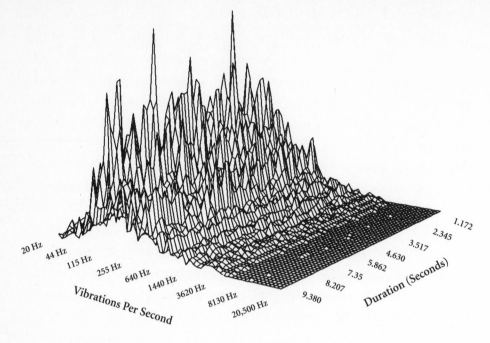

Figure 5b: Sonogram of a Washing Machine; an Enharmonic Noise.

The functions of the human brain are harmonically integrated. Electrical patterns generated in one area move through the entire mass of the brain like a tone fills a cavern. This is how a sudden sound can instantly jar muscles, eyes, voice, and emotions into concerted action. The wonder of the human brain is its ability to coherently compose so many patterns of thought and experience *at the same time.* Picture the mind as the surface of a pond. We miraculously maintain discreet perceptions of thousands of concentric waves moving through the water.

We generally associate pleasure with harmonic patterns, and displeasure with jumbled, erratic, or "noisy" patterns. Unlike the disjointed, scrambled vibrations of noise, tonal patterns set our entire body-mind into sympathetic resonance. While noise grabs our attention, tone *holds* our attention.

A tone sends a harmonically coherent message to the brain. Electrical and biochemical forces in the brain go into resonance in turn. By examining the internal structure of a single tone we will now discover how our musical perceptions reflect the interpenetrating nature of our mind.

String

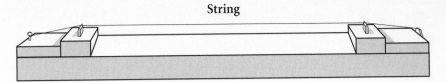

Figure 6: The Monochord.

TONE

A vibrating string actually generates a series of discreet frequencies corresponding to whole-number fractions of the length of the string. It vibrates over its entire length at one frequency, and then in half-lengths at twice that frequency, third-lengths at three times as fast, and so on, theoretically to infinity. These simultaneously generated tones are called the *overtones* or *partials* of the string. Collectively they are called the *harmonics* of the string. The same ratios occur in every resonant system from atoms to solar systems. Pythagoras observed this phenomenon in the monochord (figure 6). The *relative volume* of the harmonic partials produces the unique tonal personality of every instrument, including the human voice.

The string on the monochord, for example, while vibrating over its entire length, produces a tone called the *fundamental,* and it creates a strong pressure wave in the air (figure 7a). By virtue of the principles of resonance, the string generates other pressure waves at discreet frequencies as well.

We can view these partials one at a time by lightly fretting a guitar string. Placing a stop on a spot corresponding to one of the harmonic partials of the string will mute all the frequencies except that of the chosen harmonic partial

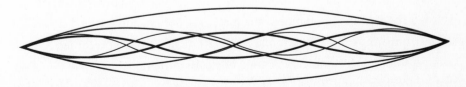

Figure 7a: Freely Vibrating String Showing First Five Overtones.

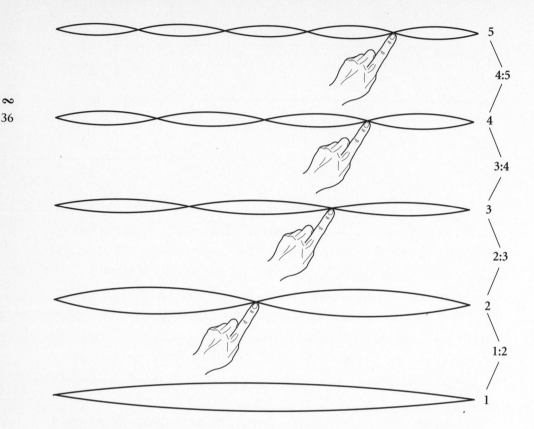

Figure 7b: "Stopping" a String to Isolate the Overtones of the Harmonic Series.

(figure 7b). These spots are called *nodes.* When all other overtones are muted, the nodes of the chosen frequency do not move, and the standing waves of the partial resonate *between the unmoving nodes.* This magical stillness within the dance of the string is the secret of resonance the Pythagoreans uncovered and described with numbers.

Instrument families have character traits that are reflected in their harmonics. This is a result of the resonance of the materials, design, and internal stresses of the instruments. A silver flute sounds different than a wooden recorder. A brass trumpet sounds brighter than a wooden horn. An upright piano sounds "smaller" than a nine-foot grand. This is due to the differing relative volumes of the partials within the harmonic series of the tones produced by the instruments. By analyzing the tones of acoustic phenomena, engineers construct synthesizers that mimic the harmonic structure of acoustic instruments.

TIMELESSNESS

The same principles at play in a solid musical tone sustain a beam of light on its journey through space. In a light beam, electric and magnetic fields oscillate in harmonic relationship and "packets" of electromagnetic energy beam into the cosmos like the tolling of a bell fills a valley. Similarly, musical tone describes a harmonic integrity of forces moving through the air. Through resonance, light, tone, and all harmonic phenomenons declare the essence of sustained power. This eternal sustaining nature inspires the idea of divine will, a spiritual force that sustains creation.

The power of tone has always been central to religion. In no uncertain terms Genesis says, "The Word was God." Actually, in the original text, "sound" was the word. Native Americans of the Lakota tribe heard the voice of God in the thunder, calling it *Wakan-tanka*. The ancient traditions of Yoga declare the sound of the letter *aum* to be the primary creative force of the universe. In the Moslem world the words of the Koran are the actual sounds of the voice of Allah.

Just as Pythagoras put sound at the center of his philosophy, Copernicus put the sun at the center of his cosmology. He was a cleric, not a physicist, and his conception was theological, not scientific. For him the eternal life-giving light perfectly symbolized the divine will, and therefore should stand at the center of the celestial realm. Whenever we create or perceive a strong tone, our musical intelligence senses a similar conception. In a solid tone, as in the light of the sun, we sense the presence of an eternal principle at work. Musical tone symbolizes the universal and timeless nature of resonance.

Musicians work to produce the clearest, strongest tone from their instruments. With lip, arm, hand, and lungs, the player initiates impulses of energy. When these impulses correspond to the structure and materials of the instrument, a good, well-projected tone results. The well-played tone literally fits into the structure of the instrument, and a corresponding resonance is produced. As long as the musician sustains the effort, a resonant tone is produced, and player and listener alike perceive a message from the divine, a whisper of eternal duration, power, and clarity.

THE THIRD CHAKRA: PERSONAL POWER

The third chakra spins in the abdominal region called the *solar plexus,* the nexus of muscles above the navel and below the ribs. This area of the body is crucial to balance, graceful movement, stamina, and posture. All physical movement is initiated from here. Our ease of movement, leverage, and physical power all hinge on the abdominal region. Weak abdominals are a ticket to backache, bad digestion, and a beer gut. Playing a musical instrument is first and foremost a physical activity, and a good tone on any instrument begins with the sense of physical balance and power that originates in the abdominal musculature.

A strong, clear vocal tone is also initiated from this region. As we breathe in, the diaphragm, the muscle at the base of the lungs, contracts and pulls downward, drawing air into the chest cavity. During exhalation the rib, abdomen, and back muscles constrict, the diaphragm relaxes, and air is expelled. To produce a good vocal tone the diaphragm must be held firm and controlled as the air passes over the vocal cords. If the diaphragm lacks sufficient muscle tone, air is expelled in a weak and uneven stream. The resulting tone is shaky. Similarly, the violinist with an unsure, jittery bow arm will produce a shaky tone.

A strong tone tends to motivate us. The firm command, the blaring horn, the cheer of encouragement, and the cry for help all challenge us to seize the moment with balance, support, and follow-through. The expressions "to have the guts for the job" and "intestinal fortitude" reflect the abdominal source of willful motivation.

As our center of gravity, and the power behind the breath, the third chakra is the gateway for physical equilibrium and stamina. It also acts as a conduit for the willful aspect of consciousness, evidenced by the imperative to *keep breathing.* Imbalance in the third chakra is said to generate greed, fatigue, fear, and violence. Butterflies in the stomach, "that sinking feeling," lethargy, and desperation are symptoms of a lack of appropriate tone in the third chakra.

Exercise 5: Root Tone

Take a deep breath and heave out a big sigh, letting it all go. Next, sit down and drop your head gently over your knees, folding your abdomen onto your lap. Take another big breath and groan out a steady "ohhhhhh." Notice the pressure in the lower belly. That's your diaphragm maintaining muscle tone as your lower back and ribs constrict your lungs. Try to keep your groan on a steady, solid pitch. Try sitting up, recreating the same tension in the belly as you inhale and intone another "ohhhhhhh."

Repeat this exercise a few times. When you sit erect, try to refine the tone. Consciously balance the tension in your diaphragm with the flow of air over your vocal cords. A deep resonance in your belly will result when the resilience of your musculature goes into resonance with the vibrations of your vocal cords. This steady sonority is a sign of willful intent in operation, indicating well-articulated third chakra activity. A good vocal tone is just a refined groan, scream, laugh, or whisper.

ELEMENT 4: HARMONY—SIMULTANEOUS TONES

Harmony is the product of relationships between tones. We saw how two flute tones generated an undertone (chapter 1, figure 5, page 14). Since frequency of an undertone is determined by the interval between the tones, different intervals create different undertones. Undertones are constantly produced between musical tones, and as they change the overall quality of the music changes. Undertones are the physical expressions of the way tones fit together. In this way, undertones *are* the harmony. The intervals between the first few tones in the harmonic series generate undertones that are part of the same harmonic structure. When we hear these harmonies and find them pleasing we are appreciating the expression of resonant relationships.

Western music is a cultural artifact that grew out of the deeply resonant Pythagorean philosophy unifying spiritual ideas with musical tone. These powerful traditions shaped Western music into a predominantly harmonic sonic system. Whereas many cultures have rhythmic-based musical forms, Western music is based primarily on the dynamics of tonal harmony. This is not an arbitrary cultural habit or bias. The micropulses within multivoiced harmonic structures fit together in elegant resonant patterns of numeric ratio. These ratios are identical to the ratios that create the power in rhythmically based musical styles. The pulses of tonal harmony are just a bit faster.

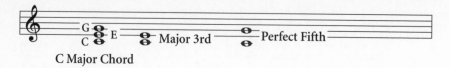

C Major Chord

Figure 8: C Major Chord and the Intervals within the Chord.

The archetype of harmony in Western music is the *major chord.* For example, the C chord, or triad, consists of three notes: C in the lowest or root position; the E two full steps above C; and the G one and a half steps up from E (figure 8). This harmony is the Euro-American musical icon of icons, our sonic touchstone. The undertone generated between the C and the G sounds an octave below the C. The tones of the major chord fit together in simple numeric resonance, creating a sound that symbolizes harmony itself.

All rhythmic patterns are simple permutations of the pulse. In a similar way the notes of the major chord and the basic structure of all tonal music are intoned simultaneously by the vibrations of a single string. Examine the harmonic series of a low C fundamental (figure 9, page 41). The emotional power of an interval is related to how the interval fits into the harmonic series. The sound created by the drone of the bagpipe resonates a sense of solid assurance. This interval, termed a *fifth* for its position within a scale (figure 10, page 41), is generated between the second and third partial of any harmonic series. The magic of every harmony is generated by the ratios between the vibrations of the tones.

We have seen that a vibrating string generates a series of tones called the harmonic series. The intervals between these tones can be represented in whole number ratios (see chapter 1, figure 2, page 5). The ratio of the perfect fifth (C to G) is ⅔. The ration of the perfect fourth (G to the C above) is ¾. These ratios are the foundation of our tonal system. These same ratios are the foundation for the *rhythmic* system of African and Latin American music. Our culture resonates these ratios at a much higher frequency, but the resonant principles at work are numerically identical.

How do spaces between tones influence the feelings resonated in musical time? Why does the sweet bluegrass harmony touch us so? What is the secret power of the unison choir, many voices riding along in powerful octave harmony? Why does

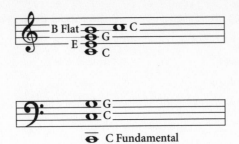

C Fundamental

Figure 9: Harmonic Series of a "C" Fundamental Tone.

Figure 10: C Major Scale Showing Scale Degrees (1–8)
and Intervals within a C Major Chord.

harmonic dissonance grate on our ears? And how do the great works of Wagner, Debussy, and even Bach exploit dissonant relationships to beautiful advantage? The answer to all these questions is revealed where we most intimately perceive relationship of any kind: the heart.

THE FOURTH CHAKRA: HEARTSTRINGS

The heart is where the body-mind feels relationship the deepest. It palpitates, shudders, and races at the thought of going on stage or falling in love. The perfect relationship is everyone's heartfelt dream. Falling out of such a bond "breaks" the heart. Domestic harmony is the ideal for the home. The revered consciousness we associate with a loving heart sings loud and clear that the highest truth is revealed through truly resonant relationships. This is the heart of the matter.

As a song touches us with a pleasing blend of voices our heart opens. It is no accident that country western music, hymns, and TV jingles lean heavily on this heart-centered element of music. To communicate affinity, love, empathy, and patriotism, we sing in harmony. Through the model of musical harmony we see that relationships work best when they are fitting, integral, and resonant in nature. Partners must be actively engaged and aware, constantly listening and playing at the same time.

We literally feel resonant relationships of all types acutely in the heart region of our body. This is the seat of the fourth chakra, the whirlpool of love in the body-mind. Aristotle revered the sensitivity of the heart. He put the seat of intelligence there. The heart chakra is central to the physiological and emotional realms of life. The fourth chakra envelops a spinning top of feelings, hormones, blood, air, and powerful impulses, all in a delicate, highly responsive balance.

The human heart has been idolized throughout time as an image of divine spirit, supernatural power, and human compassion. Every example of the iconography of the heart stems from the idea of relationship. We are encouraged to "follow your heart." What does that mean but to strive for inner and outer harmony?

What kind of relationship do you have with your neighbors? What harmonies are established between family members? Colleagues? Nations? How do these relationships effect the individual body-mind? The gospel choir, community action, and a thank-you card all reveal the power of heart-centered harmony in action. We all want to be in tune, working together, sharing the beauty we cocreate. In the harmony of life, and music, fitting together is the heart of the matter. Throughout our lives, the heart is the place in the body where we feel how we fit.

Because the heart responds so sensitively to emotional and physiological inter-actions, it is the best indicator of our performance in the temporal habitat. We can literally feel if we are in harmony or not. Resonance in the heart chakra is not a mental construct. The heart reacts directly and dramatically to changing conditions. The heart muscle is stimulated by various hormones and actually produces hormonelike substances itself. Through these biological messengers the heart is in constant communication with the entire body-mind. Like a changing tempo transforms a song, fluctuations in the heartbeat transform our experience of time.

Remember, resonant relationships occur *between* tones, forces, planets, and people. The consciousness of the heart chakra imparts to us the subtle ability to sense the resonant patterns between people, between hearts. The heart is where we sense the truest aspects of relationships. Thank the Powers that Be for that. I would not trust my mind to be as capable. Relationships assure our survival and seal our fate. The sensitivity of the heart chakra is a highly resonant and fitting expression of the inspired intentions of the body-mind to strive for harmony and love.

Some people groove to progressive jazz, while others cringe at anything more harmonically adventurous than Hank Williams. It's all about how we handle the undertones, the way the tones fit together. Emotions are undertones as well. The "vibes" we get from a situation, encounter, or relationship are strongly akin to the various reactions and impressions brought about by variations in tonal harmony. We have a word for the subtle yet insistent feelings generated by personal interaction and "charged" situations. These feelings are the *undertones* of the situation.

Exercise 6: Harmony for Two

Let's establish a harmonic relationship between you and a partner. Stand close together, facing one another. Find a moderately low pitch you can both comfortably sing with a good tone. (Remember to engage your diaphragm when you sing). Now, as one of you steadily holds this tone, the partner starts there and slowly raises the pitch in a gentle sweep. Raise the pitch very slowly. Make sure the held pitch is steady and true. Be sure to project both tones with firm support from abdomen and back muscles. A good relationship results from partners who "put themselves out there."

As the second voice moves slowly upward, the two tones create an ever-widening interval. As the interval changes, certain harmonic ratios will be generated, some pleasing, and some dissonant. Carry the tone up until you reach the octave above the held tone. Take another deep breath, sing this octave interval together, and then sweep gently, slowly, and firmly back down to the unison.

Remember, harmony results from relationship. In this case, the two tones interact in the air between the singers. You literally push the tones out into the air where they meet and mix, creating a third wave, the undertone. The changing quality of the intervals is revealed in the harmony of the tones mixing outside of the two of you. In this way all relationships create third entities with vibes of their own. The exhilaration you feel performing this exercise is the interpersonal harmony generated between the partners. This exercise can also be challenging. Relationships are work as well as play. The "steady" partner has the hardest job here. Emotions are cocreated, and as such are the harmony of souls, the sweet relationship of differences.

The "difference between the two" is what we sense and feel in all relationships. It's what touches our heart and drives us nuts. Being in love is nothing more than celebrating the certain awareness that you are creating something with your partner. Sometimes beautiful, sometimes devastating, your harmony is at all times unique in the entire world. Sing out! The harmony is happening between you. And always be willing to play the part of the listener.

ELEMENT 5: MELODY

Harmonic relationships appear on the musical score as chords. The notes are arranged vertically on the paper to represent how the tones occur simultaneously in time ("on the beat"). A melody is the modulation of tone *through* time, and is written as a series of notes written in a horizontal fashion. Musical notation pictures how long each tone in a melody lasts in relation to the underlying pulse (figure 11, page 45). Melodies combine the gutsy clarity and personality of rhythm with the primordial power of duration at the core of tone to bring us messages. More than any other element of music, melodies communicate *meaning*. They whisper, shout, cajole, celebrate, scold, and inspire. They are declarations, benedictions, love letters, and epitaphs. The composer gets his or her message across most directly with a good melody.

Melody comes from the Indo-European root *mel,* meaning "a branching." The composition of memorable melodies relies on the ability to remain true to this idea, growing and developing a sturdy and evocative structure of tonal relationships through time. To the Greeks, the eternal verities of beauty, truth, and proportion were defined by music. For them, melody was the essence of poetry, the refined music of speech.

Songlike manipulation of the voice comes before speech in the vocal development of children. Melodic articulations—with the accompanying meaning—are intoned all around us in the natural world. The songs of birds, whales, and the "speech" of dolphins show us that melodic communication predates humanity.

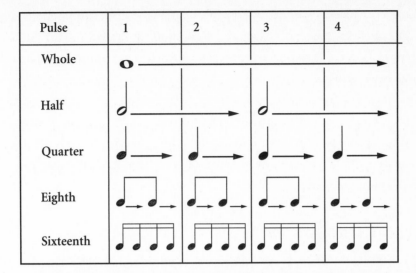

1 whole note = 4 beats; 2 half notes = 4 beats; 4 quarter notes = 4 beats;
8 eighth notes = 4 beats; 16 sixteenth notes = 4 beats.

Figure 11: Note Length Equivalents. (Notice how whole and half notes group the pulse, and eighths and sixteenths subdivide the pulse.)

The subtleties of speech are lost beyond a dozen yards. During the hunt it was crucial for early man to communicate over long distances. I think we chanted, sang, howled, and yelled hundreds of thousands of years before we talked, communicating melodically in a fashion akin to our animal progenitors.

Every melody is a unique message, a sonic statement of intent called out to our fellows. The composer takes rhythms and a series of tones and blends them within his or her crucible of inspiration, forming a temporal alloy. One melody can cut like Damascus steel. Another might be soft and lustrous like pewter or brass. One thing is certain: the slightest change in the formulation can result in a completely different outcome.

Two songs from *The Music Man* illustrate this clearly. The signature march of the musical ("76 Trombones") and a love song ("Goodnight, My Someone") are composed using the same series of notes. Meredith Willson, the composer, changed the meter of the march to a sweet waltz-time, and two unique tunes were cast from the identical notes. Just like formulating molecular compounds, when we change one element of a musical composition we change all. The two basic structural aspects of melody exploited by composers are intervals of pitch and lengths of duration of the tones.

The interplay between these attributes generates the information held in a melody: great leaps in pitch; the repetition of tones; notes sustained for several beats; quick bursts of activity. Ascending and descending "runs" and "broken chords" (figure 12) are two of the many devices a composer uses to craft the exact message he or she is after.

THE FIFTH CHAKRA: EXPRESSION

Some aspects of our resonant nature are beyond our conscious control. For example, the third chakra (will power) demands that sooner or later we take another breath. We really have no choice in this matter. At the fifth chakra, however, we have the opportunity to observe and choose how we express ourselves. My dad used to always say, "Watch your tone of voice," and, "You don't have to say everything that comes into your head." Every time we express ourselves in word, song, or deed, we are operating from the fifth chakra, reaching out to the world from the depths of our inner nature. The fifth chakra is like a nozzle. Our personal identity (second chakra) is pumped throughout our body-mind by our willful intentions (third chakra), set in relationship to our surroundings (fourth chakra), and then released through the focused stream of the fifth. By expressing

Figure 12: Broken Chords and Runs.

ourselves with our musical intelligence engaged—by acting and listening at the same time—we become aware of how we create harmony or dissonance in our relationships. As we pay attention to the incredible depth of expression available to us within fifth chakra awareness, we learn to choose from many melodic models, each with its own message.

Mantra is the practice of repeating sacred phrases over and over, resonating spiritual meaning of the words within our being. Mantra is a clear example of the musical intelligence of the fifth chakra empowering us to choose our melodic expression and taking responsibility for the choice.

In our discussion of harmony, we saw how some overtones within a single string vibrate in octave relationship. Resonance of consciousness in the chakras follow the same form. The fifth chakra spins in octave relationship with the second. At the fifth chakra we willfully express our identity (second chakra) into the world around us. The music of language gives melodic form to this truth. In the simplest example, when we speak our name our identity becomes known.

We deal with the dynamics of the fifth chakra all the time. "Words get stuck in your throat," "You're all choked up," "Things are easy for you to say," "You just have to spit it out," "You really said your piece"—these phrases articulate the harmonic correspondence between core identity and the expression of personality.

Blockages in the fifth chakra are very common. Antisocial behavior, conflict and confusion, isolation and aggressive behavior, laziness, and sloppy execution are all symptoms. Many common ills and pains come from stress in this center. If we feel like we can't get our point across to coworkers or family members, pressure builds in this chakra. The power of the will is not denied for long, however. Headache and neck pain, back problems, nervousness, and worry can all express the frustrations of blocked fifth chakra energy.

Self-expression is not only the realm of the artist. Every resonant entity from a supernova to your Uncle Fred expresses its identity. It is the *intention of creation* to express infinite examples of uniqueness through fifth chakra consciousness. Melody and song, poetry and love letters, arguments and prayer—all declare these deep intentions in no uncertain terms. Listening for the melodies in constant counterpoint all around you will train your inner ear to the resonance of your own instrument. Don't be shy! Express your Self!

Melody making, song, and verbal communication are expressed from the same region of the body—the throat. Here the double gates of the larynx modulate the unstoppable tide of the breath, shaping messages, songs, and stories. The throat is the portal where individuals bring their meaning into the human sphere. Through the fifth chakra we learn to mediate our animal nature and harness the fire of the ego. The throat chakra controls and expresses the willful force of our identity rising up from our guts like a lens focuses light. When we are unable to release and express our identity we get "choked up."

There is a direct correspondence between the center of individual identity in the second chakra and the center for expressing this identity in the fifth.

Exercise 7: Scat Attack

Express yourself in the mirror. Do not use words. Converse only with tone and a scat singer's nonsense vocabulary. The archetype for such a conversation is "Blah, blah, blah!" Modulate the tone. Go high and low. Explore the dynamics of loud and soft. Play with the emotions latent in a wide range of tone qualities. Keep up the pressure from your diaphragm. To get your message across you must always support it with good firm abdominal will power. Keep the breath going! Try different phonetics. Talk gibberish. Keep talking until you crack yourself up. Reduce yourself to laughter.

You can try this with a partner as well. Scat singer number one tells a story in gibberish for a minute or two, recounting something very meaningful and important. Use gestures and facial expressions to spice up the telling. Singer number two repeats the story back in gibberish the best he or she can.

For inspiration, listen to Ella Fitzgerald, Louis Armstrong, Brian Mahogany, or other scat singers. These great vocalists improvise amazing wordless melodies full of sass, pathos, joy, and guts.

Exercise 8: Words for the Wise, A Composition with Three Movements

1. Keep a scrap of paper and a pencil in your pocket. Sometime during the day a child, a coworker, or a homeless person on the bus will say something unique

or beautiful. These plums fall in our laps all the time, don't they? But we just don't take the time to remember them. Catch one, hold it, and record it.

2. Later, in some private space (like a walk in the park, or under a hot shower), play back one of these melodious gems. Repeat it several times out loud. Memorize it. Then put some real juice behind it. Modulate it. Express it fully. Call it out. Whisper it conspiratorially. Sing it. Identify with it. Bring tears to your eyes. Deliver the identifying feelings captured in the phrase. Make the music real.

3. Now, close your eyes, go inside, take a deep breath, and intone *aum.* Pay deep attention to the three phonemes as you slowly form the word [ahh—ooo—mmmm]. Alternate playing with your phrase and *aum* three times.

Your purloined phrase is a temporal artifact of someone's identity. Similar to a musician interpreting a score, your renditions of the phrase demands an active, expressive intent. In contrast, the sound of *aum* echoes the undivided creative force permeating all individual identities. The sound of *aum* intones a letter in the Sanskrit alphabet. In the Vedic tradition, the sound is said to be the generative force of creation (figure 13). *Aum* empties our mind of specific notions. Set in juxtaposition to this, the identifying sonic contours of the phrase are exposed like jewels on black velvet.

Figure 13: "Aum" or "Om."

ELEMENT 6: COMPOSITION AND EXTENDED FORMS

"Voice" and "vocation" share the same root. What one chooses to do with one's life is an expression of fifth chakra consciousness. With our actions we make ourselves known to the world, adding our voice to the choir. Many voices mix and blend to form the intricate beauty of a musical composition. We add our voice to the political debate, the family reunion, the pursuit of knowledge, and birthday ruckus.

Music mirrors the blending of voices in all human endeavors. Every instrument assumes a unique part to play. Together the many voices create a harmony, a counterpoint, a sonic artifact depicting human perceptions, dreams, folly, and wisdom. We may not be in complete control of our lives all the time, but we certainly want some influence over the process. Music is deeply woven into our human nature because it brings into our consciousness the temporal essence of nature itself. Music is the way human consciousness describes time.

Time being our primary element, we are preoccupied by it. We plan, scheme, regret, remember, fantasize, hope, and dream. We have intentions that motivate every action. Music is our most resonant way of expressing these intentions of consciousness. Through music our dreams become formalized in creations directly related to the forms and forces that bind the stars, spin the planets, and break hearts.

We feel the elements of music intimately. The body registers musical meaning and power in the legs, hips, belly, gut, heart, and throat. These areas respond to music. But our lungs don't choose the CD. Our butts don't plunk down the cash and buy the concert tickets. Impressed with information from the resonant centers in the body-mind, we make conscious choices with a *musical intelligence*. The traditional label for this attribute is "talent."

We have logical, kinesthetic, and intuitive intelligence. Each is an important facet of our mental capability. Our musical intelligence integrates these three powers. Musical training for children is strongly associated with accelerated academic achievement. Reading, math, and oral skills are appreciably higher in children who study music. The group dynamics of ensemble playing develop flexibility and attentiveness, the key foundations of intuition and empathy. Musicality is a keynote of the informed and intuitive mind. Exercising the musical intelligence develops a mental tone that resonates a sense of connection, belonging, creativity, and acceptance.

Athletic and musical practices engage our kinesthetic intelligence. In both disciplines mental images are expressed by the body through gestures, moves, and "plays." Musical intelligence integrates the mind and body. For more than two thousand years—from the academia of the ancient Greeks to the classical universities of Europe—musical training was required study.

The key to musical intelligence is the ability to gauge the potential influence of the choices before us. Critical thinking demands that we see relationships between forces, trends, and opinions. In this sense musical composition is the realization of one's best intentions over time. In every field of creativity, artifacts with a high degree of resonant integrity have the most power and longest effect. Witness the pyramids of Egypt, Chinese medicine (based on the chakra system, by the way), the works of J. S. Bach, the scientific method, and the Beatles.

Composers choose from tempos, rhythms, keys, harmonies, melodies, and many more options, juxtaposing chords and tunes, riffs and beats, harmonies and overtones. Improvising musicians make similar choices spontaneously. Beethoven gained his reputation by being a master improviser. Making music is a highly mental process, whether you are thinking about it consciously or not. There is no disputing the genius of a Charlie Parker, Igor Stravinsky, or Frank Zappa.

Compositional choices fall into two general categories: texture and form.

TEXTURE

Music articulates the texture of time, similar to how the fabric arts manipulate physical textures. In many cases the sonic loom is threaded with the evenly spaced threads of a beat. Over that structure the weaver (performer) sends the strands of tone, rhythm, and melody. Choosing the colors, coarseness, and lengths of the threads determines the feeling of the entire piece of material. Over time we create a weaving of textures. Hopefully it will hold together, feel good, serve some purpose, or, like a signal flag in the wind, actually mean something. Let's imagine some musical textures, keeping our musical intelligence keyed into the various musical elements at play in each piece.

A simple folk melody sung to the chords of a harp, a kazoo band arrangement of "The Star Spangled Banner," the chaotic polyrhythms of a huge drum circle, the melodic counterpoint of Bach three-part inventions, the synthesized layers of techno dance music, the vibrant strings of bluegrass music, an accordion festival, a woman singing a lullaby to a sleeping child by the fire on a rainy night—these tapestries in sound are woven from strands of musical time qualities and have palpable textures in the temporal habitat. They resonate emotional feelings.

As the musical textures envelop us we are perhaps warmed by nostalgia, prodded with excitement, abraded by coarseness much to our dislike. Musicians use the wide range of elements we have examined to weave together a composition or performance. Performances induce feelings sometimes visceral. We say, "That music makes me sick!" Textures of musical time are in turn woven into the fabric of society. We see this in the pace of modern life, the luxuries of the West, the desperation of the Middle East.

FORM

Musical compositions also fall into categories called *forms*. Two instruments playing together express the *duet* form, for example. Formal categories can be grouped into styles, and eventually traditions. You can have a *string quartet* (form) in the avant-garde style of the Western tradition. The orchestral form is expressed through the centuries in many styles from the formalism of the Baroque (circa 1650–1750) to the polytonal expressionism of the twentieth century. The Balinese *gamelan* is an orchestral form as well. The *tradition* of the gamelan relies on master musicians retaining intricate and extended compositions in the mind. Their orchestral tradition is an oral one.

Traditions can have many styles and forms. Funk, be-bop, and swing are styles of music growing out of the blues tradition. Styles of pop music such as rhythm-and-blues, rock and roll, rap, and gospel also evolved from the blues tradition.

Traditions, styles, and forms have a genetic nature. They can blend, fuse, and die through time. African pop music is a rich mix of tribal traditions and Western styles. The music of Duke Ellington was a hybrid of the blues, jazz, and classicism. Every performance from the Stone Age hunting ritual to the latest number one hit is a result of individual human choices. These individual decisions cultivate the wonderful variety of musical forms through history. The evolution of music shows us how vital and long-lasting our intentions can be. Similarly, we create lifestyles through the forms and traditions of the culture we choose to express.

THE CULTURE-WHOLE

The collective resonance of any group—a family, town, nation, school, and so on—creates what the late writer, composer, and astrologer Dane Rudhyar terms the *culture-whole*. This concept refers to the predominant resonance of an entire culture or group. Related terms are *corporate culture, counter culture, popular culture, hip-hop culture,* and *drug culture.* All these labels speak to the notion that people of common interest create a certain pervasive style or personality that is institutionalized in some form.

All the notes add up to create the impact of the entire opera. Actions and intentions of many people co-create the overall identity of a given group. Putting a plan together demands a respect for the culture-whole in which your composition is to be performed. Don't even *think* about gangsta rap for the interlude at church.

When we say, "That guy really messed with my head," or, "That movie blew my mind," we are referring to our relationship with a culture-whole. The new invention, government program, or ad campaign harmonizes in some way with the culture-whole. As we work on our plans, it is a good idea to take into account how the culture-wholes around us might respond to the articulation of our dreams and visions. This is what "taking responsibility for your actions" is all about.

A musical composition alters the temporal dynamics of experience. It is a dream of how a time and a place ought to be. All of our plans, schemes, policies, and schedules are compositions. A rock and roll show in a huge stadium, a ritual dance, a gospel worship service, and a political convention are all group dreams designed and executed with musical intelligence. The business strategy, the U.S. Constitution, the fall TV lineup, the World Series, and your plans for dinner are all closely related. They are expressions of forms, styles, and traditions filling the resonant field of conscious activity permeating the culture-whole. As in musical performance, every composition in your culture-whole is unique and will never be expressed the same way again.

A dream becomes real when a composition is released into our midst through performance. In every culture there are musical forms and conventions that are based on ancient traditions, universal ratios, and deep mysteries of the heart and mind. Every new piece of music is a new leaf on the well-rooted tree of tradition.

The evolution of new forms can be seen as cultural difference tones, complex products of one wave of tradition interpenetrating another.

Music proceeds through time like the generations of a family. This genetic nature of music has become especially evident since the advent of recorded music. One can trace the elements of music evolving into new forms, generating new traditions. The tone of Robert Johnson's blues rings out in hip-hop. The tone of Jelly Roll's jazz resonates at the core of the acoustic fusion of David Grissman. Beethoven glares out from contemporary film music.

THE SIXTH CHAKRA: INTEGRATION

The mystic traditions of India and China picture a spot in the middle of the forehead where the all-seeing "third eye" peers out of the sixth chakra with uncompromising clarity. This is the Vedic symbol of all-knowing intelligence. It represents our powers of interpretation, creativity, synthesis, intuition, and inspiration—attributes that seem to take place in our head.

The brain and the mind are certainly not the same. The gray matter is only the upholstery on which the mind reclines. The mind is our instrument of design. It articulates the overtones of musical time entering the brain through the perceptions. In a spiritual sense, the third eye is the image of the human mind in atonement, constantly turned to the light of the divine mind. It is the direct channel to and from a higher awareness of divine form revealing itself at every turn. The rays of perception streaming from the sixth chakra are the strings on which all our great plans and botched schemes are woven.

As surely as the beat draws power from the earth, the many forms of musical time enter through the shimmering doors of perception in the mind. Our brain/mind is constantly filled with visions, voices, auras, and light. All these visitations just might be the shimmering presence of the gods.

Silence frames every composition. Every element of music (and the universe) begins and ends in silence. The infinite stillness between the stars holds all the energy radiating between them. Meditation is the path leading to the silent stillness of *the now moment,* the place where everything is happening but somehow remains in stillness. The third eye (sixth chakra) simultaneously sees and illuminates the Way.

Meditation is a great tradition of temporal composition refined into many styles and forms by great minds over the ages. The goal of meditation is to silence the constant chatter of the mind in order to let the essence of stillness fill our awareness. Meditation expresses a longing to experience the empty mind, the infinite space between our ears that holds every melody, every vision.

OVERTONES OF THE DIVINE

Every physical and temporal artifact is an expression of innate human attributes. The library is an extension of our memory. The robot is an extension of our hands. Music is an extension of consciousness, the awareness resonating throughout our body-mind. The chakras represent the structure of the harmony of divine consciousness. This is the source for the eternal nature of music. This is how appreciating music directly relates to the composition of an appreciative life. Music recreates in sound the overtones of consciousness.

Self-determination, personal identity, and "attitude" are resolutely expressed in the pounding beat and banter of rap (second chakra). There is a buoyant joy in gospel and reggae (fourth chakra). Complexity and craft resonate in the virtuosity of jazz and classical music (sixth chakra). By turning our attention to this deeper resonance we recognize the sacred power within every song, every smile, every jam session and journey. Formal musical education involves years of structured ear training where one learns to recognize many specific forms of all the musical elements. To live musically we must follow the musician's example and *listen and act at the same time.* The following exercise is your first venture into the listening half of composing a life.

Exercise 9: The Listening Half

Get a pencil and paper. Turn on the radio. Channel surf from one station to the next. Listen intently as the different musical selections float by. Listen carefully. Try to discern various musical elements at play. For example, in a classical selection listen for the predominance of harmony and melody. What is the picture the composer was trying to paint in sound? What overtones of consciousness does the music resonate? In a standard pop-rock selection, notice the power of the beat, the simplicity of the harmonies. What effect does this form have on the temporal habitat? What dreams are being *formalized* in the sound? Which element (or elements) predominate each selection? Write down the elements as they are revealed in each piece. If you have an idea of the tradition, style, or form of the selections, note that as well. Train your ear to recognize musical forms. In this way you lay the groundwork for recognizing the temporal forms and textures pervading all your experiences.

ELEMENT 7: INSPIRATION

In the wide-ranging and insightful book *The Magic of Tone and the Meaning of Music,* Dane Rudhyar points out that many spiritual traditions, including Hinduism and Judeo-Christianity, claim a cosmic sound to be the primordial, causative force. He distinguishes between the sounds we hear and this spiritual vibration, or *Sound,* that is continually manifesting all creation. The *aum* and the Word of God are primal forces activating everything of this world and worlds beyond. This is a spiritual interpretation of the principles of atomic and celestial resonance we discussed in chapter 1.

Rudhyar describes the operation of Sound in terms of seven octaves of process. These can be seen as: Implicit Unity, Explicit Duality (giving rise to all discreet identities), Empowerment, Connection (Harmony), Individualization, Understanding, and Transcendence. These principles correspond directly with physical attributes of the body-mind, the overtones of consciousness in the chakras, and the inherent meaning in the elements of music (figure 14, page 57).

Music transmits the overtones of Sound into our consciousness. In this way folk music resonates one version of Sound, capturing a certain spirit, while opera echoes another. Practicing a musical intelligence helps us appreciate our feelings and experiences as overtones of Sound. As we learn to compose a resonant life we become more loving to ourselves and attentive in all our relations.

Rudhyar also distinguishes between vibration and tone. Vibrations merely excite the auditory apparatus. Our earlier definition of noise is closely related to Rudhyar's notion of vibration. Tone, on the other hand, is for Rudhyar the power of certain vibrations to transmit the deeper resonance of the creative force, or

	Chakra	Quality of Consciousness	Musical Element	For Toning	
				Pitch	Sound
7	Crown	Spirit	Inspiration	Double Octave	yy
6	Third Eye	Insight	Form	7th	ee
5	Throat	Expression	Melody	Octave 5th	eh
4	Heart	Love	Harmony	Major 3rd	oo
3	Solar Plexus	Will	Tone	Octave	ah
2	Genital	Identity	Pattern	5th	oh
1	Root	Survival	Pulse	Root	uh

Figure 14: Correspondences Between Music and the Chakras.

Sound. Tone takes on different forms from culture to culture, and can change from age to age. The same exact pattern of vibrations takes on a different tone depending on the culture-whole in which they occur. The evolution of words out of ancient roots clearly demonstrates the evolution of this aspect of tone.

For example, the sound "allah" has powerful tone for the Moslem because it communicates deeply spiritual ideas. According to Islamic faith, the words of the Koran are the actual sounds of God's voice as revealed to the Prophet after a bear hug with the archangel Gabriel. In another culture the sound of "allah" may communicate something like, "I'll, uhhh . . . ," a completely different tone within a different culture-whole.

The cacophony of the Balinese Monkey Chant has a tone that effortlessly transports the Indonesian native into ecstasy. It can just as easily chase many a Westerner out of the temple. For Rudhyar, tone is the culturally accepted medium for Sound. Tradition and ritual go a long way in defining this type of tone from culture to culture. Note that tone in this sense is qualitatively different from the physical tones of music.

The elements of musical sound are the carrier waves for specific overtones of the creative Sound within our culture. For example, the beat resonates to the forces of spiritual unity, rhythms ring out the Sound of identity, harmony sings of connection and love. Every musical style plays up these qualities in its own way. The physical sounds of the musical elements resonate in different areas of our body, and the corresponding spiritual Sound reaches into our gut, heart, stories, and inspirations. Because we are alive we have the responsibility to be a resonating chamber for the divine Sound that imbues all existence.

Musical expression is the area where vibration, tone, and Sound align in perfect resonance. We revel in it. We celebrate it, record it, ritualize it, march it, dance it, sing it, hum it, chant it, and pray with it. If in the Beginning, the Word was God, then music is the breath of God. God put his breath into man and man was inspired. "Spirit" and "inspiration" come from the Latin *spirare,* meaning "to breathe." The evolving consciousness of the universe flows into our body-mind and we are inspired. We look up, close our eyes, and thank our lucky stars with a sigh.

The elements of music assemble around the flame of inspiration in the same way planets assemble around a star. The same breath of the divine invigorates every musical expression. The baby banging his or her toy on the crib is just as inspired as the jazz artist impeccably rendering a tune. They both breathe the aroma of the gods. The garage band, thrashing about in its culture-whole, is just as inspired as the New York Philharmonic in theirs.

As a songwriter and jazz player, my moments of inspiration are but fleeting glimpses, a sonic snapshot of the visage of spirit. When music becomes transcendent, and the crowd is stamping its feet, throwing money on the stage, and I can do no wrong, the physical world seems to become transparent, and I am in "the flow." I get the same feeling making love, playing with children, hiking in the woods, laughing my guts out, careening down a rapid. At these moments all is Sound.

As a species, we have been creating musical interpretations of the Sound since before we could talk. Our bodies, and the entire race, constitute instruments of Sound. We speak music as naturally as the crickets sing in the night. We are alive, imbued with pulsing, resonant energy. We have no choice. We are inspired.

THE SEVENTH CHAKRA: THE CROWN, THE HALO

If the beat lives in the butt, harmony in the heart, and form in the mind, inspiration must live close to us but slightly removed, dwelling in the human and spiritual realms at the same time. As breath passes through our pursed lips the winds of inspiration enflame us. The gateway for the breath of inspiration hovers over our head and whispers in our ear. I say inspiration is the halo, the crown chakra, and the doorway to heaven, that place we look to when we raise our eyes in awe, amazement, and relief.

Somehow, from just outside us, inspiration makes itself present. Rudhyar postulates that the great musical artist is merely the one that gets out of the way and lets the Sound descend into consciousness. The master composer transduces Sound directly into the culture-whole. This is why musicians are so highly revered. They channel the divine. They manifest resonance. The great composers are deemed immortal.

Look to the children. They hear the voices of spirit all around them. Everything is alive, at play, dancing, and singing. The child wears the halo unself-consciously. The innocence of children inspires us because they are living their dreams, open to the Sound of the flowers, susceptible to the terror of the nightmare. For the child, dreams are real. Inspiration is only a breath away.

Our hearts are touched when we hear children sing because we sense their love of the Sound. We pound our fist to the college fight song because we are swept away by the Sound of loyalty. Everyone experiences these spiritual waveforms. Don't look now. They are right above your head, just over your shoulder.

Put your attention on the seventh chakra. Plug into a high voltage, broadband link to the source of resonance. Put on your halo. Wear the crown of inspiration. Listen. The Sound is right there, singing in the dark, spinning in the night. If you listen closely you can here it humming in the waterfall, on the radio, in the teapot, in the wind, even in that darned accordion in the next apartment.

Exercise 10: Moving As One

Every mother says, "Stand up straight!" Well, mom's advice is well taken. Good posture is the first step in wearing your halo of consciousness.

Let's practice a variation on the walking meditation from chapter 1. Stand up and begin the slow walk, concentrating on the feeling of your feet touching the floor. Lengthen the back of your neck and relax your shoulders.

Imagine your halo, a shimmering ring about eight inches in diameter. It hovers directly over your head. As you move the halo moves with you. It sort of follows you around. It is part of you but not of you. Imagine its glow, its shining translucent luster. Imagine a current moving through the halo. The current runs in both directions, pouring down into you and rising up from you. With every pulse of your step, breath, and heartbeat you connect in silent conversation with the source of inspiration. The essence of your Self and the fathomless joy of Sound mingle in the golden circle of inspiration just above your head.

Part Two

THE HUMAN INSTRUMENT

3 THE ROOTS OF PERSONAL POWER

In his book The Wisdom of the Body, physician and educator Sherwin Nuland speaks of self-awareness of the body from a clinical point of view. In his experience as surgeon and physician he sees an awareness within the body that organizes and regulates the forces that constantly challenge our survival.

> I conceive of such an awareness as part of a continuum along which may be found qualities of sentience seamlessly linking the simplest to the most complex components of the entire organism, thus allowing information to pass between them. I have become convinced that some overall impression, an awareness, of the general pattern of cellular events and organization is transmitted upward through gradually increasing levels, until it imprints itself on our very patterns of interpreting external events and is influenced by, and are the reflection of, the conflict that exists within cells, between forces that would break them down and build them up.

The "general pattern of events and organization" of which Nuland speaks strikes me as the same resonant display we see in light, hear as music, sense in the turning of the seasons, and feel pounding in our chests. The "qualities of sentience" Nuland perceives in the working of the human body I see revealed in the fabric of the entire world, and especially in the workings of music. The patterns of organization reveal themselves again and again to be variations on principles of resonance. The inner resilience of an atom is released in a nuclear chain reaction. The internal tension of a string is revealed in the tone generated by striking it. The strivings of the human mind are manifested through invention and literature. I feel that every one of these systems displays a certain form of intention, an internal predisposition of lasting effect. In these terms, atoms, cells, ecosystems, and influenza are embodiments of the same patterns that sustain the human body. In the case of the human body-mind, the presence of pattern, self-regulation, adaptation, and innovation reveals awareness, consciousness, and love.

Ecology studies the harmony between all the elements of the environment, living and inanimate alike. Dead matter is viewed as not so dead as it may seem. Just because a chunk of stone lacks big brown eyes doesn't stop it from being part of a living, throbbing biosphere.

Elemental matter exhibits the sentient qualities of increasing complexity often reserved for human "progress." Born out of the cosmic furnace, matter evolves into more and more complex structures through the explosion and reexplosion of stars. Move four or five supernovas down the cosmic timeline and what started off as simple hydrogen transforms into all the complex elements. The raw material of the universe is just as intent on complex structure as we seem to be.

Life emerged from an eddy in the current of matter, space, and time, where the greenhouse membrane of the atmosphere held in the energy of the sun. The so-called raw material had qualities of sentience that took advantage of the situation. Tom Robbins says, "Life is what water invented so it could get around."

The "opposing forces" of which Nuland speaks are at play not only on the cellular level of growth and decay, but at every level in the hierarchy of existence. Stars are born out of the forces of gravity, and they die as the exploding novas. Volcanic rock is born from the roiling depths of the earth and then is slowly broken down by the steady grinding of the elements, which are driven by the turning of the earth. The life of plants and animals runs on the alternating current generated by night folding into day. Like the binary code of the computer generating all the marvels of virtual reality, the inhabitants of actual reality are permutations of the simple on-and-off of opposites. Either the current is on or off. The river flows, or the streambed is dry. There is silence or music. When we play music we are either on the beat or "out of time."

Human beings stand midway between the grind and decay of the animal world and the realm of spirit and ideas. Muscles and organs crave gratification. At the same time, mind and soul search for meaning and inspiration. In this search we always seem to raise our eyes, look up, and sigh. Our body and mind acknowledge the World Above. Each individual is a string on the harp of humanity. One end of our string is tied securely to the earth and the other is anchored in the realm of spirit. Our musical intelligence gives us tools to compose ourselves in harmony with the overtones of our own fundamental resonance singing in the chakras.

So far, we have examined the fundamental patterns of resonance in the natural world and warmed up our musical intelligence. We are ready to use our new familiarity with musical time qualities as a guide to physical and emotional health, directly applying ourselves to the joy and discipline of composing a musical life, linking our patterns in a dance of entrainment with the powerful rhythms of the earth. The body-mind is your instrument in this performance. Accepting and articulating the resonant nature of your musical Self is the highest manifestation of the Sound that fills all time and space.

The chakras serve as our structure for this work. They are both receptors and generators of resonance. Like the atomic elements and the elements of music, the chakras do not act independently. There is constant interplay between the overtones of consciousness. Just as overtones in a string determine the quality of the tone, overtones in the chakras act in concert to influence personality and behavior. As a general plan we will move from the first through the seventh chakra just as we did in the preceding chapter, but now the compositional interplay begins. The energy of one chakra will be seen to influence the intonation of another.

THE PULSE OF LIFE

Soon after conception a special group of cells differentiate in the growing embryo. These cells are especially sensitive to gravity and they work to correctly orient the embryo in relation to the earth's pull. This group of cells eventually becomes the organs of equilibrium and hearing, giving us the perceptual tools to orient our body in space. From the very beginning our relationship with gravity is linked to the perception of sound. Tuned by the hand of gravity, the body is played like a harp, every tendon and bone growing under the touch of Mother Earth.

In the beat of music we hear the clucking of her tongue, telling us to keep our feet planted firmly on the ground. Accordingly, our first lesson will be to align the body with the forces of gravity. The basic beat grabs our attention in such a visceral way because it is in direct communication with the first chakra, the receptor for the pulse of survival consciousness.

Every overtone of awareness rides on the fundamental knowledge that we will die and our time will come to an end. Boom. Boom. Out go the lights. The stark, blank timelessness of the pulse embodies the beginning and end, the first step and the last, the cradle and the grave. Like points in mathematical space, the pulse marks out a series of points in time. The music, however, always happens *between* the beats. This is true in life as well. Our life span is the time we occupy between birth and death. Our survival consciousness in the first chakra senses this primal pulse of life and death in every step we take, and sends that beat pounding through our awareness.

In many cultures the unadorned pulse is intentionally used in rituals to resonate a deep, mesmerizing awareness in the listener. The beat of the shaman's drum links the individual to the life-and-death rhythms of nature. Many Native American songs are sung to a drum and rattle beat with no accent or meter per se. The trance-inducing drum of the Inuit is played in a driving, undifferentiated pulse. It serves as a bridge to the spirit world. The beat is the intermediary between the tribe, the land, and the afterlife.

Many of the most popular music forms stress the hard beat. Dixieland, swing, the blues, rock, rap, and techno dance music ride squarely on a wave locked into the irresistible pull of gravity. Classical forms give us many examples of the power of the beat as well. The quasi-ritualistic music of Stravinsky's *Rite of Spring* establishes raw pulse as the final altar on which the rite is played out. "Rite," "rhythm," and "river" all come from an ancient linguistic root meaning "to flow."

Every piece of music has its own perfect tempo. And every expression of life has its perfect pace. Let the beat grab you every chance you get. Listen for the tempo when you are chopping cabbage, digging in the garden, rocking a baby, stomping angrily up the stairs. Tempo determines the character of a piece of music. Our personal energy level is our expression of the tempo of life.

Some friends and I held a jam session after work. John, a roofer, said he had never played music. He was hesitant to join in. I gave him a bass drum and a big mallet and encouraged him to pound out the beat to the blues as if he were pounding nails. The jam cranked up, and John locked on the tempo, lowered his head, and dug in. The final bars brought us to a solid, raucous ending. John was completely beside himself. The next week we saw him up on a roof. Beaming down to us, he gestured with his hammer as if pounding that old drum. In the resonance between the drum and his hammer John composed his life. To compose a life one must be sure to practice the variations in the tempo of the times.

WALK THE WALK

Learning to walk is the first great independent action we take. The toddler's footfall is the initial expression of a separate, fully mobile, conscious being, no longer the captive of gravity. We establish a deeply resonant relationship with our environment through the cycle of pulling ourselves away from and falling back into gravity's arms. We push away from Mother Earth, and then we are pulled back. With every step this victory over gravity generates joy in the dancer and the gamboling child. Movement is life. The beat gets us moving! Follow the lead of the toddler grinning ear to ear. Walk! Feel the lively bounce of the earth beneath your feet. "Human" comes from a Greek root meaning "to touch the ground."

THE FIRST CHAKRA: PACING

Our connection with gravity pivots on the first chakra at the base of the spine. From the first hesitant step to the tumble into the grave we move over the earth from here. It is the fulcrum of our survival. We move or we perish. The joys of independence, the fear of falling, and our obsession with death are alive and drumming right here. You can feel the beat of these drums in your pelvis as you walk down the street. Watch your step!

   Walks can be some of the most precious moments of life. To a great extent the tempo of your steps—and your life—determines the quality of the experience. Pacing is the first lesson in the articulation of musical time. As the pulse of your steps fills your body on your walks, remember that it's only a matter of time when your foot will rise no more and gravity will have the final say. There is a best time for rushing. There is a perfect time for standing still. Walk with attention and remember the emotional resonance. Every step could be your last. With this awareness the quality of the moment takes precedence over the tyrannical ticking of the clock.

The pace of an experience is a primary defining factor in our emotional response. The composer chooses the desired tempo for the composition. We can do the same in our day-to-day expression of our musical intelligence. Every situation has tempo. Straining against the flow can easily lead to frustration. On the other hand, applying the well-timed push can save a situation from disaster. In our practice of the art of pacing we start with the beat of our own steps upon the earth.

Exercise 11: Tempo Tour

Go for a walk with the idea of intentionally playing with the tempo. Try dawdling on purpose. Take extra-long strides, hang back, and then rush ahead. Kids love this game! Educate yourself and youngsters on the variety of the pace of things. Play! What do all the various gaits and combinations of paces feel like? What does it feel like to rush? To flee? To meander? To gawk? To pause and sigh? Pick a spot and race to it. Pick another, and another. The tempo of the times is yours to create.

Exercise 12: Creekside Dance

Jog in place. Keeping the jogging tempo, get up a little higher on the toes and prance around the room. Now simultaneously slow the tempo down and lengthen your stride. Imagine you are hopping from rock to rock in a dangerous, rushing stream. Imagine the rocks getting smaller. The water is deep. One false step and . . .

The rocks are getting farther and farther apart. Take a little more time deciding where to hop next. Keep on slowing down. Hold your balance. Don't fall! You're hopping slowly from rock to rock, wider and wider, slower and slower. The danger mounts. You have no idea what lurks beneath the rushing water.

Now quickly jump to solid ground. Fall into the original jogging tempo. Notice the contrast between these two tempos. The emotional meaning of these two situations is generated by *the harmony between your pace and your task.*

THE BREATH PULSE

The pulse symbolizes the Beginning and the End, the Alpha and the Omega. The ceaseless pulse of life and death moves through us with every breath. The ability to control the pulse of the breath is our single most powerful survival skill. Breathing fully and energetically revitalizes the body and mind. Being out of breath is oppressive, and at times can actually be scary. The breath pulse is our closest rhythmic link to the joy of life and the fear of death. When we are fully inflated with air we are confident, invigorated, buoyant. When all the air has been knocked out of us we suffocate. We are pounded and buried. When we no longer draw breath we expire.

When we fill our lungs to bursting we feel a wave of energy, a rush of power and light. When we empty them completely (gasp! help!) we glimpse the black vacuum of the End. On a deep level we realize death lurks at the end of every breath. The consciousness of survival (biological sentience) rises from our first chakra and the life force literally inspires us with every breath we take.

Breath is the cornerstone of most meditative practices. Articulation of the breath in synchrony with bodily movement develops a deep resonance that touches every cell. Through nerve pathways in the hypothalamus and pituitary gland in the brain, the metabolic rate of every cell is tied directly to the amount of oxygen in the bloodstream. When we synchronize our voluntary actions with the autonomic functions of breath, the entire body-mind is in synchrony.

Physical training links the breath to the rhythms of exercise. Through diligent mental focus the athlete aligns the intentions of the higher brain functions with the autonomic functions of heart, breath, and metabolism. Professional dancers are amazing athletes in this manner. The exertion levels are incredibly high, and yet the most gymnastic of moves look effortless. Their control of the breath is a key to the power of their expression. They make it look like the dance could go on forever!

The power of breath to transform our body-mind rides on the harmony between chakras. The pulse of the breath is tied to survival awareness (first chakra). We use our will power (third chakra) to manipulate the breath, changing the metabolic pace of the entire body. The first and third overtones of consciousness mix in this intentional articulation. We can instantly change the impact of any experience through an intentional resonance of the breath.

The body and mind are intricately networked. Through bioelectric and hormonal functions, the thalamus, hypothalamus, and pituitary gland have great influence over emotional resonance. Body and mind influence each other through this complex switchboard apparatus at the center of our brain. When the body is engaged in any sort of rhythmic activity, especially deep breathing, the thalamus puts the entire body and mind on alert. Let's use the connection between breath and our emotions to get a clearer picture of our first chakra survival-oriented awareness of death.

Exercise 13: Death Watch

Stand erect with neck long, shoulders relaxed. Breathe in slowly through the nose. Imagine the air pouring into your lungs, filling you from the belly on up. When your lower lungs are filled, slowly expand your chest, keeping the shoulders relaxed. Inhale completely and hold your breath. You should get a bit of a "head rush," that slightly ecstatic lightheaded feeling.

Now purse your lips and push out all the air. Pump the last bits of air out with your diaphragm. Exhale completely, lock your throat, and hold your breath. Stand there and wait. Keep waiting.

Soon you will hear two overtones of consciousness talking loud and clear. One says, "Ahhh! I'm full and satisfied!" But soon another voice pipes up, saying, "Hey! Get real! Cut this out! Who's fooling whom!?" But *do* hold on. Wait until your dance-or-die nature is screaming at the edge, teetering over the void. Take a look into the Dark Side before you gasp for breath. The tempo of our breath is the metronome of our survival consciousness. Controlling the breath literally gives us conscious power over life and death.

THE SECOND CHAKRA: AGILITY, STAMINA, AND JOY

In Tom Robbins' novel *Jitterbug Perfume*, one of the keys to immortality was the performance of a dance practiced only in a remote corner of Argentina. The hero was on a quest to learn this dance at the source. He danced every step on his way, preparing himself for the grand instruction. It seemed to help. At the close of the book he was over seven hundred years old and still on his way. The hero got the message loud and clear: dance or die.

Dancing is a way of life for the very young. Kids don't just run into grandpa's arms, they leap. They don't walk to bed, they trudge. Charged up with anticipation or hot chocolate a child will spontaneously perform choreography spirited enough to make any ballerina sigh with envy. Remembering how to dance like a child is the next lesson for our musical intelligence.

The joy of a child's gambol through life springs from the unabashed announcement of personality through play. The dancelike body language of the youngster at play speaks in declarative statements in time. As she marches into the restaurant, the four-year-old says, "I'm hungry, happy, and I know *exactly* what I want to eat!" The natural dance language of the child is the precursor to all the physical articulations of our personality.

Psychological tones are revealed through subtle variations in everyone's step. The romp of the child, the lilt of the young lover, and the stately gait of the distinguished gentleman are all dances of a sort, each an improvised expression of how we got here and what we might expect up ahead.

We are what we do. Our temporal artifacts fill our inner life and outer experiences with the tone of our identity and personality. A different step, schedule, pace, or habit will profoundly change the musical time quality for everybody. This is why some situations can be a real drag, or an incredible rush. Practicing a new and perhaps challenging gait, cycle, or pattern in your days will change the quality of your life.

Transform every time you can into *playtime*. Give yourself an extra five minutes and stroll to the bus instead of dash. Stalk your lost car keys. Jitterbug your mate to bed. When you're feeling fatigued, make like a ninety-year-old man and really hobble to the couch. Let your sense of play modulate your habits into a new way of getting from here to there. Don't be shy. Play on! Express the many dances waiting to be released from your pelvic region. Get a new appreciation for a richer, sexier you. You'll walk through a new world, a new time habitat, exploring your personality step by step, dance by dance.

One shift in the interior resonance of an atom alters the reactivity and character of the atom. One gene can make a huge difference in the health or appearance of an animal. Small changes in the rhythmic patterns of music change one style into another. A rest here, a new note there, and a song morphs into a new song. An accidental discovery can cause a quantum leap in knowledge.

The consciousness of personal identity swirls in the second chakra and manifests as our sense of self as separate from all others. Sexuality, ego, and personality are expressed on this dance floor of the temporal habitat. But whether we know it or not, we always have dance-mates. We are not alone in the composition of life. All around us the pace and pattern of our environment cocreates the steps with us. We can't safely charge through a crowded room. Sauntering is not the best choice when fire threatens. The patterns we express harmonize with everything around us. We demonstrate response-ability to our musical natures when we listen and act accordingly, striving for appropriate harmony at every moment.

Rhythmic pattern is the basis for our most productive activities. Aerobic dance, martial art forms, sports plays, and team activity are very dancelike. We can use rhythmic awareness to tune our exercise to the natural resonance of our body. In this way our physical exercise becomes an articulation of our intentions to enhance our identity and personality through our actions.

We have seen how the spaces between steps and breaths hold different meaning. Now we will use the musical intelligence of the second chakra to co-create healthful patterns in our quest for agility, stamina, and joy, dancing with the rhythms all around us. Here is an exercise that can be done anywhere. It will help develop a dancer's approach to movement. Keep part of your attention on how this feels emotionally. We choose the dances we take through life. Any situation can be a real "ball" if you are with the music and you've got your moves down.

Exercise 14: Content/Context

Make up a simple phrase. For example: "Walking down the road." Repeat this phrase several times and perform a repetitive gesture that moves in exact time with the phrase. Tap your finger, swing your arms, and shake your head with a smile on your face. Personalize the phrase. Now you are dancing! Repeat the same phrase with a different gesture. Try these two dances at different tempos. Repeat this exercise with other phrases using more and more of your body. Pay attention to how the various movements make you feel. The rhythm and content stay the same, but a different context of experience is generated through the different gestures you use.

As the pulse of your day streams by, you make a new dance every moment. The demands of any one time or the other go a long way in shaping your most agile dance. Tune in. You can feel the ease (or stress) of your steps. You can alter a step here and there. Throw in a pause, a turn, and a skip. Your best intentions should be expressed repeatedly through productive gestures.

STAMINA

Music has always been used to increase stamina. Work songs from around the world are part of every musical heritage. Remember the Hollywood image of the drummer in front of the galley slaves? The military drum cadence sets the platoon on the march. Every aerobics teacher uses music to motivate the class. Music helps to orchestrate the subtle cycles of tensing and relaxing our muscle groups. And there are always places in the flow of the music where we can rest a bit. A musical approach to exercise can give us added stamina. We can use simple rhythms in our head in this regard.

I live in the hills of northern California and do a fair amount of biking to stay in shape. From the moment I get on the bike, I try to make my exercise a dance. I link my breath pulse to a set number of pumps on the pedals. By changing the gears, or slightly altering the tempo of my breathing, I can maintain this resonance for nearly an hour of continuous aerobic pumping. For variety—and a bit of a rest now and then—I switch to more or less pumps per breath. For example, at times I will breathe in for two pumps, then out for three. This sets up an asymmetrical flow, alternating inhalations from one foot to the other. There's a loony balance in this compound meter.

When my breath is full and I am working hard but not struggling I feel completely in sync with my body, the mountain, gravity, and the wind. Lungs, legs, arms, and back are all dancing to the tune called out by the breath. The most direct expression of my will to live ("Keep breathing!") links with the dance I am intent on performing and I am carried to a point where the body is in sublime communication with raw energy. When I lose the synchrony, when one part of my body falls out of step, it is very apparent to me that I'm working a lot harder. I feel like I'm working against myself.

Linking the timing of the breath to demanding physical exercise creates a dance. The consciousness of universal intent at the third chakra pumps energy into the center of rhythmic pattern at the second. Physical power increases. Your sense of personal accomplishment soars. A fiery source of stamina is awakened and can be applied in any demanding situation. Dance or die.

Exercise 15: Walk on the Wild Side

Let's get the first, second, and third chakra going. Put on a good pair of shoes and take a power walk. The physical dance of a power walk is basically a stride. Take steps slightly longer than normal. Posture is firm and erect. The key to good posture is to firmly but gently lengthen the back of your neck, pulling your entire spine in alignment with gravity. Engage and support the muscles in your lower torso. Pump your arms a bit to reinforce the tempo of your step. The tempo is *poco vivace,* a little fast but not too fast. Feel your toes pushing off the pavement. Breathe in deeply through the nose, out through the mouth. Take five strides for each inhalation, and five for each exhalation.

Try to keep the tempo steady. If you run out of breath, change the dance to four strides per breath, or three. If you tire with three strides per breath, slow your tempo down a bit. Tune your movements and breath for the optimum balance between exertion and exhilaration.

JOY

The essence of play is a relaxed and elegant physical expression of personality. Musicians, athletes, and children are at play most of the time. Lucky them. Everybody else is supposed to work more than play. The boss expects those eight hours at work to be serious. Playtime is seen as wasted time. No wonder our workaday world creates such tension. For hours a day we have little opportunity to actually express ourselves in the most natural, musical manner.

The beauty of playing music with other people is in the harmony. Musicians revel in the interplay between instruments. Everyone knows that his or her voice is an integral part of the whole. Personality and self-expression are the vehicles for both communication and a love of the shared moment. Children and sports team members show the same consciousness. Game players are part of the action of the whole: involved, accepted, and honored. At work we tend to lose our identity. Our personality gets subsumed into the corporate culture. Tasks are more important than the people.

We need techniques for expressing ourselves clearly and joyfully in different situations. We need to remember to play. Repetition is the first order of organization in music. Repeated patterns establish form and styles of expression. Musical styles and traditions have certain *habits.* Our life is a symphony of habits. The more we pay attention to our patterns of behavior the clearer will we perceive our identity.

Exercise 16: Your Habit Habitat

Pick a small habit you would like to break. Keep it modest, not too ambitious. Write that down. Next, imagine a habit you would like to acquire. Drinking more water? Stretching more often? Write that down. Now practice. Set a *specific* time during your day to carry out the new habit. As you do, imagine it replacing the file in your brain that houses the bad habit. Don't try to give up the old habit. Just replace it with the intention for the new.

It is important to remember that desires are different from intentions. Just as the sounds of music reveal the inner tensions of strings, taut lips, and strong vocal chords, our actions reveal our inner qualities and passions. Intentions are made real through actions. Desires are fantasies that may never make it to the surface. Dreams only make it to the level of intention when you start working on them.

Just like learning a song, establishing a new habit takes time. You are moving intentions from your upper consciousness down into the body and out to the ends of the limbs where we do the work. Be patient. The key is to use your musical intelligence to pace your new habits. Don't go any faster than you can handle. Practice success, but stick to your intentions, and visualize the good habits filtering in and replacing the old.

DANCERS, LOVERS

Besides being the storehouse for our genetic material, the second chakra is the center of the spinning wheel of sexual consciousness. Balance in this sensitive area is crucial to health and joyful self-expression. Sexual health results from holding a loving intent as the dominant tone for relationships with others. This intent is like a musician cueing his or her every action to the pulse, pitch center, or keynote of a composition, the points of reference holding the composition in resonance.

With the eye of the poet, a loving intent can be observed in nature. The moon loves the sea. We see this loving intent as the waves dance on the shore. The rain loves the earth. The bursting spring reveals this love with flowers. Symmetry and beauty are overtones of the consciousness of relationship we sense in every bond in nature. Everything is held together from the fulcrum of love, silent and immovable at the center of every relationship. Love for another human is the deepest experience of relationship we have. The sexual bond stirs up the joyful expectation that every action can be imbued with a vibrant dancelike nature. Tune in! Feel love at work in every cell of your body. Breathe deep. Feel the red corpuscles ecstatically in love with the oxygen you pull into your lungs. The essence of love is a deep awareness of relationship.

As we fall in love we effortlessly reinforce the best in our partner, and celebrate our own best intentions at the same time. Falling is effortless. We release ourselves into the silky and buoyant waters. We are in constant relationship with our inner self and all that swirls about us. We live in constant reverberation. People truly make love—create a new flower of consciousness—when they interact with the highest of mutual intentions for healing and celebration. This visceral and transcendent joy is felt in the sounds of the best music, and in the rush and tumble of sex that truly generates (makes) love.

With practiced attention we can hear the undertone created when two musical tones sound together. As we hone our attention to the tone and melody of our partner—or any relation—the more evident the intricate counterpoint becomes. The exhilaration of love comes from creating something beautiful outside of us in concert (and consort) with another. Being in love is two souls losing themselves in the harmony *between* them.

Everybody has different patterns of eating, rest, and activity. And so everyone and every couple has optimum sexual rhythms and variations of expression. Since a sex life is a kind of third entity conceived, grown, and maintained by both partners, the basic rule for sexual harmony is the same as is music: always listen as hard as you play. The harmony generated between the two soul-tones is your love life. Loving relationships are all about who's leading, who's following, and knowing when that doesn't make any difference. The following exercise is a variation on follow-the-leader.

Exercise 17: Dancing Together

Variation 1: Stand opposite your partner. Say your partner's name while taking a few steps away from him or her, being as playful, coy, or downright lewd as you like. Stop and turn to your partner. The partner, moving toward you, mimics your actions, taking the steps, calling out "Coming!" Repeat this five times with the widest range of movement and inflection as you can manage. Reverse roles.

Variation 2: Improvise with who is the leader. If you want to take the lead, simply call your partner's name rather than "Coming!" Grab the lead away quickly. Or stay with the "Coming!" response again and again.

Variation 3: Repeat Variation 1, moving as close together as you can. As the leader, every now and then say, "Coming!" at the same time with your partner, repeating the same movement and vocal tones several times in unison. Get really close for these repetitions. Perhaps include shedding articles of clothing in this dance.

THE THIRD CHAKRA: WILL POWER, MUSCLE TONE, AND TONING

We now move up to the area of the body that joins the earthbound consciousness of step-by-step survival with the heart, mind, and spirit. The third chakra humming between the navel and the lower ribs is the seat of our free will. Spinning in the solar plexus this overtone of consciousness is the most easily accessed and articulated because energy moves through the third chakra with every breath we take. All physical activity—including playing a musical instrument and danc-ing—springs from here. Firm abdominal muscles guard against backache. Good posture begins here. And the breath gets its depth and power from this area.

The third chakra symbolizes the consciousness of personal power. We have a great responsibility. We must balance the power of our own personality with those all around us. Greed, laziness, gluttony, and anger emanate from here. So do generosity, motivation, physical endurance, and acceptance. More than any other area in the body-mind, physical balance is the crucial skill to develop here. To be responsible to the earth, our community, and our own physical and mental health, the needs of the body and mind must be harmonized. We need to appreci-ate our place in the orchestra and play well. Becoming aware of the consequences of our actions is the first step.

In a musical group many times there are players who overpower others or players who won't step up and express themselves. One section of the band may listen only to itself, oblivious to the harmony of the whole. Music demands that we listen and act *in accordance*. Balance at the third chakra insures that we do not overpower our neighbor or underplay ourselves. We must blow our own horn *and* listen for the echo. We sing our part and tune into the sweet undertones of harmony. We turn on the juice and watch the sparks. Let's turn the light on in your third chakra and watch the show.

Exercise 18: Conducting Yourself Properly

Stand up. Plant your feet shoulder-width apart. Breathe in through your nose. Fill up your lower chest cavity so that your diaphragm is slightly distended. Exhale fully. Be sure to relax your shoulders and chest.

Inhale. As you do, imagine a beam of willful energy beginning to shine out of your solar plexus. Direct the beam to a specific spot in your vision. Project this beam as you exhale. It's like you are throwing a ball of energized will power out to the door, wall, tree, or whatever. Inhale. Focus on your object and draw the energy back. Catch it in another chakra, say the third eye or the heart. Hold the energy in that new place as you exhale once more. Repeat the cycle.

Now repeat the exercise. As before, the energy builds in your solar plexus/third chakra, *but before you send out the energy, route it through another chakra.* For example, feel your willful energy rising to your heart and then extending out into the world. Then draw the energy back into the same chakra. Take another breath into the solar plexus and send it out through another chakra. Keep in mind the overtones of consciousness active at each chakra. Willfully send out the tone of love (fourth chakra), self-expression (fifth chakra), survival (first chakra), and so on. As you draw the energy back to your chosen chakra, *feel the special tone of that chakra filling your entire body-mind.*

Whether we know it or not the overtones of our consciousness are always being projected into our surroundings. The energizing force for our entire body-mind is the third chakra consciousness, a spiral of power emanating from the solar plexus. Our will power, the juice behind our intentions, is generated here. Intentions are like psychic muscle tone: healthy ones keep us attentive, flexible, and ready for action. Unhealthy ones make us mentally flabby or obnoxiously dissonant like a poorly tuned instrument. We are constantly in relation in this manner. We say, "I didn't like his vibe," or "Man, that guy has a lot of guts!" These are direct reflections of personal tone impacting the surroundings from the third chakra.

Stress results from dissonance in the resonant systems of the body-mind. When a violinist puts too much pressure on the strings with his or her bow, a scratchy, atonal rasp is produced. If we do not manage our energy well we "rub people the wrong way" or suffer "burnout." Our physical and mental resonance can go out of whack. Music is our model for a discipline of joy. As we learn to act and feel at the same time the effects of our "vibes," our music, become clear. The next activity channels this crucial musical intention into every part of your body.

The first great swami to teach meditation techniques on a wide scale in the West was Paramahansa Yogananda. In his classic book *Autobiography of a Yogi,* he chronicles his path as a student and teacher of self-realization. One of his techniques shows us how we can experience and focus the creative will of the universe every day. This is a great way to wake up.

Exercise 19: Yogananda's Wake-up Call

When you wake in the morning, turn over on your back. Put your arms next to your sides. Take a few deep breaths, open your eyes wide, and blow the air out quickly between loosely pursed lips. Close your eyes and breathe in slowly and fully through your nose. Feel your diaphragm lift below your rib cage as you fill the lungs from the bottom up.

As you inhale, picture the divine will of nature as a column of light entering through your solar plexus. Exhale, keeping the vision of a pool of warm energy in your belly. Repeat three times.

Keep breathing in this manner, picturing the descending light. With each breath you will now begin to gently tense and then relax areas of your body. Start with your right foot. Try not to flex or extend any other part of your body. Tense your foot on the inhalation. Relax on the exhalation. You are filling the muscle groups around your foot with the tone of intention entering through your third chakra.

Continue in this manner all the way up your body. Tense your left foot. Right calf. Left calf. Right thigh. Left thigh. Then the whole right leg and left leg, and so on. As you breathe out, visualize a current of will power streaming from your solar plexus into the area you are working. Move through your arms, abdominals, chest, neck, and head. Try to isolate each body part, directing the stream of divine will as it enters and becomes yours. Finally tense the entire body three times.

Open your eyes wide, looking slightly up, and complete the exercise with three more breaths without tensing your muscles, deeply relaxing into the warm reservoir of will swirling in your power center. Rise out of bed in one slow and deliberate motion. Stand erect with shoulders relaxed, neck long. Take three more breaths from the diaphragm, envisioning the power of willful intention filling your body-mind.

MUSICAL MUSCLE TONE

Tone is expressed by releasing the inner tension available in a resonant system. In a musical instrument, a preexisting inner tension is required for tone to be produced. For example, a string is stretched between two points on a fret board, the trumpeter's lips are held taut behind the mouthpiece, and vocal chords are controlled as the air passes over them.

The characteristics of the musical apparatus—string, lip, and vocal muscles—determine how much tension, or load, is needed to bring tone into a given system. Slack inner tension limits the instrument's ability to produce a resonant tone. Too much inner tension and the string breaks, the lip cracks, the voice grunts. Between these two extremes lies a balanced range of tension between all the internal stresses of the instrument, bringing material and force into dynamic equilibrium. Within this range, the instrument is said to *have* tone. It is from this balanced state that any instrument—including the human instrument—releases the magic of tone, the emotion and meaning expressed from the overtones of consciousness spinning in the chakras.

Imagine your skeleton as the frame of an intricate harp. Muscles are strung like strings over this frame. Similar to the tone inherent in the silent guitar string, good muscle tone results from the inner tension of a muscle at rest. Flabby, slack muscles with little definition and slow response are like a loose string on a guitar.

This image of the string is a valuable model for the practice of developing muscle tone. Stretching will bring tautness and tone to your muscles, much like turning the tuning pegs gives tone to the guitar string. Fat content is reduced, metabolism is improved, and nerve response is heightened. The autonomic connection between your will power and your physical apparatus is polished. Reaction time and stamina are improved.

The harpist tunes his or her instrument one string at a time. The more we focus our intentions on individual muscle groups the more responsive the whole system becomes. You can accelerate the development of muscle definition and strength by learning to feel each muscle group at a time. With this growing awareness you can literally feel each group just as a skilled listener can point out the different instruments in an orchestra. Each muscle plays its own well-defined part in expressing the glorious music of the body in motion.

In Yogananda's wake-up exercise our energy was focused in an almost passive manner. What follows are exercises designed to heighten our awareness of third chakra intention *in action.* These techniques can be applied to any exercise regimen, be it classical Hatha Yoga, aerobics, high-tech machine-assisted workouts, or the daily movements of cleaning your kitchen or flipping the charts in the board room. Everything can be done with athletic intent.

The following exercise gives the general approach in the tuning of your muscle-and-tendon harp. Once you've learned the rudimental technique you will be able to apply the skills to every athletic composition you perform.

Exercise 20: Lines of Force

Stand up with your legs shoulder-width apart and your right hand stretched up over your head, your upper arm next to your ear. Keep your neck long and relaxed. Attach an imaginary string from the palm of your hand to the point of your right hip.

Keeping your legs and hips stationary and solid, gently reach up and over your head to the left, increasing the tension on the "string." Concentrate on keeping your right hip rock solid, down and away from the upward-pointing arm. At the same time stretch your hand as far away from your hip as it will go just short of pain.

Strike a balance between bending to the left and keeping the imaginary string taut. Do not collapse your left side, but lengthen it as the string stretches. Feel the lines of will power moving along the muscles connecting your right hand and hip. You will feel a delicious stretch all the way from your wrist to your hip. Maintain the tautness of muscle tone as you return to the upright position. Slowly decrease the tension on the string until your arm relaxes to your side. Repeat on the other side.

Start again. This time attach the string to your right ear with your arm completely relaxed at your side. As you lean, keep the string running taut up the side of your neck. Stretch that ear away from your hip. Keep close attention to the widening space between your ear and the point of the shoulder. Do not just drop your head over to the left; gently but firmly stretch up and over. Complete the exercise on both sides.

This time attach the string in your armpit. The stretch runs up your side. Remember that the string must be firmly attached at both ends. Keep your hips solid and firm. Do not shift your pelvis. Try attaching your imaginary string to your bottom rib. In this configuration you will feel your abdominals working hard to put tone into that string of muscles. Your attention is focused on a smaller area. Each change in intention cues a different set of muscles, a different tuning of the harp.

The benefits of this stretching practice run deep. You gain strength and flexibility. On another level you gain true inner awareness as you begin to acquire a clear picture of your interior landscape. With practice you will be able to isolate many muscle groups in your body, stretching them from tendon to tendon over the harp-frame of your skeleton. Aches and pains become manageable. In the same way a musician gains control over his or her instrument you will develop control of your body. You will learn how to feel and direct your healthy intentions directly from the center of your will out into your entire body.

TONING: ACCESSING A SPIRITUAL BODY OF SOUND

"Chant" comes from the same cognate as "enchant," the casting of a spell. Vocal toning is a discipline of enchantment that uses the resonant nature of your body as the magic wand.

Honored since the first ritual around the fire, the power of sound carries humans into a time field full of magic and spirit. Practicing sustained tone in a focused, ritualized context can give anyone access to the enduring resonance of the divine Sound, aligning our free will with the greater intentions of the universe.

There are many toning systems available to us. Among these are classical Hindu mantra, Tibetan throat singing, and systems based on the diatonic scale (white notes on the piano). These systems are rooted in honored traditions and are certainly valid, but they do not take into consideration the inherent *instrumental* qualities of the human body. The toning system I employ is drawn from the physical and spiritual resonance innate in the structure of the body-mind itself.

Like any instrument, the human body has resonant frequencies. Specific tones fit inside the cavities of every body. The pitch of the trumpet is higher than that of the trombone. It follows that a small human body has a basic resonant frequency higher than that of a larger person. The head, chest, and abdominal and pelvic cavities are set into resonance by the voice just like the soundboard of a piano is set into resonance by the vibrating strings.

Sing a low "ohhhhhh" and feel the tone in your belly. Squeal an "eeeee" and your throat and head vibrate to that bright beam of sound. A belly laugh? The name says it all. An ear-piercing shriek literally does cut into your head. The tones I recommend are pitched to the natural harmonic series generated inside the human body. The syllables employed will shape and direct the vibrations from your voice to each resonating chamber.

The harmonic series of your human instrument is the same as any resonant system. When we express these tonal relationships with our voice we are intentionally amplifying the overtones of resonance in all its manifestations, including the consciousness in the chakras. The chakra system is a bio-spiritual interface, linking our physical and spiritual bodies through resonance. Music is our most highly developed tool for expressing resonance (see chapter 2, figure 14, page 57).

Dr. Nuland's idea of ever increasing levels of sentience comes to light again at this point. The resonant forces organizing the atoms, molecules, and cells of the body eventually integrate on higher levels of organization beyond the body in the realm of ideas and spirit. Music is an open bridge to these higher realms of organization.

The spiritual realm moves into consciousness in the form of archetypes, symbols, religions, and myths permeating humankind's prayers and meditations. The third eye, acupuncture meridians, flaming hearts, and halos are examples of this expression in the mystic visual tradition. The chants, folk tunes, rhythms, and timbres of the world's music are examples of this consciousness (sentience) rising in the sonic realm.

We are creatures of the animal realm and agents of the gods, all at the same time. We are driven by gut-level imperatives just like the sea slug. In the next instant we succumb to the sweet breath of inspiration. Toning embodies the spiritual energy of Sound, imbuing our earthbound physical body with songs of the holy. The physical and spiritual bodies are harmonized through the balanced nature of musical tone.

Exercise 21: Your Resonant Tone

First of all, don't be shy! If you can talk, you can sing. Always sing with good breath support from the diaphragm in a clear, even tone. Breathe deeply and relax your shoulders. Try to hear your voice resonating off the walls. To start, find the fundamental resonant frequency of your body-mind instrument. Take a nice, full breath and sing in a full, low voice, moving the pitch slowly up and down until you feel a warm hum deep in your belly. Keep the neck long, and the chin down. Your goal is to get an even tone. This is your root. This fundamental tone will fill up your body cavity like a belly laugh fills a room. It expresses in sound the Tone of your connection with the earth wired into your first chakra at the base of your spine. Because you change every day, the pitch of this tone can change slightly from day to day as well. Find that note on a keyboard and follow the chart (figure 1) to locate the overtones of your root tone. Notice the corresponding syllables. Strike the appropriate key on the keyboard and try to make your voice disappear inside each pitch as you move through the series. If finding

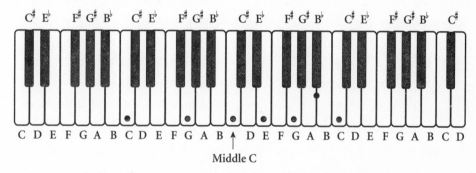

Marked notes indicate a series with the lower C at the first chakra.

	Chakra					
1	**2**	**3**	**4**	**5**	**6**	**7**
C	G	C	E	G	B♭	C
D	A	D	F♯	A	C	D
E	B	E	G♯	B	D	E
F	C	F	A	C	E♭	F
G	D	G	B	D	F	G
A	E	A	C♯	E	G	A
uh	oh	ah	oo	eh	ee	yy

Notes for Toning Exercise (left label for the six note rows)

Suggested Syllables for Each Chakra (left label for the syllable row)

Figure 1: Note Names. Tones for Toning Exercise.

the pitches is hard for you, continue to strike the note as you slowly slide your voice up and down. Listen for the relationship between the two pitches. Soon you will hear the center of both pitches blend together into one sound, the unison. Like all intentional activity, you must act and listen at the same time.

Using the suggested syllables will help focus the sound in the correct body cavity. Continue to chant these tones, moving up the spine, intoning the pitches on the chart. Picture the tones filling the resonating chambers of pelvis, gut, chest, and so on. Keep in mind the qualities of the chakras and the bodily functions associated with each chamber of the body. Change the shape of your mouth and throat slightly to direct the sound. The pitches and sounds place the tone in corresponding chambers and the body and mind harmonize with spirit.

We all hear music in our head. This gives us the ability to release the power of our toning work even in silence. With practice, your fundamental and its overtones will be alive inside of you. Soon the series of tones will be as familiar to you as "Twinkle, Twinkle Little Star." Use their integrating, calming power on the bus. You can control stress, mental fatigue, and physical exhaustion by putting your attention on the appropriate chakra even as you tone in silence. Intention is the most powerful activator of the resonant system that is your body-mind. Use it.

THE CROSSROADS

The solar plexus is the crossroads where muscle groups from the lower trunk and upper body knit together. This web of muscles literally keeps you from falling over. Good muscle tone in this region holds all the organs in place, reducing strain on the back, and places the weight "on center" over the feet.

Dancers are trained to initiate every movement from this place. Their will power in the abdomen is the starting point of their gestures. Their intentions for self-expression are initiated from their center. The tips of their fingers trace the line of their intentions as they flows across the stage. The best dancers are powerful *and* graceful. This harmony begins "on center."

Exercise 22: At the Crossroads

Stand with the feet slightly more than shoulder-width apart. Put your palms in the small of your back, resting them comfortably on the top of your pelvis. Keeping shoulders stable in relation to the feet, start to make tiny circles with your hips. Visualize the tailbone drawing a circle in the air. Slowly make the circle bigger and bigger. Keep the shoulders immobile. Use the muscle tone exercise (exercise 20, page 82) to guide you in a full performance of the movement.

Now, link the breath rhythm with the revolutions of the hips. Slowly breathe in for two revolutions, and out for two. On both the inhale and exhale repeat your name silently to yourself, focusing on the identity center in your pelvis (second chakra). Do four of these breath-cycles in one direction and then four in the other direction.

This exercise sets the lower chakras humming. Survival (first chakra), your personal identity and sexuality (second chakra), and your will power (third chakra) are all intoned in your name and sent orbiting around your center of gravity. This practice puts a multifaceted awareness of your self exactly where it will do you the most good, at your center of balance. Your intentions are focused away from your mind and into the spot where your body and the Earth are in close communication.

The root word for "guts" is *gheu,* meaning "to pour." Several offspring of *gheu* paint a family portrait of volcanic power at the base of the idea. "Geyser" is an offspring of *gheu,* and so is "fusion," the ultimate power. There is an incredible range of energy flowing through the guts, the center of will power. Stay on center. Power up!

4 FROM HEART TO SPIRIT

THE FOURTH CHAKRA: HEART OF THE MATTER

You probably know a few people who negotiate the ups and downs of life quite well. Nothing throws them off. They seem to exude confidence. They are centered and poised, ready for anything. It's not so much the outer expressions that impress us. It's the inner calm, a certain grace. Behind the persona, we hear a True Self singing a harmony of the warm heart. The resonance of consciousness humming in the heart chakra shows us the way. We know intuitively that love and harmonious relationship are the keynotes to this music of the human spirit.

The ancient Chinese considered humans to be "the middle creature," living out their days between heaven and earth, striving to balance the forces of the ever-moving male principle of heaven (yang), and the receptive female force of earth (yin). In this view we are in certain regards just like the animals, our feet tied to the nurturing soil. At the same time we lavish wealth and devotion on concerns of the mind and soul.

The lower centers of consciousness resonate the basic fundamentals. They motivate us to move about, procreate, and sustain ourselves on the planet. The upper chakras imbue humanity with ideas and religious overtones. Ethics, love, altruism, and empathy descend from the realm of spirit. We are caught in a dual fate, beckoned by both realms. It seems that for health and survival we must attend to both. The heart is the scale on which we weigh these two influences. The heart bridges the gap between heaven and earth. The heart is sensitive and responsive to all that we see and feel. This awareness defines our humanity. Our poetic nature perceives the depth of the heart's connection to every aspect of life. The heartbeat changes with every contour in the temporal habitat.

The heart does more than simply pump blood. It is a nerve center, a hormone-producing communications powerhouse, and the place in the body where two great streams of energy gush past one another and yet never mix. Hard-wired to the brain by a network of nerves, the pulse rate and blood pressure are directly affected by all the physical and mental forces acting on the structure of the body-mind. The heart, responding to these changes, actually produces hormonelike compounds affecting many critical activities in the body. And separated by mere millimeters of tissue, dark, toxin-heavy venal blood from the body rushes past bright, oxygenated arterial blood from the lungs.

The lub-dub of the heartbeat is an undertone, the harmony of the powers of the earth mixing with the inspiration of consciousness. Heaven and earth meet and sing a sweet duet in our hearts. The song reverberates throughout our body in the arteries.

Imagine your bloodstream as a pool of water. Every beat of the heart is like a rock tossed into the center of the pool. The arteries impel the blood perfectly in sync with the beating of the left ventricle, pushing the blood with a wave of bio-electric energy all the way to the tiny capillaries feeding every cell. In a truly musical sense your circulatory system fills your body with rhythm.

Our challenge is to feel the harmony of the heart every day. It only takes twenty minutes of aerobic activity three times a week to keep the vascular system and heart in reasonably good physical shape. With a little attention, we can keep our thoughts and attitudes balanced in the heart as well. The heart has the wisdom of nature. With empathy, compassion, respect, and love, the middle creature can balance the forces of the soul (air) and the body (earth). We can learn to sense and respond appropriately to these two forces, linking our best intentions with the natural balancing tendency of the heart.

THE HARMONY OF RELATIONSHIPS

A passionate counterpoint plays between our animalistic drives and the deep convictions of faith and belief. The screams of the hungry belly and the whisperings of the muse can make a rough but beautiful duet. At one moment we hear the call of the wild. The next song is the call to reason and spirit. The ancient image of the flaming heart symbolizes the power of balance and meaning available to us through devotion to the consciousness of love spinning in our heart center.

For most of us, the guts and the mind are the two dominant voices in our temporal habitat. Gut consciousness speaks from the depths of the earth. It calls out the basic beat and rhythm of survival: move, eat, breathe, or die. And we all are subject to the ceaseless chatter of the mind, filling our days with memories, ideas, plans, and images. Thoughts seem to have a life of their own. Words are charged with actual power and ideas have a compelling reality. The loving nature of the heart is often overpowered by one of these two voices. Physical desires or captivating ideas ceaselessly demand our attention.

But remember, we are not of heaven or earth alone. As creatures of the heart we are at our best when we strive to exist within a harmony of the two. With our consciousness tuned to the heart chakra, we can learn to play our part in the driving rhythms of survival while cultivating the mind *at the same time.*

The heart chakra is the harmonic center of the whole package, the place where a balance is struck between our place on earth and our part in the evolution of consciousness in the universe. Our bonds to family, mate, country, and our calling in life, are tied to our heart. As our relationships evolve we literally feel a change of heart. We say, "My heart is just not into it anymore." Our images and icons reveal the heart as a source of great wisdom, and love, the ultimate relationship. Courage means to have heart (*le coeur* in French). The words "heart" and "credo" (belief) spring from the same source.

Harmony is the musical element that touches our heart the deepest. Through the blending of tones, it symbolizes love. In the blending of musical voices we sense the perfect balance between distinct identities. The truest harmony seems to dissolve the individual tones, blending what we know to be more than one into a seamless whole. What could be a better way to soothe the heart—or care for the planet—than a life in harmony?

The healing of the self and the healing of the planet will go hand in hand. Over the past thirty years, psychologists, academics, and philosophers have forged the new field of ecopsychology. This discipline has a growing roster of practitioners in many fields who link ecological health of bioregions (and the entire earth) with the health of individuals and nations. Toxins impact not only our bodies, but degrade our sense of self. As our home dies so do we.

Environmental catastrophe has wiped out entire cultures and tribes. It will be no different for us "civilized" members of the human race. We can no more step out of our relationship with the earth than we can shed our skin. We are just as incapable of silencing the "voices in our head," the overtones of spirit permeating our awareness.

With the sound of harmony, music presents a great challenge. Can we demonstrate that the healing of the individual and the planet are integrated? I feel this mutual healing is only a matter of time. We hasten this harmonization every time we sing for joy in the shower, take those ten deep breaths, plant a tulip in hopes of spring, or celebrate the winter solstice.

THE SOUND OF THE HEART

From Dolly Parton to the bubblegum pop idols in Japan, catchy tunes and simple harmonies captivate billions. The harmonies of folk tunes are based on the interval of the third (see chapter 2, figure 10, page 41). When a backup singer in a band, or an alto section in a church choir, intones the third, the natural, internal structure of the harmonic series is amplified. That's what gives "easy listening" its name. Thirds and fifths mirror the simple, close-to-home lyrics and stories of folk and popular music, which invariably speak of the basic themes of life. Old-time gospel, bluegrass, and three-part harmony sing of the timeless relationships—home, family, the land, God, and romantic love.

Upper harmonics are rarely found in the folk music of the world. The higher partials create nonharmonic undertones that clash with the intervals within basic harmonic structures. These nonharmonic undertones give complex jazz voicings an edgy, piercing quality.

Beat-oriented music grabs us in an earthy, down-and-dirty sort of way. The sophistication of jazz and classical music sails over lots of heads, but because of inherent, harmonic relationships, sweet harmony does not demand a lot of our ears. The interval of the third plays easily on the heartstrings. The predictable cadences and resolutions of folk music the world over are familiar and comfortable. Our inner ear falls into them as easily as Gramps falls into his favorite chair.

HEART-CENTERED BALANCE

The muscle-tone exercises placed attention inside the body along the physical lines of force tying muscle to bone. The vocal toning placed a balancing resonance inside chambers of the body, stimulating the centers of consciousness along the spine. The following exercise is designed to develop your ability to discriminate between the two dominant tones of the human temporal habitat: the power of ideas, and the imperatives of physical conditions. This technique also brings your attention in your heart, the place where harmony continually resonates between what we have at our feet and what we imagine. The blend generates harmony for our Self and our world. It is a dance made from two dances, a dance of the earth and a dance of the spirit.

Exercise 23: Dance for the Heart

This activity is based on the Native American concept of the two primal forces, Mother Earth and Father Sky. To generate harmony we will set these two distinct voices in relationship and then listen for the blend.

Bend your knees, round your shoulders slightly, and lower your head as if looking for something on the ground. Imagine your heart peeking out from the hollow in your chest scouring the earth for something lost or misplaced. Hold your arms loosely at your side, elbows bent as in a jogging posture. Start to move about with a heavy step, planting each foot firmly. Count a quick one-two, one-two rhythm for each step. Pulse your whole body to this pattern.

Take four steps of this dance looking down, giving your full attention to the earth and all that you possess. On the next four steps lift your heart and face to the sky. Receive the inspiration of heaven, opening your heart to the songs of your highest intentions for yourself, your loved ones, and the world around you. Continue in this cycle for a while. Play with the two voices channeling the two intentions. One reflects on what is at your feet. The other opens us to messages from the realm of pure consciousness.

Every now and then bring yourself to a relaxed upright posture. Continue pulsing in place to the rhythm. Put your attention in your heart. As you exhale feel the two voices mix and blend in your heart chakra. You are grounded, rooted, and determined on one hand, and translucent, impressionable, and insightful on the other. Imagine these two versions of yourself blending in your heart. Imagine a pure resonant tone emitting from your heart. Direct this beam of intention toward someone or something you love. As you inhale, receive love from this object of your intention.

Repeat these steps. Dance to Mother Earth. Reach to Father Sky. Hear the harmony in your heart. Send it on.

Many forms of music rely on restatement and recapitulation. Themes are expressed over and over in various arrangements. Changing the instrumentation, range, tempo, or key of a musical phrase can influence subtle levels of meaning. Let's revisit a previous theme of the heart chakra.

Return to exercise 6 (page 43). While intoning the intervals with your partner pay close attention to the emotional qualities of the changing harmony. Feel the effects of the changing relationship in your heart center. In the dance of relationships this subtle harmony is playing about you all the time. Your relationship to your surroundings change moment to moment. With a musical intention you can feel this in your heart, the receptor and generator of love consciousness. Groundedness, joy, stress, unity, power, impasse, attraction, peace—all these feelings are expressed in the changing harmonies of the interval exercise. Listen up!

THE FIFTH CHAKRA: THE CHANNEL FOR SELF-EXPRESSION

We saw in the toning system that the second and fifth chakras share the same note in octave relationship (chapter 2, figure 14, page 57). This correspondence resounds in several layers of vibratory symmetry. At the sexual-biological level our identity is encoded *internally* at the second chakra. And the message of individual identity is expressed *externally* through words and deeds spinning out from the energy at the fifth chakra. Our personality is pumped up from the depths of our being, passed through the heart and then ushered into the world by the consciousness of self-expression moving through the throat chakra. *Expression of identity* is the overtone of consciousness moving here.

Obviously our voice is a big player in all this. Our words and speech are the primary modes for making our personality known. Language molds the pathways and topography of our conceptual landscape. If we don't have a word for something it barely exists. The way we spend our time, our habits, impulses, opinions, and diversions all expose facets of our personality to the world. A culture as a whole communicates overtones of consciousness as well. How do the songs of an agrarian culture resonate in the world? How do the themes and forms of consumer-based progress harmonize with other cultures? Can the bottom line and an all-pervasive faith work in pleasing counterpoint?

KEYING IN TO YOUR VOICE

Our voice reveals more about who we are than any other expression. To put our best intentions forward we need to be comfortable and facile in our verbal interactions. When we are ready and amiable in relating to others we are invigorated by the counterpoint. Conversations become jam sessions. We cocreate productive, dynamic relationships. The relationship between sexual identity and vocal expression can be painful at times, especially in romantically charged situations. We can easily be tongue-tied from embarrassment or lack of confidence. The blockage in our throat can reach all the way down below the belt.

The healthy expression of the personality depends greatly on the flexibility and range of the voice and the discriminating ear that is its master. At its roots, communication means "with an equitable exchange." Using the voice effectively requires receiving information and expressing oneself at the same time. The art of communication is the basis for healthy culture, be it the internal culture of your mind or the corporate culture at work. Conversation is the music we make every time we open our mouths.

The power of a single voice, resonating through a culture at the right time, can change the course of history. Elvis Presley's voice captured an entire generation.

His phenomenal popularity in his own time—and for decades to follow—was a result of his voice. He was the first artist to bring the primal power of the Afro-American beat into the white mainstream. He forged a bridge between the white world of melody and the shake-your-booty world of black gospel and R & B. You could feel it in his voice. It came bubbling up from his gyrating hips and streamed over our temporal habitat like a river of lava.

Hitler, Mussolini, Churchill, and F. D. R. had powerful styles of oratory that moved nations and the world. Evangelists, actors, singers, and newscasters have voices that resonate with meaning. The sound reaches down and grabs you, compels you, influences you. More than any other means of expression the human voice channels personal identity into the world's awareness. And an individual can surely change the world. Certainly actions speak louder than words, but very often actions follow directly on the echoes of words both well chosen and ill advised.

The voice is as unique as a fingerprint. It is legal to videotape a person's image anytime without sound, but capturing an individual's voice on tape always requires special permission.

Animals definitely respond to the tone of voice. A friend of mine can chase off the hungriest raccoon with her own low and vicious growl. To these aggressive critters human words usually have about as much effect as spitting at a hurricane. But her well-placed guttural utterance—even at low volume—will send them scuttling into the blackberries.

My father had a memorable voice. My boyhood home was long and rambling. My brother and I shared a room at one end. Several doorways away, my dad often sat in the den, working at the desk. We would talk, laugh, and goof-off long after bedtime. Dad would hear us and call out through the house, "Boys!" with a slow, rising inflection. That's all we needed. We knew significant actions would follow swiftly on the heels of that one word. We clammed up, giggling into our pillows.

Clear and thoughtful use of the voice expresses your identity, revealing your best intentions in a musical, melodic fashion. Stress and confusion often result from speaking without thinking. Running off at the mouth, mumbling, nervous chatter, and overblown diatribes belie an imbalance in the fifth chakra.

On the other hand, a heartbreaking confession, the well-placed word, the sharp and timely reprimand, and the whispered promise all resonate from a point of correspondence between the personality and the intention to express one's Self artfully. The voice is the messenger of the self. A healthy respect for the musical power of the voice gives your personality range, depth, and subtlety. The following ideas are pointers for expanding your vocal range. Try them out. See how they make you feel. Speak up! As you develop your voice the fifth chakra opens and expressiveness on all levels expands.

VOICE TRAINING: LISTENING

Observe how personalities are revealed through speech. Certain phrases ring incredibly true to the personality of the speaker. Steve Martin's "Well, EXCUUU-UUSE ME!" is a perfect minimalist tone poem expressing his entire smarty-pants stage persona in three words.

Try to catch personal melodies as they fly by. Play with repeating them later, imitating the speaker as best you can. Try to emphasize the dominant features of the voice. Does she say "ah" a lot? Is he always talking out of the corner of his mouth? The way people shape the tones of speech reveals their personality. Every guffaw, mumble, sigh, and snort exposes their identity to every ear prepared to notice.

We all have picked up vocal patterns over the years. A certain laugh, a cadence, a phrase, or an all-pervasive pattern of modulation and accent are often borrowed from one voice into another. As children we learn to speak through simple imitation. We imitate not only the words but also the tones we hear. I can hear my mother's voice in my own at certain times, my father's at other times. I laugh like a friend from eighth grade.

Intentionally imitating voices is an efficient way to get inside another person's head. Through imitation you will become quickly aware of a brilliant world of melodies playing all about you. By experiencing another person's vocal melodies you will expand your own range of expression.

A buddy and I performed improvisational radio theater for years. We talk so much alike that family members are fooled on the phone. I am sure that to a great degree personalities and self-images are formed by the resonant forces within the tones of speech we hear and end up making our own. Just as cultures brew predominant musical forms, our personality is cultivated in the music of our speech.

RANGE

Cast about in your memory for distinctive personalities. What were their dominant characteristics? Remember the pace, pitch, clarity of enunciation, volume, and so on. How was identity expressed in the sound of the voice? Put that expression in your voice. Expand your range. Exercise your Self. I'll never forget the music of "Boys!"

Well-executed self-expression grabs our attention and earns our respect. We admire athletes and people in great physical shape. The articulate actor, lawyer, musician, politician, and media personality also command our respect. This next section coaches you to exercise your vocal skills, expanding your concept of how you can express yourself.

Technical vocal manipulation, like calisthenics, will broaden your range of vocal expression. Pacing, volume, pitch, and enunciation are the basic elements of speech patterns. Here are a few simple etudes to help you expand the musicality of your speech.

Exercise 24: Vocal Calisthenics

Warm up: start with a soft, very low tone on "ahhh." Very slowly raise your pitch as if imitating the sound of an air-raid siren starting up. About mid-range change the phoneme to "eeee." Keep going. Increase the volume and breath support. Go all the way up, as high as you can go. SCREECH! Now slowly come back down, all the way to the grunt. Repeat several times, taking less and less time to complete the siren's call. That's your extended range, probably close to three octaves. Singers spend years training these three octaves to perform.

For the following exercises use this sentence for the score: "There is no possible chance you can convince me of anything."

Pacing: Repeat the sentence at medium volume and with the tempo in a monotone.

Changing nothing else, repeat the sentence several times, increasing the pace each time, saying it faster and faster until the words start to be garbled. Now repeat the sentence at a slower pace, going slower and slower until the words begin to modulate and blur. (The slower you go you will notice that it is harder to maintain the monotone.)

Volume: Using a normal inflection, start by repeating the words at a slightly louder than normal volume. Repeat louder yet, changing nothing else. See how loud you can get. When did the volume start to influence the meaning? Now go the other way. Repeat the phrase, getting softer and softer until you are whispering. How did the meaning and personality of the words change?

Pitch: Pitch (coupled with volume) is probably the most revealing aspect of the human voice because pitch modulation is clearly a product of varying degrees of inner tension. Keeping an even, near-monotone articulation, repeat the entire phrase starting at different places all over your range. At this point do not modulate from word to word. Maintain a normal pace and volume as you change only the register in which you speak the entire phrase. Notice the tension in your throat, lungs, and belly as you move from register to register.

Enunciation: Clear consonants and resonant vowels articulate distinctive images. Slurring words, talking into our teeth, and talking so fast the words race by all contribute to a blurry rendition, a fuzzy projection of our best intentions—a bad first impression.

Repeat the sample sentence using varying degrees of clear enunciation. At one extreme, slowly and carefully clip every consonant; move your mouth and tongue in an exaggerated way, sculpting every letter of every word. At the other end, see how little you can move your apparatus and still get the words out. Take it another stage further; mumble to the extent that the words dissolve into a garbled slush. Again, concentrate on only the enunciation aspect; keep the pacing, pitch, and volume at a middle setting.

MORE VOCAL TRAINING

We have applied the four elements of speech over the entire length of the sample. Now take an element and change it word to word, or throughout parts of the sentence. For example, try increasing the volume of words within the phrase. Or start out mumbling and by the end refine the enunciation to "broadcast quality." Play, experiment, and practice. Invent your own sentences. Compose yourself.

Besides increasing your range of vocal expression, voice training will automatically increase your ability to hear the personal messages other voices send out. Human speech is certainly one hallmark of the species. The more we can appreciate the power and subtlety of the voice, the more healthy and human we become.

Our actions also speak volumes about our identity and our chosen life-path. The history of the English language gives us a hint into this other level of expression moving through the throat center: "voice" and "vocation" are from the same root. Words conceptualize our intentions. Actions articulate them.

HABITS

Signature rhythmic patterns and other musical elements differentiate one tradition, style, or form of music from another. In the same way, the patterns we display in our life-composition distinguish us from the next person. Common patterns of behavior distinguish one culture from another. Our lives are compositions of patterns and habits developed over time. Body language, vocal patterns, interests, obsessions, family dynamics, friendships, social patterns, and our choices in music and lifestyle are the songs we sing. All these are habits. Using a musical attitude as a guide, we learn to recognize and studiously practice the habits and patterns that truly express what we most value in our personality. Attributes of personality are ingrained because we express aspects of ourselves *repeatedly*. We fall into rhythm after rhythm throughout life. Music demonstrates that we have the power to "change our tune."

We learn patterns that serve us somehow, and then we stick by them, even if their time has past. Situations change and the old patterns are not in tune anymore. Often we keep hammering away at old tunes even though the underlying beat or harmony has changed.

The musical model for composing a life demands that we listen and play at the same time. Your heart will tell you when your intentions and expressions are out of sync with the harmony moving around you. Your mate, child, personal appearance, or body will tell you sooner or later as well.

We learn our basic habits and patterns early in life. We create many of them to get the attention and love we crave from our primary caregivers, siblings, and close friends. As our life changes, the old ways of getting and giving love and support change. In order to get the strokes and juice we want out of life we need to be prepared and flexible, ready to put down outdated riffs and pick up new harmonies, melodies, and rhythms. When the personnel in a musical group changes, the good players open up and pay attention to the style and expertise of the new members. In order to play together, we have to listen!

Daily practice is the best technique for trying out new melodies for your voice. Consistency is more important than the actual length of time you spend at this. Do just one of the exercises in this book every day at the same time and in the same location for three weeks. Build a new habit day by day. Bring flowers to your mate every Sunday for a month. Turn off the TV and take a walk after dinner one day a week. If you have a child, have the youngster read *you* a bedtime story. Move things around. Try out a new temporal arrangement. Live in it for a while. Listen to your heart. How does it fit? What is the harmony? New habits and patterns express facets of your self that you may never have been aware of before! Jam on.

Everyone needs to develop a diversity of patterns. If one pattern changes, then others can take over. If our identity rides on just one tune, one rhythm, one instrument, then our identity is limited to the expressive nature of one song only. It is natural to deeply identify with patterns and rhythms formed over the years. When the deepest patterns change, the resonance of the unfamiliar music can be life threatening. Retired males are the group most prone to commit suicide. For many people work is life. The "empty nest" syndrome is tough on women and men alike.

Strive to be a multi-instrumentalist of your soul. Establish a diversity of active, habitual, rewarding relationships. Don't settle for diversions or distractions. Use a well-tuned heart to find harmoniously expressive ensembles of fellow players. Keep playing! There is danger in a monoculture of consciousness.

Recorded music shows that one person's voice can sweep over the world. On a smaller scale everything we do reaches out into our temporal habitat. Our callings rise up from the identity center and pass through the heart on their way to interactions with other callings. Our words and our deeds are rich with heart chakra resonance simply because once they are expressed they instantly establish harmonies with others. Musicians listen to the patterns around them and adjust their actions to maximize the pleasures of making music. We can follow this clear example by adjusting our actions to maximize our ability to make love in all its forms.

THE SIXTH CHAKRA: CHANGE YOUR MIND, CHANGE THE WORLD

Experience fills the mind like the vibrations of the strings fill the body of a guitar. Just as the shape of an instrument determines the quality of the sound, our personal tuning shapes every bit of information we process. The basic configuration of the mind is carved out by the powerful forces of genetics, parenting, childhood experiences, surging hormones, and significant events.

The smaller contours of thought—day-to-day moods and concerns—are cluttered with everything from the last TV show you saw to what you ate for lunch. In the midst of the canyons and mountaintops of your mindscape, remember that feelings, opinions, and reactions to all types of stimulus can be strongly influenced by the intentions. You can change the topography. You can make your own way in the world.

Most everyone knows a born-again Christian, a convert to vegetarianism, a recovering alcoholic, or a five-year-old who has recently changed his or her mind in a radical and all-encompassing way. The same information is getting to these people, but their minds are modified to accept or reject information in a different way. These revolutions show us that radical change is possible for anyone. Changing the way we process information can and does change the world.

When we process experience through a mental configuration based on compassion and inclusion we send into the world a harmonious resonance that amplifies the compassion. In this way we make love with and for the world.

When we process information through a system of cynicism, personal indulgence, and national chauvinism, the world around us resounds with these dissonant projections. Our dominant attitudes shape our internal mind-space, and then in turn shape the world. The way we tune the overtones of consciousness significantly influences the way we process information. This context has immediate and ultimately overwhelming influence over content. Reacting with resentment and anger to a difficult situation will produce one set of reverberations. Seeing the same situation as a challenge or a lesson will resound completely differently.

Both self-awareness and insight into others grows as we learn to recognize the way mental constructs corrupt, enhance, or otherwise influence the information and feelings under consideration. Listen carefully to two people recounting the same event. You can get a hint of the different interior configurations in their tones, inflections, tensions, and pacing of the voices.

One emotional or intellectual approach will not always serve you best. By practicing new mental approaches to your time habitat, you can negotiate conflict, challenge, shock, elation, ecstasy, or one-too-many margaritas from new and diverse points of view. Stay light on your feet. Try a new dance.

About every two years or so while I was growing up my mother would go on a furniture-moving binge. One time, after moving the couch into four or five positions, I realized something: we were not just moving furniture; we were reconfiguring my mother's concept of space. Once the new setup was in place the contour of space and time shifted. We had to learn a new way of moving through the house. Looking back, it seems that these periodic polar rotations continually imbued our home with a lively nature that echoed my mother's ready-set-go personality.

By changing attitudes and establishing new habits, we can filter and amplify the overtones of consciousness spinning throughout our body and mind. We can orchestrate our lives just like a composer chooses the correct instruments to realize his or her score. Our task is to orchestrate our perceptions and actions into a composition, an expression of life as art.

COMPOSE YOURSELF

Our perceptions are hard-wired into every part of our body-mind via the switchboard in the thalamus. This egg-shaped mass in the center of the brain routes incoming signals to the other areas of our brain. Physical processes and thought patterns cocreate our experience. The constant "inner-play" between brain and body creates the body-mind, the human instrument of amazing dexterity and consciousness that constantly weaves the inventions, dreams, pain, elation, and all the things we do, know, and feel. The mind seems to reside in the head. All the information seems to be buzzing between our ears.

However, the human mind is infinitely greater than the lump of flesh in our cranium. The mind is connected to the environment of ideas, history, fantasy, and fear that we all create together in the temporal habitat. The sixth chakra represents the whirling vortex of this mind-center, the Great Synthesizer, where all the bioelectric energies of our being harmonize. The third eye peering out from the forehead symbolizes the all-seeing consciousness of the divine mind, the source of self-awareness, intelligence, insight, and revelation. The sixth chakra is the portal where dreams and physical forms dance together in a timeless rhythm of wholeness and integrity.

The toning system places the seventh harmonic partial at the sixth chakra (chapter 2, figure 14, page 57). When played with the lower tones in the harmonic series, this tone generates a desire for movement and resolution. It "tilts" the sound of a major chord into a new key. In this role the tone is termed the "dominant seventh" interval. The addition of the dominant seventh to a major triad generates a cyclic harmonic movement that shifts the tonal center of the music to a new key. The other relationships inside the chords are the same, but the seventh creates a harmonic imperative to move from one tonal center to the next. This harmonic movement is called the dominant-tonic relationship. The dominant chords (V^7) are based on the fifth degree of the scale. The tonic chords (I) are based on the keynote, the first degree of the scale (figure 1, page 105).

The seventh generates a tonal phenomenon not unlike a quantum shift in the atom, where an input of a specific amount of energy creates a specific shift in the internal resonance. When the seventh is added to the root, third, and fifth, tension builds between the intervals. A quantum leap to a new key occurs and resonant patterns align to a new tonal center. This harmonic movement, prevalent in many forms of music the world over, exemplifies the capability we have to orchestrate quantum leaps of consciousness *at will*. The mind does its best work when it follows the example of the seventh, demonstrating facility and ease of movement from one point of view to the next.

⌐ Indicates the dominant seventh tone. When added to a tonic major chord (I), this creates a dominant seventh chord (V⁷) in a new key.

Figure 1: The Dominant-Tonic Harmonic Relationship.

Sixth chakra consciousness integrates, modulates, and transforms information from the body and the surrounding environment. It is the seat of reason and the touchstone for intuition. The integrated mind can modulate any situation into a new configuration. The third-eye consciousness inspires us to meet influences head on, with the confidence and facility to move forward and sustain harmony. A cultivated mind is fertile and well prepared to compose the songs of the future from the echoes of the past.

ORCHESTRATING YOUR INNER VOICES

Every sound in every piece of music is chosen by the composer for the emotional impact inherent in the sound. The sounds are orchestrated and balanced in relationship to one another in order to express the composer's intentional emotional message. For the listener, an internal sounding board is created in the mind from experiences, attitudes, education, and moods. If the listener's sounding board is culturally tuned to the composer's intent, the music resonates the consciousness of integration at the sixth chakra. The listener is said to be "touched" by the music.

Mental health is closely akin to the art of orchestration. Balance is the key. Imagine all those voices in your head as sections in the inner orchestra, playing the composition of your life. The trumpets announce your grandest plans and deepest trials. The harp whispers sentimentally in your ear. The percussion section pounds out the demands of work and responsibility. We maintain balance in this tumult by intentionally composing ourselves. We can arrange and conduct the various voices. We can choose to devote our attention to the ones that best serve us, and mute the ones that throw us off track.

We use our various modes of intelligence in this ongoing task. We dodge the careening vehicle with our kinesthetic intelligence. We arrange a hectic schedule with our linear, logical mind. We "go with a hunch" and intuitively extend ourselves to stranger. All the while we are receiving and managing the various messengers and cargoes streaming into our awareness by means of the musical mind that recognizes the various tempos, patterns, tones, harmonies, and melodies swirling all around.

All events have structure and form generated by the relationship between the overtones of consciousness. The challenge of mindfulness is to discern these forms as they come our way and balance the voices in the composition. The composer knows the expressive range of each instrument and uses that tone at his or her discretion. Our innate musical intelligence gives us the same power over the forces acting on us from the inside and from without. We have the compositional power to choose anger or patience, frugality or self-indulgence. We have the discretion to choose meaning over image, value over wealth, time over money, love over infatuation.

Take the time to examine the content and import of the objects, forces, and choices entering into your awareness. Is that new car really important for your survival (first chakra)? Or does it simply stimulate your ego (second chakra)? Do you place your work at the core of your identity (second chakra)? Or do the relationships and feelings between you and your loved ones take priority in your life (fourth chakra)?

Television and computer screens cultivate image over substance. Modern culture has made ideas more important than survival, peace of mind, self-expression, and love. The terms "mind game," "head trip," and "la-la land" indicate mental states where the mind can become inappropriately dominant. Artful composition demands discriminating choices, the separation of technique and effect. As you examine the flood of input entering your body-mind, strive for balance. Your health depends on it.

THE VOICES OF NATURE

Ecologists tell us that diversity in the biosphere insures health and stability. The fabric of life depends on the strength of many threads. For example, monoculture—the domination of a single species in a given area—creates the danger that the demise of one life form could spell the end for all the life in that region. When a great diversity of forms is flourishing, the end of one does not mean the end of all. With many interconnected strands, the net of life remains healthy even if there is a rip in one area. Similarly, cultivating a multitude of voices in our external environment and inner life will impart vigor and stability to one and all. There is power in the "open mind," the alert third eye. When an opinion, attitude, habit, or myth is challenged or shattered, the diverse, open-minded personality can take another view, modulate to a new, more harmonious key.

Appreciation of diversity in the natural world seems to cultivate tolerance and acceptance. Strive to practice disciplines honoring the vitality of the many voices rising up within you. Through sympathetic resonance we gain a growing compassion and respect for the voices of other people, cultures, and even other species.

Early human culture was inseparable from the natural world. But in the last two thousand years a powerful myth of a separate human reality has grown dominant. The scientific method bulldozed its way into every aspect of life. We assume that mind power can control everything. This strange variation of sixth chakra consciousness permeates our perceptions in the same way superstitions permeate other cultures. Under the dominance of the mind we have become isolated and dangerously out of control regarding our impact on the planet. Like a finger muting all overtones of a string save one, the dominance of the mind has dampened our awareness of the call of the earth, our own personal power, our sense of unconditional love, and our ability to express ourselves. We crumble on the inside and run amok on the outside. We are left with a jumble of manufactured images reverberating inside our own lonely heads.

INSIGHT

A better use for the mind is akin to the service performed by a lighthouse. We can cultivate a mindfulness that illuminates and guides at the same time. We can look inside to examine our True Self. And we can turn our attention outward to know the world *as it is*. We can use the considerable power of the mind to discriminate and choose. We can harmonize moral, spiritual, and practical knowledge.

Musical compositions give voice to one instrument and then another. A composer's intent is expressed through the blending of voices. The great Impressionists such as Ravel and Debussy took the art of orchestration to new levels by using innovative combinations of instruments. Their revolutionary use of extreme high and low registers, mixed timbres, and tonal clusters prepared the Western ear for the electronic soundscape to follow. Their genius applies the power of insight to the mastering of musical form.

We can use the same sixth chakra power to form our lives, to compose our selves. Whirling within each of us is a True Self waiting to be composed and expressed. It is important to exercise every instrument of the internal orchestra, from the physical muscle and bone all the way up through the spirit. Ultimately, though, the mind makes the choices, puts the ensemble together, and picks the tunes. Art does not happen by accident.

Whether we are aware of the process or not, each of us projects our selves into our family, hobbies, causes, relationships, or job. The self can be released through creative endeavors or physical exercise. We may sing our song in front of an audience or in front of a mirror making faces with a three-year-old. Every conscious choice or knee-jerk reaction takes form somehow in our surroundings. To live musically we must take responsibility for the fact that every thought, word, and deed resonates beyond our Selves. Most of the exercises in this book have been working the individual instruments in our orchestra of Self. It is now time to engage the facility of insight, the consciousness of the sixth chakra.

Traditional folk and tribal music is generally composed by ear. New ideas are intuitively expressed within a well-established style and simply remembered through repetition. This is the oral tradition. On the other hand, the great works of Western culture are invariably written down, using the logical intelligence to formalize the music in every detail. We will use a combination of the two modes to develop our musical intelligence.

Every great musical composition has an inner structure that rests on simple themes. The composer expands on these themes, constantly referring to them as

FROM HEART TO SPIRIT

the piece unfolds. Keep the source of your best intentions at the front of your mind. Stay true to the simple resonance of each tone of consciousness we have amplified with the previous exercises. Listen for the harmony. How does it all fit? Are you composing a frantic monkey chant or a mythic opera, a splurge of disco or a hymn?

Exercise 25: A Harmony of Thoughts

Keep a small pad and pencil handy. Every so often, quickly jot down a few words or phases reflecting things that demanded your attention in the past few hours. Be specific, noting at least one dominant quality of the interaction. Home maintenance is different than the idea of a new home. Completing a business deal is different from pitching one. A gourmet meal is not the same as porking out on french fries.

At bedtime do a quick rendition of the heart dance (exercise 23, page 93) as a warmup, and then review your list. Use your mind to hold each experience in the objective illumination of the third eye. Starting at your root, pass the experience by each of your chakras, repeating their keynotes one at a time. The experience will harmonize differently in each area of your consciousness. Where is the dominant harmony of each activity? Is there a dissonance generated here and there? What is the distinctive tone of your experiences in relationship to your awareness?

Do you crave a vacation in order to express your freedom or to recharge for another great push needed to keep your business alive? Does your fear of gaining weight resonate as a health or self-image issue? Our life is a changing symphony of harmonic relationships. The consciousness of mind gives us the power to change our part in all this, altering the resulting harmony. We cannot control all the currents of life, but we do have the choice to compose the tones and arrangement of our part. And that's half the battle.

THE SEVENTH CHAKRA: INSPIRATION

Inspiration is the sudden realization that something meaningful and resonant is imminently manifest. It is the crucial spark or flash that initiates every articulate expression. If we are prepared and diligent we just may have the tools to fan the sparks into life. Where does the spark of inspiration come from, and how can we be a lightning rod for its charge?

The chakra system puts the portal for inspiration just above the head in the crown. In a previous exercise we visualized the seventh chakra halo and moved under its luminous presence (exercise 10, page 59). We will now examine how this whorl of consciousness serves as the source of energy that sets our body-mind instrument into resonance. Inspiration is the bow moving on our strings and the wind in our flute.

The toning system puts the overtone of the second octave at the crown chakra. Through octave harmony the crown corresponds with the earth at the root chakra and our personal power pumping in the solar plexus. If the three tones were sounded together they would seem to dissolve into one another. When musical tones sound in octave harmony they form the unison: *uni* (one) *sonus* (sound). The octave correspondence of the first, third, and seventh chakras symbolizes that our physical existence, our will to live, and the divine are overtones of one resonant whole that is our personal expression of consciousness.

In meditation and prayer we see our physical form, actions, and feelings in the light of this radiance. We are in a relaxed state conducive to true and lasting health. We move through the reefs and channels of life like a wave moves over the seabed. Resonance carries us even beyond the "end" of our life span. The echoes of our lifelong composition resound beyond our time.

In the freely resonating string we see that all the points dividing the string into the various partials are constantly moving. We can "stop" the string at one partial, creating the standing wave pattern of a single overtone. But in its totality only the end-points of the string are truly still. Tension is placed on the string at these end-points, thus giving it tone.

In our toning system we employ harmonic ratios to resonate the consciousness within our body-mind. The power of physical tone sympathetically resonates feelings and insights associated with the chakras. These tones stimulate our body-mind at consistent locations and at predictable harmonic ratios. The various feelings we experience moment to moment are melodies composed of tone. Physical tones resonate in the cavities of our physical instrument. The tones of conscious-ness resonate in our feelings, intuitions, and moments of inspiration.

Picture one end of our fundamental tone rooted in the stillness of the earth. The other end is tethered to the stillness of heaven. The tension between the two creates our unique sense of time and our innate musicality. We are "the middle creature," rooted in the earth and looking to the sky at the same time. Like every piece of music, we are born from and shall return to silence.

Sometimes it seems like quite the opposite. In the midst of a lively conversation or a dramatic event, inspiration may strike. But think back. Isn't there always an instant of balance, lucid insight, shock, or joy when the world dissolves and the new thought descends into your awareness? When I am playing music, totally engaged and active, inspiration can grab me and I sense a liftoff, a warp in the space-time, and a suspension of reality. Certainly at the end of a great perfor-mance, in that moment before the crowd starts to applaud, inspiration hangs in the air, sifting down into everyone's crown chakra. We are at one with the moment, still and receptive, grateful to be alive and together for that instant. What a time!

STILLNESS

Stress is rampant in modern life. We often feel like there is just no time to unwind, no way to reduce the pressure, no place to truly relax. The images we see in the media put true ease and peace beyond the reach of many people. Not enough time, money, or stock options. Inspiration? Fat chance. We are inundated with schedules, commitments, bills . . . you know, *reality.*

But a frame sets off every picture in the gallery. Every sculpture is surrounded by space. Every frame in an I-Max film clicks on and off, a stab of darkness inserted between every image. If we do not orchestrate silence and stillness into our life all becomes a blur. The edges get smeared. The most precious things lose their meaning. We cease to understand the significance of our efforts. All the overtones of our personal instrument and the wondrous variety of our culture mix into a mush. Stillness, silence, and a bit of the void is a necessary part of any-thing meaningful. Without the stillness at the end-nodes, the strings go slack and no music can be made.

Should we continue to look for more input, sources, partners, collaborators, and new experiences? Of course! But stimulation is not inspiration. Inspiration enters in a brief break in the action. These moments take your breath away, replacing preconceptions with the intentions of pure consciousness. This is like a divine injection, and it is much better to be centered and still while you get the shot.

Many say we can't control inspiration. It is a random occurrence, out of our hands. We imagine that if we keep moving, moving, moving, we increase the chances of finding the right moment, the right opportunity. We work like crazy to make it happen, and then we can only hope it *might* happen. What did we really expect anyway? Everyone knows inspiration is a product of chance, and perhaps brilliance. Geniuses are inspired. But we don't have to settle for accidental magic. Training full attention on the still point over one's head will attract inspiration like a door ajar attracts cats. Silence and stillness are the doorways to creative expression.

The overtones of consciousness we have been experiencing are accessible through the silent doorway standing open above the head. This is the great mystery that mystics and scientists all ponder. Physicists are mathematically certain that the *infinite mass* of the universe emerged from a *single point* in space. For the mystic, the infinite source of spirit and creativity is at the still point, the empty threshold, the silent end of the string.

We need to practice being at the still point. We must make silence a permanent guest in our temporal habitat. This practice will maintain the tone of our fundamental resonance, setting up the overtones of health, identity, stamina, a loving nature, clarity of expression, and insightful thought.

Even in a complete absence of audible sound, life still hums beneath the silence. The famous composer John Cage went into an anechoic chamber at Bell Labs. The small room was designed to be as close to soundproof as possible. Even the noise of Cage's own breathing was swallowed by the chamber. Cage commented that he still heard two sounds, a low churning white noise and a high whistle. The technicians told him this was his blood circulating and his nervous system firing.

Exercise 26: Carrier Waves

Find a very quiet spot. Return to this spot for fifteen minutes at the same time three days in a row. Listen for the sound of your blood and your circuits. Do this every week for three months.

These next two activities are best learned with a partner. Have someone read the instructions to you as you perform the exercise.

Exercise 27: Tin Can Telephone

Imagine your chakras strung like bells on a string. Your string is anchored at the ends in earth and sky. Starting at the first chakra, ring each bell three times. Imagine the straight, taught string suspending the bells directly above each other. Like a tin can telephone the bells send subtle vibrations through the string to all the other bells. As you toll each bell, name the key concept for each chakra bell: (1) survival; (2) identity; (3) will power; (4) relationship; (5) self-expression; (6) insight; (7) spirit.

Keep the string singing. The songs of the bells draw inspiration down from the portal above your head. Ring the bells from the bottom up, top down, and then bottom up once more. The vibrating string is an antennae picking up the tone of the inspirational silence holding all the bells in relation. The intention is there. Stay tuned.

Exercise 28: Crowning Glory

Stand with feet together. Keeping the top of your head over your feet, gently undulate your spine, hips, and thighs, shifting the positions of the chakras side-to-side, front to back. The crown chakra and the feet remain stable. You may tilt your head from side to side a bit as you swing out your hips and shoulders. But keep your head directly under the halo just above the top of your skull. Imagine all your overtones of awareness moving and sounding in relation to the silent end-points rooted deep in heaven and earth. Turn your attention easily to each chakra. Keep no particular order. Every now and then your attention will fall on the crown chakra. At that point stand still, close your eyes, and immerse yourself in the stillness at the threshold of the open door. Imagine yourself above your body looking down. The string of bells continues to sway and oscillate beneath you. You know that there is a very special harmony resonating in the person below you. But you are now in the silent place beyond conscious awareness. You are at the portal where anything is possible because nothing is happening. Take three deep breaths.

Repeat this exercise three times, ending with three final breaths.

Part Three

RITUAL, RELATIONSHIP, AND REVELATION

5 A RETURN TO RITUAL

The doors to the great hall swing open. Elegantly attired attendants usher the hushed crowd to their appointed places. The air is shimmering with expectation. All eyes follow the leader as he steps into view. The musicians rivet their attention on his every move. He waits for the moment of absolute silence, gives a determined glance at his performers, and raises his arm, signaling the beginning of the ... of the what?

This description could fit a Balinese shadow play, an opera in a grand theater in Europe, or a ceremony honoring the African gods in a *condomble* ritual in Brazil. The deep respect so apparent in all these scenes grows from the nature of ritual and mystery surrounding our love of music, and our need to share this love.

In *The Lives of a Cell,* Lewis Thomas speaks of the genetic imperative for music that permeates the human species, "The need to make music, and to listen to it, is universally expressed by human beings. I cannot imagine, even in our most primitive of times, the emergence of talented painters to make cave paintings without there having been, near at hand, equally creative people making song. It is, like speech, a dominant aspect of human biology." Rituals have created eons of musical intention, binding cultures to the cycles of nature.

During musical performances we suspend our links to the everyday experience of time and ride a common wave. Cultural and religious rituals the world over draw their power from this communal experience of musical time. As in music, the ritual experience unites us at specific points in cycles of time with common intent. Rituals are born and continue to thrive because the harmony of the group sustains the inner resonance of the individual. The sacred rite of the world's religions and the throb of the all night dance rave plug into the same source—the power of musical time qualities resonating overtones of consciousness spinning through our body-mind.

In the past, every area of life revolved around the songs, dances, litanies, and incantations of ritual. The beat of the drum and the waves of melody and harmony can return us to this powerful source of physical and spiritual sustenance so obscured in our image-driven post-modern world.

In this chapter we relate the power and practice of ritual to the nature of music. We will show how our own home is the most natural place to use our awareness of musical time. It is at home where we can cast a circle and set aside a little sacred ground for ourselves in the midst of the chaotic day-to-day hubbub. A ritual resonance can bring magic and wonder into the life of youngsters. We will also outline activities to help reestablish ritual connections with the seven aspects of consciousness associated with the chakras.

SIGNPOSTS IN TIME

Throughout history, every aspect of cultural life has been marked by ritual. Celebrations of the seasons, feast days, and historical events define ethnic identity, national values, and spiritual callings. The word "ritual" comes to us from a Latin variant of *ar,* the root word for "harmony" and "art." By establishing meaningful patterns in our life, and revisiting them on a regular basis, we ritualize our experience. We return to the resonant power moving through all of nature. The songs and dances that are central to rituals around the world give us vibrant models for imbuing our individual lives with a deep ritual resonance. Rituals serve as signposts in the temporal habitat of cultures, and cultures are created through repeated patterns of habitation, commerce, religion, agriculture, and artistic activity. Just as instruments resonate characteristic timbres, individual and cultural identity resonate from ritualized patterns established over longs cycles of time.

When a need arises in a culture, new rituals are designed and celebrated. Unheard of until the late 1800s, the famous Ghost Dance of the Plains Indians grew out of the ultimately fatal threat to their culture from encroaching Americans.

With a practiced attention to personal stresses and challenges, we can change our pattern of life at will to serve new needs, intentionally composing new patterns when necessary. By living musically, tuning in to the overtones of awareness singing in our body-mind, we become more graceful and expressive while responding to change. The true ritual is any pattern of life that we willingly perform in order to bring overtones of a spiritual nature to our families, homes, communities, and the earth.

Like the primal pulse of music, rituals gain their influence through the power of repetition. Like the beating of a drum, rituals are performed again and again on a precise frequency, sending waves through the culture whole. The same phrases, the same steps, the same litanies are repeated over and over, creating century-long compositions of deep meaning and undeniable power. Like a beam of light pulsing through space then finally striking the surface of a vibrantly alive world, ritual consciousness is revealed as it manifests in song, dance, words, and deeds, ultimately illuminating a culture.

Tribal chant is a clear example of a flowering of ritual culture. Often the music is composed of short melodies repeated again and again. The diversity of African chant, linked to the drum and other percussion instruments, offers many cultural blossoms in sound. The liquid sounds of the *mbira* (thumb piano) and light voices of the Xona [Sho-na] from Zimbabwe differ greatly from the powerful *bata* drum and full-voiced chant of the Yoruba in Nigeria. The message of repetition inherent in the beat itself drives the message of the ritual deep into the hearts and bodies of the celebrants. The beat returns. The seasons return. Ritual is a returning to the sacred—a regular and deeply emotional attachment to forces that sustain physical and spiritual health. Bringing musical intention and pattern into our daily lives will bring the powerful message of ritual back home.

We are all "wired" by genetics, fate, and social and family structure. Our basic personality is well established by the time we can ride a bike. But as we grow and mature, it becomes apparent that we can intentionally practice new patterns to shape, enhance, expand, and metamorphose the raw material. All of us have talents worth developing, and negative tendencies worth watching. Patterns carry meaning and consciousness. Habits resonate aspects of physical health as well as emotional and spiritual overtones.

Rituals stay alive through a deep connection with the underlying aspects of consciousness empowering the ritual activity. Sports rituals are about power (third chakra). Sacred rituals are about spirit (seventh chakra). Family rituals are about identity (second and fifth). Without clear connections to the spiritual tones humming in our body-mind, any ritual can devolve into sterile habit. Our choices—or tacit involvement—set our course.

Life does just not "fall together" or "fall apart" like rocks compressed and then ground to dust by the simple passing of time. At every turn there are musical, creative choices going on, whether we are aware of them or not. Cultures evolve and endure through ritual. Individuals grow and mature through intentions actualized in patterns of behavior. Music demonstrates that our creative choices determine the dynamics of our experience.

THE DEMISE OF RITUAL CULTURE

Tribal cultures retain a sense of time that includes ages past and ages to come. Through the links to the ancestors and the bonds of survival rooting them to the earth, they live in a musical time that is rich and deep. Their dances are often heavy on the beat, low to the ground, rooted in the soil. A symbol for this type of culture could be the drum beating out the rhythm of the dance. The drum speaks with the deep voice of the ancestors. The beat returns joy to the village. In a terrible loss for the vitality of the entire planet, ritual-based cultures are being muted and dispersed.

A new culture of the individual has come into being, taking sway over the old ways of the clan and tribe. There are two primary forces forging this new culture. The first force is the Judeo-Christian-Moslem promise of a personal relationship with a godhead. This is a theme that has removed each one of us from the ritual circle. We don't need the village anymore. We are free but isolated, spiritual mavericks on a solo journey.

The second force is the siren song of money. In the past our survival was tied directly to communal work in harmony with the earth. These links have been superseded by the power of cash. We don't grow our food or barter for goods, we simply buy it all. Money puts more stuff in our hands than we could ever make for ourselves. With enough cash we have the power to obtain anything we might imagine. Why bother going to the sacred fire on the days appointed by custom, history, and celestial rhythms? We can just watch it all on TV. We order our life over the phone. We even gain salvation online, twenty-four hours a day.

These forces have ripped us from the resonant time fields of ritual. One serious effect of the cult of the individual is the undermining of cultural links to the past and the future. With such wide-ranging individual freedoms, all of us, especially children, are set adrift in a mono-dimensional present with no view of the times gone by, and an unclear vision into an amorphous future. Ritual culture has been trivialized into fashion seasons, network premieres, and holiday decorating schemes. We would gain much through a return to patterns and harmonies that truly sustain our physical and spiritual vitality. We can start by creating a ritual culture in our homes and communities. This chapter contains tools for casting new ritual circles. These tools will also help you recognize the old circles that will never be obscured by the glitz and blare of modern life.

THE AGELESS PULSE OF RITUAL

Studies of many indigenous cultures by the Storyscape Institute in San Francisco show that areas with intact, ritual-based cultures maintain biological diversity and ecological vitality much better than regions where the culture binding humans to their locale has been diluted or gutted by "progress."

The power of ritual comes by means of returning again and again to energetic points in time that are naturally imbued with significance. The Solstice. The first day of spring. The morning hug. Wednesday night story time. Full moon walks. Every ritual captures the essence of the power of return, the same power that pulses in the beat of music. The ancient Greek root of the word "return" is *tornos,* a tool for drawing a circle. We need to provide for our families and communities the tools that will trace the circles in time, bringing us back again and again to something real. We need a rhythm of experience that sets hearts and minds in phase with our fellows, in tune with the land on which we live.

With considered intent, every repetitive act has the potential of becoming a ritual. We have seen how the musical elements resonate aspects of awareness in our body-mind. Rituals do the same thing at very long frequencies. Through repetition they bring musical qualities to life over days, months, years, and generations. Earthiness, clarity of mission, perseverance, love, beauty, transcendence, and inspiration all flow from ritual behaviors. Moving from this place of purpose and trust, normal routine can be transformed.

Although we were all tribes-people not so long ago, we can't hope to bring the magical tribal powers of our great-great grandparents back to our midst. But we can ritualize life as we live it now, celebrating the birth and death of each day and the rise and fall of the seasons. With ritual intent, every greeting can be a chant to love, every good-bye a benediction, every meal a feast of the gods. We have the responsibility to erect signposts along time's long road for our children, and their children to come. We can compose attitudes and activities that will establish a rhythmic, ritual awareness in youngsters. Whether we are primary guardians or not, we short-change the future if we do not sustain and amplify resonance in our relations with the young.

Every ritual has a traditional place such as the sanctuary, the holy grove, the sacred ground. The essence of ritual, like the power of rhythm and song, draws from the beauty of repetition, the return to familiar territory. Our most well known territory, the place to which we return the most often, is our home space. If we are to recast the sacred circle, home is the place to start.

HOME AGAIN

Home is the place where our efforts should most purely express our truest intentions, creating a harmony that includes every aspect of our life, even our death. The actions you perform over and over again ritualize the space between the walls. Habits, chores, prayers, and routine determine a cadence, a harmonic structure to your home. The actions you perform in carrying out these intentions compose the themes, movements, suites, and symphonies that make up the concert program that is your life. Dedicated care and feeding of the home-space clothes us in a musical time quality of warmth, sustenance, satisfaction, and security.

In many cultures the home is guarded by a shrine or altar. A candle may burn continuously at the door. There may be a fetish statue to which a daily homage is offered. The altar is not moved. It lives in its own sanctified corner of the house. Every person entering or leaving bows to the shrine, and in this way acknowledges the spirit of the place. The entire home is "altered" by this ritual attention, sanctified by gestures of faith and thanksgiving. A musical time-field of stability is intoned, a time territory that is filled with ritual intention. As the family shrine is addressed each day a rhythm of devotion is sustained over days, weeks, years, and generations. Like the beat of a ritual drum, this pulse becomes an extension of the heartsong of the people. Arrivals and leave-takings are the steady strokes on the drum of home.

Many of us have our own altars: the wall of family portraits; the shelf of treasured momentos; the shrine to our chosen deities; the vase always filled with flowers. Daily attention to the altar of your choice will resonate deep within your time habitat. Paying attention to the object of your devotion sets up a musical wave of intention connecting you with something greater than yourself. This I-Thou relationship creates a harmony within the walls of your home, a harmony of spirit.

Playing music in your home on a regular basis will sanctify your home. The seven elements of music emphasize different aspects of consciousness. It follows that the music we choose, and the time we choose to play it, go a long way in determining the musical time quality of our home. Decide what aspect of consciousness you want to resonate. Refer to the "Suggested Listening" section at the end of the book. Many styles of music are listed, noting dominant musical elements. References to specific artists are included.

The materials of a ritual are always chosen to serve a specific cycle of time. So determine the best times to play your chosen sounds. Fill the space between the gypsum, plaster, linoleum, and countertop with the music that fills your heart, your gut, or your mind.

Is the TV soundtrack—that modern sonic icon of mediocrity and malaise—hanging around your house like a sleepy vampire bat in the shadows? In contrast, the *cantina* music beaming from every door in Mexican towns paints sound murals of unrelenting exuberance. Replayed again and again, a song or style of music seeps into the space as surely as the furniture polish soaks into the coffee table.

And know that musical time qualities are resonated by all kinds of vibrations. Invite friends and family into your home to soak the walls with laughter, sweat, sidelong glances, and lively argument. Bathe the home in regular doses of appreci-ation. Rearrange furniture. Keep an eye out for the perfect addition to the decor. In this way the housewarming goes on. It becomes a fire that you stoke on a ritual time frame. Whoever enters a space so served cannot help but feel at home them-selves. They sense the echoes ringing subtly around the room. Somehow, out of the corner of the eye, they catch a fleeting glimpse of a shimmering shadow. Could it be the dance of spinning sunbeams coming through the kitchen window?

RITUALIZE!

Many things dearest to you are performed only at home. A home is imbued with personal energy and spirit, a singular music. Ritualize your life! By setting the things closest to your heart into a resonant pattern, your practice becomes musi-cal by nature. If you meditate, pray, do Yoga, or play an instrument, try them out in various locales, then choose the place most conducive for these activities. Ritu-alize the space on a regular basis. It is more important to your musical sense of time that you do things regularly for five minutes every day in the same place than sporadically for an hour here and there. The sense of return is the key to the rewards of ritual. In this way, watering plants, petting the cat, sweeping the porch, mowing the lawn, or practicing an art form can all become ritual cycles of caring.

The musician strives to express the essence of the music with every note. In rit-ualizing our life we must always have a clear awareness of what element of con-sciousness we are trying to resonate. Every intentional repetition of a task imparts a musicality to the time in which it takes to complete, charging the elapsed time with the quality of the intention itself. This is how housework can become a musi-cal activity. As we intentionally clean and tidy up the space, qualities of order, con-venience, clarity, and simplicity flow from our intentions, changing the quality of the time spent by everyone who enters the space. In this way mindfulness and musicianship are one and the same. Work reveals the qualities of our intentions just as the drawing of the bow over the strings reveals the tones within the violin.

So much of our time at home is spent on chores. Chores done mindfully can have a cumulative affect of refining our space beyond the obvious. They can take on the quality of ritual. They can become revelatory rather than obligatory, exposing a welcoming space for our friends and ourselves, a place of repose and celebration. Each time we make the bed we can invoke the quiet repose we feel when we lie down there. With every weeding of the flowerbed beauty is revealed yet again, fresher, deeper, and truer. "Chore" comes from a word referring to a piece of wood turning on a lathe. The essence of the work at hand is always spinning in the same space. The way we touch this whirling potential determines its shape and function. This is all about paying attention and acting with intention, the two keynotes of musicality.

The future belongs to the young. We may or may not be parents, but our actions resonate into the culture and are picked up by the impressionable hearts and minds of the children nevertheless. Our most intentional practice must be undertaken when considering the ripple effect on the next generation.

RITUALS FOR THE YOUNG

Everyone somehow senses that the most natural and beautiful aspects of humanity are embodied by musical expression. An infant bangs on a piano with joyous abandon, obviously reveling in the surge of tones. The sounds may not be all that pleasing, but the joy of the sound embodies the bright overtones of the child's spirit. At every stage of a child's growth, spontaneous expressions of spiritual Sound can be seen.

Even before kids walk we see them dancing when music plays. Music is an instinctual activity, generated out of the interplay of gravity, our bodies, our immediate surroundings, and our ability to sense and respond to the changing quality of time. Moving with the beat feels good. Watch a toddler wave his or her booty to the Rolling Stones or Vivaldi. Is there any doubt that this is a good time?

Repetition is a favorite musical device (or weapon) employed by every child. Who hasn't been driven mad by the I'll-repeat-everything-you-say game? Repeating nonsense phrases or the punch line to a silly joke gets kids excited. It's a mini-ritual of ecstatic mirth. They return to it again and again. Don't shy away from the deep resounding joy blooming from the repetition of a glob of gibberish. Join in! Revel in it. Sing their tune until they tire of it. This childhood phase will pass all too quickly.

PLAY

Taking the time to play music on a regular basis ritualizes a part of your day. This is especially true if part of your family hasn't been born yet. Pregnant women: sing your child a chant of encouragement, healing, protection, or gratitude. Invoke ritual intention at regular times, such as when you work out, do a household chore, walk to the office, or prepare a meal.

Play music at regular times for yourself and your family. Link music to significant cycles in the young life. Music-time is a signpost in the vast landscape of this huge chaotic world. Babies are new arrivals from a dimension beyond time. They grew up in a water world, and are pulled down by dry, hard gravity. Lift them up on a wave of music day after day after day.

LIMITS

A ritualized approach to time includes awareness of how to end things. Children respond well to appropriate limits. Be honest with children about the beginning, middle, and end of things, especially playtimes. When asked, "When are we going to play?" raise your head out of your preoccupation, think for a moment, consider your schedule, and give an honest answer, looking directly at the inquirer. And then live up to your eye contact. Be ready to play at the agreed upon time. Before you start, though, invoke your prerogative as the adult maestro of the situation; pronounce the conditions of ending. Don't be shy; the young player will respect a firm hand if the obvious intent is to instruct and inspire. By practicing performance with the young in this way, we show by example how limits can enhance and intensify experience. A musicality of action sets moments apart from one another, as clearly separate and unique as day and night.

One ending technique is to determine how long you will play. Make eye contact and slow the pace down a bit, changing the quality of time from playtime to honesty-time. "We will play until eight-fifteen." Get a positive agreement with eye contact, or maybe a high five. This artful pause frames the experience. The honesty of the moment sets the playtime apart, casts a spell, and creates a ritual. A clear ending is also a beginning, the dawning of a new "now."

As kids grow older they automatically start to declare their own territory. Since the advent of recorded music a hundred years ago, music has become an emblem for the emerging youthful identity. And kids need it to be loud. It is their right. They need to experience the threshold of aural pain. It helps them develop a sense of limits. Experimenting with volume is one of the earliest and most formative adventures in self-determination taken by the young. Help them establish these limits. Agree on a specific time to blast the tunes. Set off the ritual space for this crucial declaration of temporal territory. This can be either a set block of time— say, 4:30 to 5:30—or a set length of time to be scheduled on a daily basis. Do not change the length of time. This would be like establishing a treaty with the natives and then taking some of the land away later. Teens especially need to know that their sonic space is inviolable. Even if you limit their access to loud music they will respect you for acknowledging its value to them.

TEN DEEP BREATHS

The rhythm of the breath is a powerful tool for orchestrating life. "Take ten deep breaths" is the best music to calm any savage beast. Take them with the over-wrought child, mate, or coworker. Share the musical time together. If you mumble comically on the exhalation, soon, no matter what turmoil seethed before, the musical quality of the time will change. Laughter will bubble out under the breath like a chuckling bassoon under the violins. But keep going! Take all ten breaths. And wait to hear the silence together at the close of this little duet. If your are not laughing together after ten mumble-breaths, keep mumbling for ten more.

TIME ENVELOPES: THE WAVE PACKETS OF LIFE

Physicists have come to conceive of light—and all electromagnetic phenomena— in terms of "wave packets." Light seems to travel in discreet units called *photons,* which are massless bundles of energy. These bundles exist at certain wavelengths and power levels. Some radio waves from outer space are miles longs. Other forms, such as x-rays, are very short. The frequency and amplitude (power level) of the various forms of radiation determine the attributes of the wave packets. The various forms deliver different messages: infrared warms; ultraviolet kills.

Every musical event occurs in what sound engineers term a *time envelope.* Like wave packets, the shape of the envelope determines the meaning carried by the sound waves. The development of electronic music helped label the four stages in this process: attack, sustain, decay, and release, or ASDR (figure 1). Understanding this structure of musical events can help us sharpen our attention to the shape of the longer cycles of ritual. Since every sigh, love affair, childhood, career, or geological era expresses musical qualities, the ASDR model informs us of a basic form to reality itself.

The attack phase lasts from the beginning of a musical event to the point were optimum resonance is achieved. Remember, most tones start with a burst of noise and static as the string or air column changes from one configuration to the next. The full resonance of the tone occurs in the sustain phase. The decay phase begins when the tone starts to decrease in intensity or volume for the last time. The release phase is the last articulation of the tone just before it returns to silence. When the activating force is removed from an instrument, the instrument resonates for a while on its own, ringing like a bell. Or perhaps, like the metal chimes of the Balinese *gamelan,* each tone is intentionally muted, and the resonance of the instrument is cut off abruptly. These presilence articulations mark the release phase of the tone.

There are also natural dynamic limits to instruments defined by the intrinsic qualities of the materials at play. A violin just can't be as loud as a trumpet. Living musically encourages us to recognize and emulate the dynamics of the time enve-

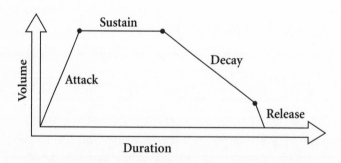

Figure 1: Envelope of a Musical Tone or "Sound Event."

lope model. This involves exploring the very farthest reaches of our limitations, racing along the borders of experience.

Music-making is risky. At any moment you can break a string, crack a note, or have your voice go hoarse. I heard a live recording of the famous cellist Yo-Yo Ma on which he got so excited playing he fell over backward. He picked himself up and jumped right back on beat. Life is the most instructive on the edge. Go there. Take a look. Stick your foot in. Dive in. Take a child with you. Or your mother. Walk up to the precipice. Hold hands and look into the abyss with the ones you love.

We are instruments ourselves. Our bodies, habits, and devotions send out tone after tone into the music of family, community, and culture. The practiced articulation of our instrument is our goal. Since every event in the time field follows the ASDR form, using it to analyze our performance gives us insight into how we are doing.

Are we taking a long time in the attack phase, scurrying around out of resonance? Do we love the sound of our own voice, indulging in our own sustained dominance in the situation? Are we clinging to the past as one moment inevitably decays, transforming into the next? Can we hear the echo, the reverberations of our actions as we release our articulations of time into the silence?

Repeating the same action over and over drives the quality of that time into your body, mind, and spirit just as the ritual chant drives the essence of sacred intention into the soul. Clear intentions turn the random bluster and spark of noise into music. Different actions, just like different instruments, songs, or styles, all have a message for us, as well as for those around us. Music shows us we can either "fake it," playing the songs of life on the fly, not bothering to honor the music enough to learn it, or we can practice, study, rehearse, and perform with intent. Practice and performance require some kind of study plan, a constant return to the discipline and joy of ritualizing our temporal faculties.

Here is a program designed to develop a sense of ritual in each of the seven chakras.

THE FIRST CHAKRA: ROOTS IN THE EARTH

The loss of ritual has uprooted our bonds with the earth. The idea of homeland really doesn't have much meaning for many of us. Only a fraction of Americans live in a setting where the land has significant influence. The term "sacred grounds" more often than not refers to a coffee joint. But there is no denying that we are dependent on the earth for our survival. All life grows out of soil and water.

The sense of place central to tribal and agricultural people is essential to our survival as well. Lacking it, we lose respect for where we live, namely the earth. This tendency leaves us "ungrounded." We think food comes from the store, and water from the tap. The stress-related illnesses and syndromes so prevalent today are caused to a great extent by a lack of connection to the source of life.

Out of touch with the earth, we are literally "at loose ends." Our fundamental connection to the source of survival at the first chakra is severed, and we flail about like a kite without a tail. The following activity is a guide to a path down into the earth, a way to maintain an internal resilience that only a deep connection with the earth can provide.

Exercise 29: Your Personal Underworld

Find a spot where you feel connected to the earth. You will recognize this spot simply through the intention of looking for it. Once you have found it, keep its location secret. This is your doorway into a powerful reality. Picture this spot as an entry hall, an atrium into the heart of the earth.

On a regular basis, find a half-hour to visit your spot. Once every two weeks might be possible for many people. Sit erect in a comfortable posture. Close your eyes. Breathe gently. Ask for entry into the lower realms of the earth. If you don't sense a response of some kind in a few minutes, get up and go about your business. Try again later.

But keep coming back to this spot. Sit in the same place, facing the same direction. Calmly ask for entry each time. Your intent will eventually open a path for you. Tell your body you'll be back soon. Rise and leave your body behind, watching it recede as you slowly go down the path. You will come to ten wide stone stairs. Take each step slowly and attentively. You will come to a door. Go on through. Who do you meet? Let them guide you. Get to know these characters. Trust them. Go for a trip. Ask a question. Expect an answer.

Come back to the doorway. Slowly mount the stairs, keeping a clear picture of the things you have seen beyond the door. Climb to the surface again. There is your waiting body. You look so safe and calm, don't you? Gently slip inside. Start to breathe with yourself. You have come home.

THE SECOND CHAKRA: IDENTITY

We have explored the power of rhythmic pattern in previous exercises. We have seen how identity is linked to the rhythm of our steps, the tone of our voice, and the way we hold our body in relation to gravity. Setting aside a time and place for actually playing rhythms with others brings the consciousness of the second chakra identity center into direct temporal relationship with your fellow players. Communicating to one another with rhythm can be the best ritual of all.

Our words are truly musical in nature, perhaps the most ancient of all our tonal artifacts. But they are cumbersome and thick with layer upon layer of meaning. When dealing with emotions—especially with kids—try stepping off the sticky verbal flypaper. Jump into the musical time-field of rhythm and harmony. Nothing communicates joy or diffuses anger and frustration better than dancing like crazy or pounding on a drum. We can proclaim our essential identity through rhythm with no loss of clarity.

DRUMMING

Sturdy drums and hefty sticks should be as ubiquitous in our homes as fresh fruit and hot water. Have a ritual space reserved in the home for noise and drumming. Design a special sacred ground where letting off steam is the order of the day. Make it kid-friendly even if you are the only kid around.

Drumming is something everyone can do. Play with others. Hand off control of the tempo and volume. Steal it away. Share it. Through music, power dynamics between people can be explored and changed without the encumbrances of logical thinking and a lot of blah-blah. Consider your responsibility to the future and include kids in the drum circle. After a child is about five years old he or she is totally equipped to stand as an equal to an adult in a simple pound-out-the-beat drum session.

Kids are destroyers. Match your materials with the potential forces that may be applied. Get drums with sturdy cowhide or extra-strength synthetic heads. Discarded plastic food buckets of all sizes are available at restaurants. Use mallets rather than sticks, as they provide a greater variety of tone. These can be expensive, so make your own. Wrap hardwood dowels with electrical friction tape to ensure a firm grip. Drill a hole halfway through a hard rubber or synthetic ball and use two-part epoxy to glue it onto the stick.

Try out the drums with some kids. Explore the range of the tones. You get the loudest and most resonant tone by *bouncing* the mallet off the head. Discover the tones at the edge, in the center, and those that resonate under various levels of force. Run along the edge of your rhythmic identity. Play with mock anger, sneakiness, and frenzy. Do this out in the open so everyone can learn to recognize each other's intentions and style. Call out, "I'm taking over! You better follow me!" or, "No! Not any faster! Please!" Be firm. "Stay with me now! Come on! LOUDER!!" Make a space for "bad" feelings to speak out.

Be aware of tempo. A slow, steady beat resonates different emotional overtones than a flurry. Hold the same pattern until you feel the rhythmic message moving through body and mind. Holding the beat for a good while prepares a group for ritual transcendence.

Try simple articulations. ONE two three four. ONE two three four. Or try this: ONE two three FOUR ONE two three FOUR ONE two three FOUR, and so on. Call these articulations *out loud* as you play. In this way your logical, sequential mind is linked to the visceral muscle memory of your body. Say the articulations slowly, then faster and faster. Each new tempo will have a new "feel."

Take a little time to get into the physicality of the strokes. How can you make your sticking patterns more efficient? A good rule of thumb is to try alternating left to right as often as you can, always starting the pattern over again with the same hand. Then listen with your heart for the message of the drum.

Pacing is all-important to the ritual experience. From the grand unfolding of High Mass to the aerobic drive of a basketball game, pacing is a primary compositional element. In the musical context, the intentional manipulation of the beat tells us that we can determine our own pacing. You don't have to be dragged into the whirlpool of frenzy. You can avoid tire spinning. With a little practice you can pick up the pace of the whole game. You can be in control. Why do people drum their fingers and tap their foot? Impatience? Nervousness? Boredom? The tempo of a beat is a carrier wave for time quality.

Exercise 30: Pacemaker

By intentionally "drumming" with any part of your body you can quickly change your mood by changing the pace of the moment. If you are bored, put your hand under the table and evenly and firmly massage the side of your thigh, like you're tending to a small injury. Lean into it. Your body-mind will pick up on the pulse and send synchronizing messages darting through every center of consciousness, repacing the whole animal. Keep up the pulse until you feel yourself moving into another time-field, your attention returning, your intentions gaining the appropriate resilience.

Exercise 31: Pumping Up

Do you need extra energy fast? Stand up and bounce on your heels for a count of fifty. This will send a new energetic musical pulse through your system from the ground up. Draw the energy up from the physical activity in your lower chakras to your third eye. Tune your body-mind to this steady, grounded pace, then pump it up!

MAKING LOVE, MAKING MUSIC

The second chakra is the home for our sexual identity. And we literally owe it to ourselves to approach sexuality from a ritualistic frame of mind. Our rhythms of courtship and lovemaking develop as we mature. One person's style may be light and lilting. The next one's may be insistent, dynamic, and even overbearing at times. There is no limit to the range of style, pace, and rhythms in romance. In the realm of love we know that many different patterns can combine ever so musically. No other area of life demands more acute attention. To make and accept love musically one must listen. Every gesture is a question. Every glance is an answer. Every touch is a melody, every response is a variation. Attended by respect, support, and passion, love evolves between people like a great symphonic theme, encompassing variations of every tempo, every timbre, and every expression. The keynotes may change. The instrumentation may alter. But with deep intention and practiced skill, the themes of love are maintained.

The music of love flows best when both partners strive to always hear their own tone in the mix. The harmony of loving hearts and bodies—just as in music——is generated *between* two strong voices. Partners must always sing out and hear the other's music at the same time. One voice can be dominant only through the willing subordination of the other. When one player feels like the other is not listening, half the music is wasted.

Expressions of love should always have overtones of ritual musicality. Every aspect of our body-mind should come into play. Diversity in the natural world insures survival of the whole; variation, trust, and creativity in love sustains the bonds that hold two hearts in harmony. Use the breath, the voice, and every muscle and bone to express the highest intentions of your desires. Trade off leading and following. Use rhythm and the physical resonance of the whole body. Dance! Always strive to act and listen at the same time. In sexual matters and in every aspect of deep relationships, making love and making music are closely related. We succeed best in both activities when every overtone of consciousness in our body-mind is intentionally brought into play. Listen. Sing. Embrace. Play on!

THE THIRD CHAKRA: POWER

Breath is the channel for power at the third chakra. Physical stamina depends on a healthy cardiovascular system, well maintained with the cleansing fire of aerobic exercise. Rituals feeding the third chakra should always involve the breath. Make the time to play, run, bike, or even sing to the point of breathlessness. Do this together with those you love. Establish a ritual connection at this central power point.

One reason choral music is often chosen for ritual is that everyone in the choir is breathing as one. After the stirring game of tag, or a power walk around the block, synchronize your breath with your playmate. Look into each other's eyes and sanctify the moment with a unison breath or two. Get on the same wavelength of life force. Inspire yourself! Pass it around!

The next exercise becomes a ritual act, an opening call to worship, and a closing benediction to any energetic group activity such as a rambunctious game of tag, a jog around the track, a game of racket ball, or a hike up the hill.

Exercise 32: Windjammer

This is a way to experience a harmony of wills. Two people (or more) engage in active exercise. Then, gather close enough to each other so you can hear the breath. Breathe in unison for a while. Inhale and exhale as one for ten cycles. This is basically a huddle. Break the circle and go about your romp, whatever it may be. Continue with the activity until you are in the aerobic state, huffing and puffing but not completely winded. Come back together and reconnect the breath rhythms once more until everyone has "caught" his or her breath. Repeat three times: huddle, exercise, breathing to a calm place. Do this whole activity with an intention for sharing a resonant, energetic, powerful time.

THE FOURTH CHAKRA: RELATIONSHIP

Rituals celebrate heartfelt relationships between people acknowledging a special time and place. Rituals reiterate long-standing intentions, sending the same signal through the time field again and again, singing a variation of the heartbeat itself. The feeling the band gets when it locks onto the beat is the same feeling you get when you sense an emotional resonance with a dear friend—you know *he* knows that you know what he knows.

All our relations—love, fright, excitement, apprehension, and deep relaxation—are played out in the rhythm of our pounding heart. Any ritual designed to foster harmonious relationships needs to center on the heart. We will investigate the musicality of relationship in greater detail in the next chapter. Here is an exercise to get your ready for the more in-depth work to come.

Exercise 33: An Empathy Symphony

Go to a familiar place: your home, a favorite park, your school, or your workplace. Take a deep breath, expanding your ribcage, bringing the air fully into your chest. Exhale slowly, keeping the chest lifted. Repeat this "heart breath" three times. Continue breathing in this way as you focus your attention on various objects around the scene. As you do, remember a feeling associated with that object. Breathe that feeling into your heart three times. Keep the chest expanded and open. Find another focal point. Breathe in an image, a feeling, a memory. Breathe out while holding the feeling in your heart. Take three breaths.

THE FIFTH CHAKRA: EXPRESSING YOUR SELF

The themes of a lifetime are composed minute by minute, and over decades. Through the years, the rhythm of lifestyle and habit generate one's personality. The attitudes we assume, the food we eat, our style of dress, our spiritual observances, our tone of voice, and the relationship our body has with gravity all reverberate through the corridors of our life. Through actions, choices, and mostly our voices, we project physical and psychic themes into our surroundings. These themes are expressed through the overtone of consciousness whirling at the throat chakra.

The songs we send into our midst are most often improvised without a thought. Our expressions reverberate with temporal qualities such as tidiness, elegance, funkiness, calmness, frenzy, simplicity, overbearance, confidence, love, and so on. The lessons of music show us, however, that clear intention can add artfulness to our lives.

This can be as simple as choosing music appropriate to our intentions. The world of recorded music is so diverse and eclectic today you can find musical accompaniment for any personality or attitude. Music clearly sets the tone for your temporal environment. What reflects your identity? What music might you play to gently push you in another direction? Once you're well awake in the morning, try playing something with an easy walking rhythm. A nice jazz ride, or the gentle lope of reggae. Maybe you would prefer big band or Baroque? When you get home from work do you need to relax with a Brahms *largo* or recharge with some Chicago blues? What better furnishings for your home than the appropriate sound-stimulus!

A sluggish morning person can intentionally energize his or her space. For the hyper type, the well-chosen musical selection can mellow it all down. The quality of your time environment—your constant home—can be readily changed. Intentions are key. Give in to the music and let it mold you. Refer to the "Suggested Listening" section at the end of the book for various sonic furnishings for the times of your day. Country punk by Jello Biafra and Mojo Nixon, women's world beat by Pele Juju, space jazz by Rashelle Farrell, vocal chantlike orchestrations by Bobby McFerrin and Voicestra, polka meets garage band thrash in Those Darn Accordions—the choices are limited only by your willingness to listen.

You will discover that you can actually change your pace, intensity, mood, and delivery through this musical ritualization of your time. Is there really a need to rush so? What are the benefits of dawdling? There definitely are some, but do they serve your needs at the moment? By actively listening to the tempo of your actions you can learn to choose the best pace and intensity, gaining a basic element of control over your life.

Slowing things down just a bit reveals qualities hidden within the simplest tasks, such as raking leaves, sweeping, or wiping a window. Most physical actions are oscillations by nature, resonant from the get-go. By slowing things down intentionally just a tad, we expose temporal contours just under the surface. We can watch ourselves performing. We thoughtfully approach the chore as it spins on the lathe, enhancing the shape of things as we work.

Other cultures exhibit a basic pace much slower than the whirl of our thrill-a-minute feel-a-thon. In a tiny Mexican market I watched a fourteen-year-old boy load my few items into a bag with the care of a jeweler setting stones in a tiara. I noticed this tempo everywhere I went in that country. Even in busy situations, the pace of the culture resonated care, respect, and appreciation. Notice the music around you. Practice and play your favorite themes.

TRANSITIONS

When a horn player moves from one tone to the next, his or her tongue and lips significantly interfere with the smooth flow of air passing through the horn. This is the attack phase of the ASDR form. When the fiddle player changes the direction of the bow, the string goes into a convulsion or transient waves, dragged out of free resonance by the abrupt change in the force activating the string. An oscilloscope would show a burst of white noise at the start of these musical events.

The articulate musician is able to minimize the jumble of nonresonant, transient waves at the beginning of each tone.

This control is really a manipulation of time itself. To have well-articulated control over tone, one must focus one's attention ahead in time, aiming the entire body-mind at the resonant center of the next note in the series lying just past the noise.

All temporal events connect like the notes in a melody. There is a little jumble of noisy static of some sort between every experience. Every movement from the known to the unknown releases protests on some level. The easygoing person is admired because he or she, like the articulate musician, moves in acceptance of this state of affairs, unperturbed through change, reaching ahead, moving on, seeing the real issue. How we move through change into resonance reveals our level of facility on our instrument. The great musician can actually play with the noise latent in the attack, gaining great depth of expression by turning jarring forces to his or her advantage.

One powerful practice aid in the expressive articulation of change is the sense of humor. The full, round laugh is one of the most resonant expressions in the human vocabulary. Keep that theme in your head. It can harmonize with just about anything. Tragedy plus time creates comedy. Humor cracks open a door into a realm where the pain of an experience is transformed into laughter. Here is a ritual designed to allow you to open that door at will.

Exercise 34: Laughing Out Loud

Transport yourself to a "bad" time, returning in memory to a sad or frustrating moment. Bow your head with your eyes closed for a moment. Gently smile as you shake your head from side to side with this bad time in mind. Keep shaking your head. Smile. Go on, smile! Now chuckle out loud. It may feel dumb or forced. No matter. Go on! Laugh out loud a bit. Keep thinking about that really, really bad time. Build the laughter. Act out. Let time wash away the hurt and see the ridiculous aspects, the stupidity, the delusion and irony. Laugh until you actually feel the true humor in it all.

LET THE DANCE BEGIN

After a long day we can feel drained. We imagine we have no more energy under our skin. But our physical body has enormous reserves of energy. Hormones and neurotransmitters are ready to throw open the doors to those energy reserves. After hours of work or study it's more than likely our intentions are tapped out, not our raw power potential. Five minutes of intense leg-shaking to up-tempo ska, hip-hop, rock-a-billy, or a good polka band will put the edge back on the moment. Our center of gravity will once again tap into the earth, and resonant movement will tune the senses. A bright spot of clarity will be shared, bringing a bit of light to the rest of the evening. The idea is to get up and dance on the tips of the toes. Grab your spouse, offspring, or wild-child self and move! Making this kind of house party a regular habit will bring a ritual power to an otherwise lackluster time of day.

THE SIXTH CHAKRA: PICTURING THE SCORE

The sixth chakra symbolizes the integrative power of mindful awareness. All the elements of time and space are "seen" by the perceptive consciousness. The conductor of an orchestra has a written document that symbolizes the all-seeing eye of the composer. This is the score.

The written score is a crucial element in the Western musical tradition. We live by rule of law. We respect the written word. The manuscripts of the musical and literary greats are prized possessions. The score of a great composition is the physical record of the creative act of "catching" musical forms as they emerge from the spiritual world of Sound into the acoustic realm of the sounds we hear. The composer "plays" with an idea for a while until it becomes well defined enough to write down. Ideas are caught, manipulated, discarded, and then finalized into the score.

Let's move through a compositional process to create a score for a new life-performance based on your improvisations over a week's time.

139

Exercise 35: Score One for You

Using the following chart as a guide, keep a log of your significant activities for a week (figure 2, page 141). Make note of when you started and stopped the activity. The more specific you can be, the better. You are creating a temporal sketchbook, a record of the times of your life for that week. Try to do this in "real time," jotting down your entries as they happen. Or take time at the end of each day to do this. Once your events have been logged, go to a specific place. Settle in and relax. Now, without a lot of thought, quickly associate each entry on your list with one of the seven aspects of consciousness (the chakras). Where did each activity register on your body-mind instrument?

Review the list again. Rate each entry with a number, 1 through 5. Five signifies a highly meaningful experience; 1 denotes an experience that meant very little to you. Strive to recognize the intrinsic quality of each entry. Be discriminating. Meaningful experiences are not always enjoyable, lengthy, or lucrative. A number 5 might fall next to a tragedy, or a glance.

Your log of events is now organized by overtone of consciousness and significance of meaning. Review your list once more. Cast your memory back to the time of each event. Try to remember your intent at that moment. With one word, record that intent next to the entry. Try to be accurate even with this one word. Discern devotion from caring, stamina from health, generosity from goodness, determination from perseverance.

Examine your log now with all this information in front of you. Where did your best intentions come into play? Where were meaningful events accompanied by inappropriate intentions? What is the dominant overtone in your week of experience? How would you take this score and arrange it for the clearest, most harmonious rendition of a week of your time?

Choose a handful of these entries that you feel deserve to be ritualized into the score of your life. Put them on the calendar. Practice daily.

EXPECTATIONS AND THE FUTURE OF RITUAL

Rituals are rooted in the past but always look to the future. The past spirals in, the future spirals out. Ritual behavior uses experience as the foundation and expecta-

Day	Activity/Event	Chakra	Rating	Intent
Time				
Start:				
Stop:				
Time				
Start:				
Stop:				
Time				
Start:				
Stop:				
Time				
Start:				
Stop:				

Figure 2: Sample Log for Exercise 35.

tion as the springboard into the next ritual cycle. This is why repetitive musical elements like the beat and chant are central to ritual. The basic musical time qualities inherent in repetition are evident in a frantic dance step as well as the cycles of astronomical time.

Expectation is the basic emotional attribute of musical repetition and ritual power. As we ride on the cycles of the beat—or the seasons—we feel the contour of time envelopes and we sense the coming arrival of the next measure of time. When time fulfills our expectations it is always sweet music to our ears. When the expectation is not answered it is as if the drumhead shattered or the singer choked. We are wrenched out of time.

Expectation is founded on past events. When we hear three evenly articulated pulses we naturally expect the fourth to land in step. For ages, composers have used the power of expectation to draw us into the music, captivating our musical time sense. We wait for the resolution to the phrase, the answer to the melody's question, the harmonic cadence, the final crashing bar.

In the longer envelopes of ritual cycles we anticipate the coming of spring. We fantasize about our birthday celebration. We hope for good returns at the stockholder's meeting. The more we can realize the ritual dynamics underlying our lifepatterns, the more practiced in the musical life we will become. We can choose the rituals we engage in on the basis of the musical qualities they embody. The year-end audit does not resonate like the yearly fishing trip. What is your highest intent for your life? Ritualize *that*.

PRAYER

Prayer is a singular concept. It has very few related words in English. The word "prayer" comes from the ancient Indo-European root *perk,* meaning "to ask." The magic of prayer lies in this root meaning; to ask implies there will be a reply. And one must listen to catch any reply. Prayer is simply the act of bringing a question into the open. If we pay attention, we always perceive some form of direction guiding our next step, our next performance. Because listening is such a part of the musical art, every time a musician plays a note it is a prayer in this sense.

For the musician, the answers come back in the echo, the harmony, the motion of the maestro's baton, and from the joy of the audience. The artist is a seeker whose every gesture is a prayer to the gods of inspiration. The answers to the artist's prayers come only if he or she keeps listening and playing, aiming his or her intentions into the next cycle. On a cultural level, ritual is the living embodiment of this technique of listening and playing at the same time.

Call-and-response is a universal form of prayer. Rooted in ancient rituals in every culture, the dynamics of call-and-response set up a powerful circuit of energy between a central priest and a congregation of participants. As individual members of a congregation, we naturally identify with the single voice of the priest, shaman, or gospel singer calling out the entreaty. That single voice could be ours. When the group responds, it symbolizes the joyous voices of the Heavenly Host answering the call. The community is transformed, cast as the Source of the answer. This reversal of roles magically informs us that the answers to our questions bloom inside our own hearts.

A ritual does not simply mark time like a birthday. Many cultures believe rituals must be completed in order for the cycles of nature to continue. If the sacrifice is not made the harvest will not come. The seasonal celebrations are not just an excuse to party. They are the responsibility of the caretakers of the earth.

Rituals grow in the human time habitat for very good reasons. They are manifestations of our unique position as the middle creature. We are influenced by a biological imperative to connect our animal and spiritual natures. The Druid ceremony in the sacred grove and the country line dance are playing from the same score. Ritual, performance, and prayer are pervasive manifestations of our true nature as temporal beings. Turning patterns of behavior—the habits, schedules, and routines of life—into ritual will return us to our true selves.

Exercise 36: Out There

This is a two-part exercise. Stand up in the largest room of your house. Close your eyes. After an interval of silence to frame the exercise, ask this question: "Where do I go next?" Breathe in and out. Open your eyes. Focus very closely on the first thing you see. Inhale, exhale, and then take three slow, firm steps toward that point in the room. Inhale and exhale again. Close your eyes. Spin around slowly in place a bit. Stop spinning. With eyes closed repeat the exercise, starting with the question, "Where do I go next?" Repeat seven times.

Go outside and do the same exercise, except this time ask, "What is out there for me?" As you breathe in and out with your eyes closed, notice a sound. Before you open your eyes, turn toward the sound. Open your eyes and try to locate the source visually. If you can't spot it, no matter. Take your steps in the direction of the sound in any case. Repeat this one seven times.

You will always get an answer. The insistence of the pulse of time gives us no choice. We always move toward the source of *something*.

6 HARMONIC RELATIONSHIPS

Our day-to-day experience is filled with resonant relationships. Physical objects, living beings, and aspects of consciousness influence each other and change as a result of the interaction. All relationships rely on an exchange of energy. To be expressive and sonorous, the relationships of music must operate in resonant correspondence. In a similar way, when forces and materials relate in an integral fashion, a harmonious musical nature is revealed in communication on the biological, conceptual, and emotional levels. Relationships in the musical art shed light on all our communications, including our dependence on the earth for survival, our exchanges with loved ones and coworkers, and the dialogue we carry out with our inner voices.

The linguistic history of the word "relationship" shows us that balance is the key to all relationships. Ancient financial transactions were done with scales and weights. *Tel* is an Indo-European root word referring to the act of balancing weights on a simple scale. Derivatives of *tel* have to do with money and payment, such as a "toll." A Latin cognate, *tolerare*, means "to bear," or "endure," as in carrying a weight, hence "tolerate."

There are many derivatives of *tel* in several languages. All these words have at their core the idea of balance between one value and another. English descendants from this idea include elate, relate, translate, legislate, and superlative. Notice how the phonemes of *tel* were reversed over time to become "late." This retrograde modulation is very common in the evolution of language, and is also a typical device in musical composition, where the notes of a melody are played in reverse.

In ancient Greek, *tantalos* was the word for the standardized weights used on the balance scales. This is where we get the word "talent." Talent is seen as a given quality, fixed and immutable. A talent is a recognized value by which related things are measured. Our talents are always available to us but not always used. Talents gain importance as one puts them into practice through dedication and perseverance. A talent may be set aside or ignored, but by definition talents always remain available. They are seen as the gifts of fate and genetics. To ignore a talent wastes something of intrinsic value.

In every relationship there is always give and take. To judge the value of any situation one must watch the scale of relationship as it swings, putting out more talents as needed. Hiding talent away removes the possibility of balance. Fixing the scales or cheating the balance will inevitably extract a toll. Relationship—the balance of talents—demands that we tolerate the inevitable swings, the ups and downs. We should actually embrace the swing. These ups and downs communicate a high degree of elation in and of themselves. Many people crave the inevitable roller coaster of love, seeking out affair after affair. The scales never lie. We will prosper to the extent that we trust our talents and keep them out in the open. Where is the fulcrum in this system? And what force pulls so evenly on both sides of the scale?

THE FULCRUM OF LOVE

In our examination of the forces moving through the body-mind we saw that the heart was the pivot point between the earth-bound rhythms of nature and the ethereal songs of the spirit. When life is in balance our heart is at ease, relaxed, poised, receptive, and expressive. The consciousness of harmony and love swirl at the heart center. It follows that we stand to relate best when we are tuned to the overtone of consciousness singing in the heart, for it is here where we literally feel our physical and spiritual natures balancing on the fulcrum of love.

Personal relationships are sturdy when love is the point of reference. The sweet music of loving communication is obvious to us. Loving expressions create concentric waves of joy. We can feel the resonance. We feel the waves of elation in every one of the seven centers of consciousness. We ride the wave of pleasure from physical action and sex. Hearts aligned to a common inspiration take our breath away. The counterpoint of bright conversation engages our voices to speak truly of our visions and ourselves. The "aha!" moments of shared insight stir up new brainstorms. The deep hum of group prayer and meditation carries our awareness heavenward.

The value on the scale increases as we invest more and more into our relations. Don't be shy. The fulcrum will endure. Like a solid beat or a well-tuned instrument, love will resonate strong and true. The system is so simple: two sides of a balance swinging on a common point of reference. But what pulls on the scale of love? What force causes the scales to swing in the first place?

Our awareness of our own death puts a constant pull on the scales of love. When we see that we have a limited time to play on the wide lawn of the earth, love soon becomes a matter of life and death. The tug of death pulls on our heartstrings and we swing away on the ups and downs of life. Trusting the fulcrum of love we can strike a balance between the mysteries of the unknown and the celebration of the present moment. Music demonstrates the same dynamic. Balance is the key to every aspect of music. When balance is lost, the violin's tone goes slack, the rhythm falters, the style disappears or mutates.

To ascertain the value of any relationship, one must actively participate in the process. Weigh in on the matter. Watch for the swings as more or less talent rides on the scales. We are best served by being patient as the arms swing on the fulcrum. The system is alive, dynamic, and musical. With a careful and confident hand we can attend to the constant movement of talents riding on the fulcrum of love.

STRIKING A BALANCE

The musical art describes many aspects of this lifelong balancing act. Like attending to loving relationships, music demands a constant, willing participation. From note to note the process never ends. Expressions like "being in tune," "staying on the beat," and "speaking in a clear tone" make perfect sense to us apart from the musical context because our musical nature is second nature to us. Everyone has an intuitive understanding of what is demanded by the harmony of life.

Sections of musical ensembles are dynamically balanced to create the desired texture of a musical work. In smaller groups, like a string quartet, melodic lines intertwine to express the intricacies of counterpoint. There is nothing more ecstatic than musicians weaving and flowing playfully together. The boisterous romp of the Dixieland band, the delicate maneuverings of a Mozart flute duet, the break-neck buggy-ride of the finger-picker and the fiddle player, the luscious, fiery harmony of the *salsa coro*. Musical ensembles are embodiments of the best possible group dynamic. Counterpoint, balance, and interplay create the composition of our inner life, our family dynamics, and the wider cultural identity.

Remember my roofer friend, John? The guy who couldn't play music? All he needed was the chance to lower his head and dig in. When given this chance, he sensed that the group would gladly follow his lead. He found his perfect relationship. He balanced a natural talent he used every day—pounding firmly and accurately—with a loving and accepting situation. His musical joy was potent, virile, and sexy. He was in love. Like a bird riding the air, he sailed on the waves of musical time one stroke after the other.

Every moment of the day we have the opportunity to strike John's perfect balance. Musical moments like John's touch people deeply every day. Lewis Thomas' notion that making and listening to music is a biological need of all humans reminds me of a Gary Larson *Far Side* cartoon picturing a caveman band. Skin-clad players stare blankly at sticks and rocks held heavily in their grubby hands. Before them stands a conductor with a raised baton. The score on the conductor's music stand has but one crudely drawn eighth note. Larson's image is of the musical Big Bang, one primordial WHAM of a relationship that may be all that those cavemen can handle—for now.

Larson captures a snapshot of humans on the fulcrum of musical time. It's the image of one instant when everyone acts together. In his comic vision of the so-called uncivilized past, one note was all the poor slobs were capable of. And yet that one note says it all. If we can start out together, why wouldn't we evolve together, in love with music forever, moving through the eons to techno-pop and Mahler? Getting everyone's attention for the initial downbeat is the first accomplishment. Sustaining the synchrony of love is the true miracle of humanity. Practice makes perfect. Somehow we're still at it.

INTONATION

The first relationship our body-mind addresses is the position and awareness of our physical being in space. No matter where you go, there you are. With every pain in the back, stubbed toe, or traffic jam, we are struck with the blunt fact that we are physical beings tripping through a physical world. To be loving and communicative we have to realize that our reactions to our physical reality—inner and outer—register on everyone around us, and on the entire surface of this delicate frog pond of a planet we call home. Intonation with our location is the initial and constant musical act. Let the pull of the earth have its way with you, and notice how the dance goes. Fall in love with every place you are. Tune in to how your body fits with your surroundings. Practice your body-mind intonation.

Intonation most commonly refers to the musical act of "playing in tune." Two notes of exactly the same frequency are in tune. Intervals in pleasing harmonic proportion are said to be in tune as well. Intonation demands that instruments be played in reference to a tonal standard. This standard can be an internal and relative one, as when all six guitar strings are tuned one at a time in reference to the lowest string on the instrument.

Being in tune can also mean playing in accurate relation to an external standard. In Western music this standard is typically the frequency of 440 vibrations per second. This is the pitch to which orchestras and electronic guitar tuners refer. Without this point of reference, or through lack of attention to it, harmonies are corrupted. Being out of tune for any length of time is far worse on our Western ears than playing an occasional wrong note.

Musical intonation is a constant balancing act. Each note is tuned as it is articulated. The musician instantly raises or lowers the pitch to match the prevailing harmony. Only keyboard players and percussionists are excused from this duty.

Everyone knows intuitively what "being in tune" means in everyday life. On the internal, personal level it means to act in accordance with our best intentions, our truest love. Being in tune with our external surroundings implies an instantaneous adaptability. The in-tune person demonstrates a keen perception followed by flexible, effective, and appropriate action.

This moment-by-moment active awareness is the essence of musical intonation as well. Musicians are always sliding around, getting back in tune. When a player moves from one note to the next there is always an instant of adjustment when the tonal center of the new pitch must be found as soon as possible. In our composition of our everyday lives, this tuning process is going on with every step we take, every new situation, emotion, or experience we encounter.

Exercise 37: Spot On Again

Stand on one leg. Stay balanced. Hop to the other foot. Stay balanced there for a moment or two. If need be, jiggle around to stay in that position for a bit. Now, with strong intention, hop to the other foot, landing in a slightly different facing. Balance. Hop and change. Face in a new direction. Concentrate on the differences in the space as you hop from foot to foot. You are balanced and in a different place each time.

The maestro will correct the viola section when he or she hears a sour note, but how do we stay in tune at work? During an argument? Throughout a love affair? Where's our maestro? Is there a standard for personal intonation? Where is the "440 Hz" of the everyday? How do we learn to hear it? The therapist, pastor, or well-meaning friend may say, "Be true to yourself!" But how do we hear our true voice? What is the technique for keeping our body-mind in tune?

Musical relationships are dynamic, changing, flexible, random, and even chaotic at times. In performance the musician is constantly slipping all over the place. Tempo is a fluid standard, very much a product of the audiences' reactions as well as the players' efforts. Live performances always speed up and slow down through the course of a piece. So in the middle of all this sloppiness, where is the point of reference?

Musicians pay constant attention to the effect of their actions. This is the secret of musicianship. Good musicianship demands that one act confidently, and then observe the interactions with fellow players. Music teaches us that we can express a deep personal intonation only when we are willing and eager to adjust to others in the spirit of love.

Just as great performances express the inner truths of a composition, our actions express the inner truths we hold in our hearts. Simply "having feelings" does not manifest love, no matter how deep these feeling may register inside. To have meaning to another, feelings must be expressed in word, deed, and action. The printed score remains silent until the bow strikes the string. Love is made—actually formed, congealed, and manifested—only through active, productive relationships. Sections of musical compositions are called "movements." Love is said to move hearts. We stay in tune with our highest self—and the loves of our life—when we move with intent, in tune with our inner truth, while at the same time paying close attention to how others react.

Through practice and dedication, musicians discover the joy of their voices through the feedback they get from the appreciation their music generates. They constantly listen to the music and intentionally blend their music with all the other expressions moving around them. With a critical ear and a balanced intent, the resulting music embodies intonation on every level. This is the elation of a perfect love. Musicians always take a moment to tune up before they play with others. Out of respect to our fellow participants in the music of life, shouldn't we take a moment now and then to tune up our body-mind instrument?

Exercise 38: Personal Intonation

Stand erect with relaxed shoulders. Sing a low "ho," feeling the vibrations in your pelvis and belly. Now raise the pitch a bit and sing "ha." Feel that tone in your solar plexus and chest area. Raise the pitch a bit more and sing "heh," as in "heck." This resonates in your throat. Sing a bit higher with the syllable "hee" ringing in your head. Finally, smile really big and sing "yyyy." This vibration should almost take the top of your head off. You are using body cavities to resonate several distinct ranges in your voice.

Repeat the tones, paying attention to the subtle feeling you get as you sing in the different ranges. Look for signs of darkness, clotting, and blockage in the various cavities resonated by the tones. Also look for brightness, release, and joy. Tune into the darkest and the lightest areas, and the associated sound and range.

Now you are going to intentionally transfer some of the good feeling in your clearest area to the clogged, dark area. Take a deep breath and sing the tone associated with the clear area. Feel the strength and clarity ringing there. Now switch immediately to the dark area, singing its associated tone and syllable. Feel the clarity of the first tone imbue the tone of the dark area with fresh energy. Repeat this two-tone song seven times.

You may be moving from low to high pitch ranges. Or the opposite might be true. The key here is to perform with intent. You are activating a healing relationship between two areas of your body-mind.

An advanced version of this technique uses the tones of the harmonic series specifically associated with each chakra. For this you substitute the nonspecific pitches with tones of the harmonic series appropriate to your fundamental tone (chapter 3, figure 1, page 85). Moving energy between these seven tones "fine tunes" your personal instrument, resonating every overtone of consciousness throughout your body-mind *at will*.

THE HEART OF RELATIONSHIP

For anything to be truly rewarding and joyous, we say, "My heart has got to be in it." We have seen how the heart is the place where inspiration from above and physical energy from the earth meet to manifest art, culture, and the bonds of love. The heart is the fulcrum for all relationships.

Lena Horne, the acclaimed actress and vocal stylist of the mid-twentieth century, suffered from a common affliction: stage fright. Like Jackie Robinson in the world of sports, she was always painfully aware of her role and duty in the struggle of the black race. Lena was a pioneer in the world of popular entertainment. On the handbills for musical showcases in Las Vegas her picture was bigger than Frank Sinatra's. Through it all she struggled to keep a clear view of her responsibilities to her art, her race, and her family. And yet with all her success, before nearly every performance she struggled with shortness of breath, heart palpitations, and cold sweats. Why would such a great talent be so stressed in front of an audience?

In his book *The Language of the Heart*, James J. Lynch reviews the considerable research on the relationship between human communication—mainly speech—and the health of the heart. It has been noted for decades that blood pressure and heart rate will generally rise during speech. Physiological factors such as constriction of the airway and unevenness of breathing were taken to be the cause. Lynch's research, however, showed that the physical mechanics of speech do not by themselves cause a change in the vital signs.

By studying various populations such as prisoners, schizophrenics, high blood pressure sufferers, and others, Lynch determined unequivocally that the crucial factor in changing heart function during conversation is what he terms the "social membrane," the place where the self, projected out through the voice, meets the world. Moving personal messages back and forth over this membrane is a natural cause for stress.

Understandably, Lena Horne's social membrane was extremely sensitive. The thought of putting her talents on stage caused her heart to race, her skin to crawl. She knew that a big, white world was out there ready to judge her, and by inference, her people as well. This star performer had good reason to get the jitters. Her social membrane was highly vulnerable and under attack.

As we reach out into our surroundings with our voice, a fight-or-flight mechanism is triggered throughout the body-mind and the heart starts to work harder, readying us for the applause or the retributions. Lynch not only found that talking to someone—and especially a group of people—elevates cardiac activity, he also found that listening in an active and attentive way lowers the stress on the heart, sometimes below resting-state levels. Talking and listening emerge as the two sides of a balance. One side raises us up, preparing us for risk; the other side lowers us down, grounding us in the safety of taking in information that may serve us in the future.

The sensitivity and responsiveness of the heart to human contact—most often through conversation—show that there is indeed a membrane of interaction where our entire being strikes a balance of relationship with the many other selves we contact every day. If these interchanges are truly reciprocal, heart rates and blood pressures reflect an easy give and take. If one is nervous, always "second guessing," or concerned about how they are "coming across," the heart is in constant fight-or-flight mode, and cardiac activity remains high.

Physiologically we are all on stage simply by opening our mouths to speak. We get nervous, love-struck, embarrassed, tongue-tied, and clumsy because we want so desperately to cross over that social membrane. We want to gracefully strike a balance. We want to relate. And the storms of hormones stand between. We fear intolerance. We are afraid to place ourselves on the scales of love, dangling there for all to see. The outside world is often cruel, thoughtless, judgmental, flippant, or just downright stupid. No wonder the heart pounds and the ears ring. No wonder we blush and sweat and stutter. Our heart feels the influence of others through the social membrane, and races in response.

But at every turn in the conversation we have the chance to rest, sit back, and open up our ears. When we truly listen we automatically drop our defenses and become receptive. We demonstrate a simple trust. We give ourselves over to the other for a moment. The self is no longer on the starting blocks. Paying attention allows the emanations of someone else to pass over the membrane, informing us of the other's perspective. We say, "I get you now." The heart calms, but only for a moment. When the conversation turns our way, we're on the spot once more and the heart picks up the tempo. Is this what the expression "life's ups and downs" is all about?

Here is where music shows us the technique for balancing all of this. The more we listen as we play the calmer and more confident we become. Through an engaged attention to the talents and expressions of others, we are informed and inspired. We strike a balance between what is going on around us and what we have to offer. Music demonstrates that listening is the key to good relationships, facilitating an easy flow of information across the social membrane. Without the relaxing effect of the open ear we would always be on the defensive.

This dynamic nature of relationship is exemplified in many aspects of music. The call-and-response forms of gospel singing—rooted in the sacred chants of the African homeland—move through musical time like a spirited conversation. In classical music, the conversational element is most evident in the compositional device of the *sequence*. The violins might state a phrase. Immediately at the end of the phrase the woodwinds may take up the same melody starting on a different note, or in a different register. Note-to-note relationships within the two phrases remain very much the same, but the change in timbre from one group of instruments to the next sets up a conversational quality. Depending on the emotional nature of the melody itself, these exchanges can take on significant power and effect.

The musical model exemplifies the best ways to project one's self beyond the delicate membrane separating us from the world. We succeed in health and creativity when we act forthrightly with clear intent while noticing the effect our actions have on our surroundings, and then adjusting our subsequent actions to further our highest intent.

Willing harmony is the hallmark of love. Moving from your heart-center communicates that you honor an inner resonant awareness. This is similar to a group of musicians playing accurately to the beat. This kind of intonation puts opinions, reactions, emotions, and transitory situations in perspective. Heart awareness will create a magical atmosphere, a subtle and comforting detachment from the swirl and bumps of life. The scales may fly up and down day-by-day, moment-to-moment, but with an eye to the balance point of love, challenges and triumphs become the rehearsals for the larger performances of life.

ACTIVE LISTENING AND THE "I-MESSAGE"

To help others more clearly understand where you are coming from, the best approach is to express yourself in terms of what you are feeling for yourself at the moment. Express your feelings from your point of view. Say, "I imagine that you mean . . . ," or "When you say that I feel very . . ." Don't second-guess the other person. All you can truly say is how you feel. Tell the person how his or her words affected you. Do not accuse him or her with something like, "You really are trying to . . . ," or "That doesn't make any sense . . ." But you can say, "That makes me feel like I've just been insulted," or "I'm getting really mad right now!"

Other examples include: "I imagine you to feel . . . ," or "I have a hunch what you're saying is . . . ," or "I feel you're telling me that . . ." Reiteration communicates that a message has made it over to your side of the social membrane separating you from the speaker. This feedback relieves the natural fear of isolation we all must confront. The barriers relax. The fight-or-flight reaction inherent in all exchanges is lessened. The heart calms and talents are placed on the balance in a relationship of mutual respect. We are playing together. This style of communication echoes the call-and-response form of music. In both cases, listening is the foundation for understanding.

Here's how reiterative, active listening works. Listen for what you recognize to be the power points. Then give the speaker a concise echo of what you think you heard. These power points are the keynotes, the patterns, the melodic seeds, and the structural foundations of the speaker's message. The speaker will eagerly correct you, or add a missed theme. He or she wants you to understand. Your mutual intent for understanding works as your bond. Notice how similar the sounds are in the words "intonation" and " intention." We speak music.

This I-Message approach is key to more intimate communication as well. When your mate is flaring, sputtering, fuming, and going off about some upsetting matter, listen through the sparks to the power points. All you may clearly receive is the flash of raw emotion. Fine. That's a kettledrum-on-the-downbeat kind of place to start. Say, "It seems to me you are really upset about something right now. Honestly, it scares me, but I feel something's really got you teed off. Tell me again. I want to know what it is." Your statement about how you feel acknowledges the raw emotion of the moment without accusations or defensiveness. That's all anyone ever really wants anyway. We all need the assurance that we are not out there all alone. This is a musical act of atonement; the art of two hearts reaching out across the scary gulf of isolation we first recognized in our youth when we saw death for the first time.

ACTIVE LISTENING AT WORK

The orchestra is a clear example of a productive, mutually rewarding team. The composer defines the tasks needed to perform the score. Every player has a role to play on an instrument suited for specific musical tasks within the entire composition. In a similar way, team building in the workplace starts with defining relationship between roles and tasks.

Productive teams work best when many small tasks are defined so clearly that collectively they meet a larger goal. These tasks in turn define roles needed to complete the tasks. One person can fill more than one role, serving many tasks. Tasks are best assigned to the appropriate players. For example, the "money-minder" should respect his or her position and not assume the tasks of the "idea-person," whose job is to tell the "implementor" how to realize the idea for less money.

At work, as in the musical group, capable individuals filling specific roles through agreed-upon tasks carry the common goals forward. In the best teams there is a procedure for cross-referencing. This is the brainstorming session, the jam, the place for one player to make suggestions to another. This happens in musical groups as well. Many rock, jazz, and folk ensembles create their music together, without a score, relying on the interplay of the groups for their inspiration and guidance.

In this way, everyone knows how one's role fits in relationship to others. The action of the individual player "locks" with others. A resonant reenforcement results and everyone's work gets easier through harmonious support. The joy in this kind of setup comes from a mutual self-respect, a musical appreciation for each other's voice. Inappropriately jumping over to another part only confuses things. Members of a well-defined, smooth running team know that they are working in relationship with others, and everyone is working toward a common goal.

PUNCTUALITY AND PACING

In music and sports rhythmic accuracy between players shows humans at their best. Every physical movement demonstrates loud and clear the synchrony of mind and heart. How can we reflect this beauty, elegance, and virtuosity in our daily comings and goings? For starters, simply be on time. Punctuality is a musical attribute. It brings people together at the same place at the same time for the same reasons.

The beginning of an event is crucial to meaning, impact, and style. Every encounter, date, consultation, appointment, or excursion will start off better if it starts on time. My mom's backyard tennis lessons taught us to aim our approach to the ball so we would be at our set point before the ball arrived at our feet. In this way we stayed in control of the game. Being on time provides a strong advantage in any situation. Arriving a little early is even better. This is the first step in a musical approach to time management. Musical time management doesn't stop with simply being punctual; you have to stay in step.

Maintaining an accurate tempo is the first requirement of the ensemble player. Remember, the pace of musical time—so connected to our bond with the earth through gravity and our footfall—determines the initial emotional response.

Linked physiologically to the heart and the breath, the tempo of music—or of an interview, meeting, or coffee break—sets the mood, style, and motivational guidelines.

The length of a pendulum sets the tempo for the clock. Likewise, the tempo of musical time is determined by the swings of the arms on the scale of relationship. How long does it take for things to swing back and forth? The solid relationship established by a punctual beginning must be diligently maintained through attention to the pace of events. In music making, with practice, this becomes automatic. A good player easily locks on the tempo within two or three beats. Unlike the steady push of the beat in music, however, the tempo of life is constantly changing. This requires constant awareness of, and appreciation for, the constant change of pace.

You have arrived on time, prepared for the downbeat. What happens after the music starts and the inevitable push and pull of interacting social membranes gets underway? Do we just go along for the ride, or can we actually influence the tempo? Listen to a great jazz group for guidance. Often the soloists will break into "double time," or stretch out a phrase over several beats, playing with the melodic pacing.

In the same way, you can alter the tempo of your relationships. Slow the tempo of your words or actions. Take the lead in a discussion through astute listening and facile interjection. These tempo moves can be made only in constant respect of the group. At the moment you decide to take the lead and change the tempo, can you reasonably expect a willing accordance on behalf of your fellow players? You must listen and sense the group's level of willing harmony. You will not succeed by simply blasting in. Without the support of players ready to follow your lead, you are going to look like a blowhard. The moment of change usually falls into a sliver of silence. Listen for a conclusion, a cadence in the conversation, or the end of a phrase. Enter confidently (but not belligerently), employing the tempo and tone appropriate to the message you are trying to get across.

This attentive clarity gives actions an elegant musicality. A great performance, be it at the hands of an athlete, musician, or parent, relies on the way intent is revealed through actions. The silent awe at the close of the concert, the soothed child, the bottom line of the ledger in the black—all these are artifacts of intent. When we make our best intentions obvious, support flows to us like roses to the feet of the diva. We become irresistible. We are appreciated. We increase our self-worth.

But good intentions alone often pave the way to disappointment. The internal conviction to do something is never enough. Straightforward action must follow the desire. The music in the string is only expressed when the string is well tuned and well played. My dad used to say that the two hardest things about playing the trumpet were getting it out of the case and getting the butt on the chair.

Exercise 39: Flying on Time

Find a feather. A piece of down is the best. Hold the feather over your head. Pick a spot about ten feet away from you. Let the feather fall. Keeping your eye on the feather, arrive at your chosen spot exactly when the feather hits the floor. Repeat seven times.

SUSTAINING LOVING INTENTIONS

By arriving at encounters on time, dedicated to remain in tempo, your intentions are put into clear relationship with others. Your timely presence—and remaining present—communicates your intentions even if you never open your mouth. The social membrane is activated and energized simply by your commitment to reach out with your attention. Your heart races and your arteries contract during conversation because you are pushing yourself beyond the limits of your silence. And it is scary out there. When you are truly ready to listen, the intentions behind your attention will be clearly felt, and people will be drawn to you. Your attention is your gift. And every mutually attentive person will appreciate the gift and return the favor.

If you want to speak meaningfully in an ensemble, you need to have a good notion of your place, your role, your message, and your melody. What have you to say about the situation? What instrument are you playing today? What kind of tone will you strike? What talent do you bring to the relationship? What aspect of consciousness informs your approach? You will best serve any ensemble by expressing your truest personal tone and inner harmony. Use the awareness resonating in your heart as your guide. Let your heart inform you, then listen for the fit, the harmony between your voice and all the others.

Many forms of music demonstrate how various voices weave a tapestry in sound. Afro-Cuban music is a dynamic example of this. Every player has a distinct sound and a discreet rhythmic "pocket." The *timbale* plays in one niche, the *conga* in another. The distinctive quality of each instrument's sound is linked to the pattern each instrument plays. The distinct timbres and rhythmic patterns of the various parts give the music a complex, layered sound. Everyone has a role to play as distinct as the instruments themselves. The vibrancy and raw liveliness of the music grows out of all these parts remaining true to their roles. To communicate well we must talk *with* others, not just *at* them. Communication is a musical counterpoint, an exchange.

The root of the word "communicate" goes back to specific customs of exchange in the Roman Empire. The *munus* was the practice of providing spectacles and entertainment for the populace in exchange for fealty to the Empire. If a community paid its taxes, the Empire would stage circuses, gladiator battles, or other events, and everyone was happy. The people got their roads and aqueducts and the Empire got its cut. Eventually, the idea of the munus mutated to mean "the exchange of ideas." Linguistically speaking, communication is by definition a two-way deal, an exchange both parties can live with.

Relationship and communication share the ideas of balance and give and take. These notions fit perfectly with the workings of music. Earlier we discussed how harmonics are generated between the nodes on the string. We examined how rhythm moves between the beats. In the improvising group, players exchange melodic ideas back and forth across "the changes" that remain constant. The magic of each piece of music is made between the silences before and after the performance.

At every moment modern life asks us to carry a part in a variety of resonant ensembles. The more we appreciate the value of our voice in the total harmony, the more we realize that we are all in love together with every flower, every stranger, every child, every Monday. Communicating from the incorruptible fulcrum of love enlivens the whole range of our relationships.

TOGETHER WITH LOVE

Musicians play with each other through the medium of sound. The music created by two mutually inspiring players is like the love created between truly harmonious lovers. Musicians say, "I am playing music *with* you." Lovers say, "I am in love *with* you." The players generate the music between them and are surrounded by their creation. They are with the other players *in the music.* In the same way, deeply harmonious people generate love between them, and live in love with the other. The best loving relationships generate the music of love in the home, in happy children, in beautiful creations, good works, community cohesion, and all the other songs and dances of hearts living in harmony. There are many forces, places, people, and spirits that accompany the double concerto of love. To live by the romantic notion that "you are all I need" is an act of exclusion. Defining love strictly by the shared emotions between two people isolates lovers from all the other accompanying orchestras available to them. As a matter of fact, if love is truly moving between two people, the nature of harmony dictates that a third tone, a third entity, is always created. Listen for the harmony you are cocreating; that's the music that both of you are in love with.

Your loving nature is manifested in your life's essential work—your best expression of your talents. Being in love with someone involves sharing these expressions on a visceral and spiritual level. This pursuit is an engaging, irresistible, and active adventure. Passively watching a movie about the great outdoors doesn't really share the love of nature. The joy of nature is intoned in the huffing and puffing as you hike together up the trail. Love of your home is not expressed through repeated reminders about doing the chores. Love is made when you work side by side to create a welcoming, comfortable space.

Work hard. Stand close. Feel the breath, smell the sweat, sense the harmony in the joy of shared effort. Being in resonance with one another is all about being at the same place, doing the same thing, at the same time, with the certainty of shared intent.

Exercise 40: Scales Study

This is an exercise for two people designed to light up the heart center. Stand opposite each other, close enough so you can easily join hands. Each person places his or her right hand, palm up, in the palm of the other person's left hand. Imagine your hands to be the two scales on a balance. Gently tilt the scale back and forth. Each person exerts gentle pressure to bring the scale back down.

Keep swinging the scales. Imagine your heart to be at the center of this action, the pivot of the balance. Imagine an axle connecting your two hearts. Your pivot points are one.

Now, taking turns, put something of yourself in your right hand and push the scale down. As you do this, name this talent. It may be "sense of humor," "my singing voice," or "anger at my father," anything that you feel strongly influences who you truly are. Pivot back and forth as these qualities are placed on the scales. See how things balance out.

RELATIONS AT HOME

Early in the morning you walk briskly over the grass. The sun sews diamonds into the dew. On the drive to work, the turns in the road remind you of how it felt to slide down grandma's banister. The wind touches the leaves on the alder trees and a tumult of silver dollars chime in the breeze. How come you never noticed those trees before? At the office, a colleague transforms three weeks of mutual toil into triumph with just the right smile. That evening at home, your daughter's voice meanders out of the shower. She veils the whole house with the liquid incense of her song.

These moments of resonance come to us out of the blue. They are surprising, even inspiring. We crave these enchanting time-jewels where the music happens all by itself. We want them to be around every corner, at every turn. We hunger for that magic source of nourishment and refreshment—that familiar, natural gift that seems to effortlessly fall into our lap. We feel this kind of love the strongest in that place we call home.

"Home" springs from an ancient root, *kei,* meaning to lie down, or to bed for the night, to rest with your beloved. In Old English, the words for home and hamlet were the same. To go home again was "to haunt" a place. Ghosts never leave home. In Greek, a related cognate, *koiman,* means "to lie down," to rest. This produced the word for the final resting place, the cemetery. The home, then, is the comforting place where the beginning and end of our life blends in that sweetest place, home sweet home.

Our true home is not defined by the walls or carpets that surround our physical bodies, but by the feelings we experience when we are there. The home is not the bed, but the delicious feelings of release and safety that sweep over us when we lie down in fatigue or passion. At the truest level, home is a quality of time, a musical harmony of familiarity we can carry with us wherever we go. Home, the old saying goes, is where the heart is. Isn't that everywhere we go?

The home is much more than the physical trappings. Home is the quality of the space between the walls, the light coming through the window, the familiar creak in the floor. If we take an empty apartment, fill it with beautiful things, and then never fill the spaces between all those things with caring actions, repeated on a regular basis, the physical objects become the literal trappings of our life. We are imprisoned by stuff.

Next to our own skin, our home is our most personal space, our most intimate temporal environment. Configurations of objects, personal habits, and patterns of style create the relationships that give a home unique character, personality, and "vibes." Orchestrated musically, home maintenance schedules can actually draw you into a loving relationship with your surroundings. Productive habits become musical patterns, rhythmic signatures defining the character and personality of a home. The living patterns created within the home are like the rhythmic patterns associated with a particular style of music. As long as the patterns are fittingly repeated, the inherent attributes are maintained.

There is a counterpoint between the materials of the home-space and the energy filling it. The physical materials of the home are like the brass of the horn. Your activities in your home act as the musician's breath filling the instrument. The relationship creates a tone, a timbre, a composition of caring and perseverance. Entire towns in Mexico are handmade. The streets are cobbled. The houses are built with hand-molded bricks and mortared with concrete mixed with a shovel. The relationships between people in Mexican towns I have visited seem to reflect this solid, intimate construction style. There is much handshaking, friendly smiles, and many laughing, easygoing children in the streets.

Look for ways to paint your walls with music. Fill the spaces inside the walls of your home with ringing laughter, beautiful colors, and clean lines.

Exercise 41: Some Musical Homework

Play music in your home on a regular basis for a week. Play it loud enough so when you put your hand to the wall you feel the music resonating there.

Tend some sort of living environment around your home on a regular basis for two months. For example, window boxes, houseplants, a flowerbed, a garden, or a lawn.

Call from one end of the house to the other with a family member or friend. Pretend you're cowboys conversing over the herd, or auto mechanics at the speedway. Put conversational inflections in your speech, but speak *fortissimo!* Use your belly muscles to pump out a good strong tone to your voice. Listen for the echo off the walls and feel the space resonate.

Put something unique, humorous, or downright nuts in the envelope with your rent or mortgage payment for six months. Get more outrageous until you actually get a reaction from the landlord.

Put a flower by your bed every night for two weeks (use a new flower every night). Notice it when you get up.

Do one chore at the same time every day for two weeks. Schedule at your leisure. Mark "down time" on the calendar and make no plans for filling it up. Give yourself the gift of freedom.

RELATING WITH THE EARTH

Driving from my home into town one morning, I crested the 2,500-foot ridge to gaze down onto the fog. There were scores of mountain peaks poking up through the mist, islands in a white sea. The wind was stirring up the surface of that endless fog-ocean, teasing out horsetails and feathery angel hands. The sun came up over the far ridge and all at once those swirling plumes were gilded with rainbows. I looked down on a fantasia of pastel holograms. The vision of light and wind and water sparked the uncanny realization that I live in outer space. Right here under my nose, the cosmos presented a great spectacle. I had no need to travel through vast reaches to enjoy galactic visions.

The music of the earth runs through everyone's head now and then. No one is immune to awe or irony. The logger cutting down the two-thousand-year-old redwood will tell his or her kids about the grandeur of the forest with as much awe as the tree-hugger. We are all involved with the earth, wrapped up in her sweet veils simply by being here. We feel it every time the ocean invigorates us, the raging river scares us, or the budding flower humbles us, and every time an epidemic devastates us.

The music of the earth emanates from the land in every neighborhood. High profile ecosystems like redwood forests get a lot of coverage and can capture the attention of even the most jaded city dweller. But aren't there lots of precious and threatened temples of the earth close to Manhattan—even in the middle of the city itself?

A friend of mine moved from the backwoods to a suburban town. In his subdivision there is a small park built around a nearly obliterated seasonal watercourse. He spends weekends landscaping the creek side with native plants. Does his concern with grasses and perennial shrubs compare to the century-old effort to protect redwood trees? His landscaping expresses in leaf, root, and stem the harmony between his intentions and the ground under his feet. The millions of dollars and countless hours of sacrifice poured into forest preservation—and recently, restoration—are expressed in the grandeur of the groves that will stand forever. Are the individuals battling for the redwoods doing more significant work than my friend? No comparison need be made because both enhance reverence for the planet.

Relationship and communication with the earth—as well as with people—develop most authentically in close proximity. Cultivate your love of your home ground through gestures, actions, monuments, and physical effort. Dig in. Give a little. The beautiful lesson flowering in all this is that the earth does not forget. She will return your care or your indifference. She will bloom, flourish, fruit, and shade your brow. She may also starve us, fry us, drown us, and bury us under landslides of mud and ash. She never ignores a relationship. She's always listening. And she responds every time.

The emerging field of ecopsychology shows how the connections to our surroundings influence our mental health. Looking at a polluted river actually feels different than looking at a pristine one. Our body-mind registers these things because we are born of the earth. "Human" is from the same root as "humus." From dust to dust. Our feelings for the stream are time-qualities of the moment, the harmony between the observer and the environment. The very idea that the atmosphere itself is poisonous or weakened cripples our age-old communication with the earth. How can we feel at home when the ground we walk on may be toxic? Where does our heart find rest?

Just as active listening relaxes the heart, dilates the arteries, and opens channels of reception, so can attentive appreciation of the earth allow the music of nature to filter into our awareness. What is the vacant lot telling you? Have you listened to the place in your backyard where you dump your oil? Does the trash by the side of the road ever call out to you? Do you ever stop and pick up a bit of it? My dad always told me, "Leave a place cleaner than you found it." Willie Smith, a cook I used to work for, said, "Clean as you go." Good advice. Good practice. Once upon a time, the earth seemed so huge! She could easily swallow all our trash. But the earth is crowded now. Everybody is tossing trash into someone else's yard, forgetting that the earth only has one yard, and the fence is the ozone layer.

Exercise 42: Earth in the Balance

Grow something—lots of things if you have the room. The time you spend communicating with the living world will feed you like a favorite melody returning again and again.

Notice natural light. Move furniture to bask in it. Trim the shrubs to let it in. Get up early to walk in it. Remember the moon. Take a night trip out of the city to find the stars again.

Choose the cleanest way. Buy "green" products. The extra expense is a tip of appreciation to the businesses that are trying to market a new kind of respect for our earthly home.

Find yourself in the real world. Somewhere close by is a nook or cranny in the time-field of nature that resonates deeply for you. Find it. Plan an excursion. Take some friends. Don't forget the kids and the picnic. Look for the music of the earth in the cracks in the sidewalk. When you wake up at three in the morning, notice how much quieter it is.

Keep ecopolitics close to home. Every environment—especially cities—includes the human species as well.

Do a personal energy audit. Repair. Reuse. Recycle.

Share the big picture. Contemplate and take action on environmental concerns in terms of the overall quality of life in your area.

We live within the membrane of a single pulsating organism. Humans might be carrying the brain material of this planet-animal. The computerized info-web we are now weaving into every corner of the world seems like the beginning of a planetary nervous system informing us, changing dreams to actual forms. Your choices do affect a greater system. Every action you take etches one more note in the score for the composition of our future.

REFINING YOUR PART

A tiny change of accent within a simple rhythmic time pattern turns a cha-cha into a tango. In the personal time-field, a change of emphasis can change a thoughtful desire for cleanliness into the nail-biting compulsions of the "neat freak."

Notice how you form your energy into patterns. What are your favorite dances around the house, the office, or the social scene? What aspects of consciousness are you expressing? Are your actions simply habits eroded into your time-landscape through thoughtless repetition? Musical creativity comes to life by sensing and doing at the same time. Notice who is listening to you.

When we are first learning to practice a musical life—or practice an actual musical instrument—we must slow down in order to notice what we are doing. In our personal life this can be especially pleasurable, because as we slow the pace of our patterns we find more opportunity to fall into the places between the hidden corners. We find the unnoticed shaft of light, the sound of the wind in the trees outside our bedroom. And inside the silence is where the music happens. The more we use the silence the more defined our part in relationships become.

All great musicians show an artistic evolution throughout their career. Beethoven's First Symphony and his last quartets show a growth from a classical musician providing appropriate court music for his patron to the visionary standing on the edge of the new Romantic musical era.

Miles Davis took a similar place on the frontiers of jazz. From the be-bop of the late 40s to the funk, soul, and hip-hop grooves of his later years, Davis cut a deep swath through musical time. Great musicians do not get stuck. Their patterns are always evolving, regenerating. The genetic material of one opus is handed down to the next in a new form, a new groove.

As we form and practice our relationships, it is important to keep our minds open and free to the new permutations that always arise. These new versions usually arise from "mistakes" or "problems" in the performance of existing patterns. The solid groove can easily turn into a rut from which we may find ourselves struggling to escape. When people say "Oh, God, I'm really in a rut!" they usually are referring to the way they are spending their time. The pattern is not serving, but wearing them down.

But casting off that old, grimy, oh-so-comfortable coat for a new one is tough. It took me three years to chuck the bed that was giving me backaches. I drove an unsafe car for sixteen years because it just kept going. Our habits create a niche in the temporal habitat that define who we are. Our patterns establish how we relate to other members of the environment. We say, "It's going to be hard to find the time for that," but the most meaningful time management is not the scheduling of elapsed time, it is the composition of musical time qualities. One moment of intimate harmony can change the composition of an entire lifetime.

In our discussion of musical elements, we learned that the beat could be articulated into infinite patterns using accents and silences. Subdividing and syncopating the beat further expands the possibilities of rhythm. Very simple shifts in the pattern of rhythmic figures create a radically different dance. A very simple theme can be a touchstone for an entire symphony. One moment in your life can become a reference point for the composition of every loving relationship in your life.

For the human animal, establishing time niches is just as important as staking out geographical terrain. I have a friend who has a very high-stress job as a lawyer. The job includes a commute that is over an hour long. When his kids were just toddlers, he made "Dave Time" a regular theme in the rhythm of his family. When he arrives home from work he gives everyone a big kiss and a hug, then he retreats to his lair, a small room separate from the house where he can wind down for twenty minutes or so. He indulges in music at high volume, a beer, a nap, a phone call. It's "Dave Time." His wife handles the two boys, knowing her mate stands a much greater chance of emerging as a fully functional dad if he can tune in to his own muse for just that little while. His time has become as accepted as washing hands before dinner, as much a part of the day as the bedtime story. His after-work niche in his temporal habitat has been successfully ritualized, sanctified as Dave's and Dave's alone. This is one note in Dave's personality, and in the symphony he composes with his family.

COUNTERPOINT: VOICES MOVING TOGETHER

Stable patterns within the home and the wider culture give everyone, especially children, a sense of security. We develop our personality through patterns of behavior in relationship to events such as "Dave Time." The frantic, unpredictable, deritualized lifestyle of our post-modern world does not lend itself to regular daily rhythms. Family activities are a scheduling nightmare. Many families rarely eat together. This is like a band where everybody is playing but nobody is listening. They may be on the same stage, but there is little or no sharing. This is a very lonely kind of music.

Our personal music only really comes alive when someone else appreciates it. A powerful creative current is generated through the relationship between the player and the listener that is "unplugged" when one acts in solitude. The audience brings openness, expectations, knowledge, memories, and a critical ear to a musical performance. The players bring talent, passion, and experience. This two-way relationship swings on the scales of love.

There is an intimacy that comes from sharing the special quality of any time— a good laugh, a good cry, a long, long time staring at the stars. When we are truly at the same place at the same time with loved ones the bonds of intimacy are electrified through musical resonance. Hearts and minds reinforce one another. A spiritual union is forged.

The art of musical counterpoint creates similar magic through the blending of melodies, and demonstrates in sound the perfect dynamic for a relationship. For me, Bach and Dixieland jazz are the clearest examples of this. In both forms we hear individual lines moving together, dancing over, under, and around other voices. Each instrument maintains integrity and direction, and yet is in balance with the other voices. This gives the perfect model for personal interaction. Every voice must be composed to express a unique attribute of the music, always in balance with the other voices.

A family, committee, string quartet, or dance class are all *polyphonic* in nature. In polyphonic music there are several (at least two) voices projecting, each carrying a discreet musical line forward. Each instrument has limitations of range and tonal quality. Each group member has physical limitations, talents, emotional range, and stamina that help to chart the course of any collective expression. The various voices intertwine like the voices in a fugue, or the sections in an orchestra. Harmony is maintained to the extent that all members are able to clearly discriminate their voice among the many. There must be a balance between parts. Everyone must know and feel that everyone appreciates his or her part in reference to the composition. The basis for the art of group musicianship—listening while playing—serves as a model for productive group dynamics in every form.

Many voices can exist in apparent dissonance if there is an inherent harmony of intent. In one section of Beethoven's Third Symphony, the composer sets many voices running in rapid counterpoint. Every voice plays true to the key of the piece. Then at one climactic downbeat, the voices simultaneously arrive at a series of driving accents, and these pounding chords break every rule of harmony in the book. Every note in the entire scale is sounded at once! Playing the chord on the keyboard would require no technique at all. You could use your forearm.

Each melodic line in the counterpoint of voices speaks of Beethoven's consistency and power, but they arrive at a unique singularity in the temporal habitat of classical music; a crashing dissonance, a true post-Romantic "cluster chord" of pitches, decades ahead of its time. The chord is hammered again and again, the sound letting us know that, yes, this is exactly the intention the composer had in mind. This moment in the Third Symphony is the perfect model for the group process of "agreeing to disagree."

When individual voices hold a common and clearly defined point of reference—in the Third's example, the keynote—diverse variations of interpretation are more readily accepted by the group. Conflicts and clashes are heard and actually embraced by the group out of this mutual respect. The key, in short, is the key. What is the keynote of your various ensembles? The business has the product line and the bottom line. The non-profit has the mission statement. The family has the bonds of love. The construction crew has the blueprints.

Every group forms and stays together only because of a mutual respect for some central idea, whether this idea is directly expressed or not. The more in tune we are with the keynote of a group, the better players we become. No matter where our individual melody takes us, we will play in counterpoint and harmony.

THE FLOW AND THE LEADER

Whenever we are in close proximity our feelings influence the other's experiences. We are constantly swinging on the loving scale of relationship. Back and forth. Give and take. Call and response. Upbeat and downbeat. We are always in the pull of love's gravity. This constant fluctuation is the basic component of "the flow," the smooth current of life on which we all want so desperately to float.

Flow happens in a classroom, on a bus, during a chance encounter with your nemesis, at a family reunion, with a goodnight kiss, at a sales meeting. Keep listening. The perfect expression of the moment starts within the silence surrounding the moment itself.

To get into the flow, one must pay attention to how combined forces excite and resonate the total structure at hand. Flow is an essential aspect of sports. A team develops momentum during a game when every player feels the play-by-play progressing toward an inexorably victorious future. Certainly the players can't know if they will triumph or not, but the *feeling* of being in the flow certainly resonates that way in the gut. Teammates see each other moving in harmony, paying attention, and playing with shared intentions.

To get into the flow of a song, the jazz group uses an arrangement outlining the melody and chord structure of the tune. This is the lead sheet, or chart. For musical veterans, however, it is possible to be so familiar with the standard tunes and the group's intentions that spontaneous improvisation progresses naturally in a spirit of mutual respect. The accomplished musical ensemble, the productive work group, and the harmonious family all display this deep sense of direction, which leads to productive and inspiring work. In a word, improvement. The music of language is singing again. Hear the sounds of "improve" and "improvise."

To assume a leadership role in all of this, one must adhere to the true nature of the flow. *The I-Ching,* the ancient Chinese *Book of Changes,* teaches that the great leader recognizes the will of the people, and through word and deed demonstrates the people's inner longings. When the people see the leader demonstrating his or her heart's desire, enthusiasm and support for the idea flow naturally. Being a true leader depends mainly on how one listens rather than how one acts. This effective leader does not try to drag people this way and that. Progress is made most readily when the tendencies of the whole are directed and focused. The visionary leader puts a knife's edge on common knowledge. Innovation comes most effectively from creative permutation. The people are the deep wave. The leaders are the crest. The leader is the brightly waving flag. The people are the wind. The virtuoso soloist getting all the accolades exists only with the support of the accompanying ensemble.

In personal interactions, business ventures, family matters, and all forms of relationship, the hallmark of leadership is openness to the inner truth of others. The leader draws out that which is there already. Gratitude, loyalty, and mutual respect are the harmony-tones playing between the leading personality and those ready to be led. Be a leader. Encourage love. Reach out through the membrane at the far edge of yourself. Pass the words, the touch, the look, and the music over to the next one. Then relax the tension on the social membrane. Let the other one return your gift embellished, polished, and appreciated.

The flow comes when we see all the little actions become one grand undifferentiated gesture. With practice, all the thousands of individual notes making up the composition merge into a single gesture, an integrated artifact in time. Every kiss, fight, twilight, and dawn blends into a life, a love affair, a career, the work of art.

Exercise 43: Practice Tips for the Flow

Picture It. You are contemplating an upcoming situation. Go over various scenarios in your mind. Create a picture of the most rewarding and most practical procedure and outcome. Move through the scenario step by step. Think positively about your contribution in real terms. Ask yourself, *What can I do? When will I do it? What won't I do?* Be realistic and confident. Run the story line over in your head. Observe yourself in the scene. Are you being realistic? Are you being yourself? From which body-mind center are you acting?

Ground It. The situation is at hand. Set the stage with the other participants. Share expectations and game plans. Agree about responsibilities and expectations. Discover the keynote, your common point of reference. Encourage participation and show respect and appreciation for all contributions. Balance the talents. Set the scale.

Be On Time. Be ready when the curtain goes up. Have your instrument tuned, your music on the stand, and be attentive to the music poised to be expressed. Chart out the course. Create a timeline. Then be flexible.

Share Yourself. Acknowledge others as you play. Make eye contact. Challenge yourself and the others to act promptly on common goals. Search out the joy, humor, and risk. Channel nay-saying and ego-waving into practical, concerted effort focused on moment-to-moment mutual success. Look for the laughs.

Maintain Perspective. Every single action is part of a larger composition. Point out to your fellows when momentum is gathering or waning. See all the tedious, repetitive, mundane tasks as links along a temporal chain tethering the intentions of the group to the ultimate realization of the score. Remember to use silence and stillness to frame every event. The widest perspective is gained at the very edge.

Take Pleasure in the Moment. This is perhaps the most important and the hardest. With plans laid, perspectives framed, and all the other groundwork done, every action, task, and interaction will feel the best if it is done strictly for its own sake with no ulterior motives. This is the joy of effort, the rush of the moment, and the grease for frictionless forward motion. The spading of the ground and the planting of the seed are best enjoyed with no hope for a harvest. What if the grasshoppers come? Or the deer? Or the moles? Taking pleasure in the moment frees you to enjoy it all—even the dirt under your fingernails.

Schedule Leisure. Time outs are part of any successful game plan. When recreational activities are applied correctly and regularly they rebuild and maintain the engines of your ingenuity. Use downtime for "going in" time. Recreate your self through exercise, prayer, meditation, vocal toning, or even a dose of a mind-altering pursuit such as extreme snowboarding or *salsa habanero.*

Check Expectations. When that one thing you had your heart set on doesn't work out, remember: you are now free to do anything else in the world.

Aim Yourself in Time. Look ahead. Plan a course that carries you to a definite end. Don't leave live wires dangling, pivotal issues unattended. The flow can only happen with smooth transitions from one gesture in the time-field to the next. Keep track of elapsed time, but first of all, stay open to all the qualities of musical time that may come up. Always make a polite, graceful, and direct exit.

KEEPING THE CHANNELS OPEN

In the film *Amadeus,* Frederick the Great, on hearing an early Mozart symphony, exclaimed to the boyish composer, "Too many notes, Mozart!" Many modern rock guitar players have flapping fingers but no soul. Guard against your own overplaying. Be sure every gesture communicates your intent. Watch for the audience reaction.

Too much information—too many notes—will go beyond the limits of audience comprehension. Some styles of music seem foreign to us simply because we do not have the experience needed to understand the meaning of the sounds. We can get into the flow only if we have the appropriate boat for the current. Our ability to handle information depends on a resilient and responsive instrument— and a practiced hand on the controls.

The idea of flow implies that events and intentions travel through a channel of some sort. In our post-industrial world the river of electronic information seems to be the big flow. The current in this river is pressing ever onward and rising, threatening to breech the banks. For information flood-management purposes, we need to admit that there is a limit to the amount we can process. Any given wire can handle just so much electric current before it burns up. Our personal ability to handle information runs on similar principles.

The mathematics of energy exchange (thermodynamics) and information theory use similar constants, logarithms, and equations. In the family of science, heat loss (entropy) and information static are first cousins. Usable energy and information are closely related mathematically. The relationship between our internal wiring and the flow of information and energy determine our stress level. The information (or energy) flowing through a system can be used to do work. In terms of information, when you try to pump too much through a system you get static or interference and the channel breaks up. When a system cannot handle the voltage, the wires heat up or burn out, and energy is lost, randomized as heat into the environment. In the family or business relationship, "burnout" is possible as well.

Pacing and clarity are the keys to efficient information processing. Don't put too much on the table. Family schedules and professional agendas need to be well structured, keyed to core values, realistic goals, and attainable practicalities. Bring all the crucial players online to help process the information. Watch for the signs of channel breakdown: blurry eyes, fidgeting, drumming fingers, slouching, impatience, and anger, for example. Control the pace so that everyone can incorporate the information. Look for nods of understanding, note taking, eye contact, frowns of concern. Watch for involvement. If it's not evident, the information is going into an overloaded system and is being lost.

Information moves in discreet bits just as energy travels in quanta. The efficient transmission of information through any system is tied to the internal transmission rate of the system. Stress management is primarily about creating and maintaining resonant relationships between the amount and the rate of information. This is all about pace, finding the right tempo, and staying on it.

Exercise 44: Tempo Minder

Your personal pace can be conducted at will, steadied, or changed altogether. Sit up straight with your feet flat on the floor, lengthen and relax the nape of your neck, and let your mind sink down to the base of your spine. Concentrate on those two little bones that you sit on (your "sit-bones"). That's where your weight is resting right now. Breathe slowly and fully, dropping your shoulders. Notice the line of gravitational force that comes up from the sit-bones and shoots right out the top of your head. Keep your back easily taut, like the lowest string on a bass fiddle. Let your breath drift over that string. Listen. Listen.

Now decide what tempo you would like to assume. Do you want to pick up your pace or slow it down? Choose carefully. Start to tap your thumb on your leg at your desired tempo. Imagine yourself walking at this tempo. How does it feel? Is that your perfect pace for the moment? Try a few tempos until the perfect one resonates for you. Start to take a virtual walk at that tempo. Use your mind's eye and imagine yourself moving through your next slice of life at that new tempo. Play on!

Relationships are never static or predictable; constant adjustment is the rule. At best, these adjustments are creative and innovative. A ship moves over seas that are sometimes stormy, sometime placid. Every relationship also moves through a course in time. We should look at relationship as a quality of action similar to musicianship, seamanship, or leadership.

SPIRIT RELATIONSHIP

In all our relations, the spirit of love is generated when individuals move in true harmony with other people and forces. From a spiritual point of view, the world is imbued with love all the time. This love is visible in the return of the seasons, in the delicious fragrance of a summer rain, and the soft purring of a sleeping child. This is the love the earth has for life. We are awash in this all-pervasive higher love. As we teeter from one step to the next we are falling in love all the time.

By honoring the musical spirit of loving relationships we can move toward our heart's desire like the great composition moves to the final cadence. Moving gracefully in this way requires practice. We must devote time to the attainment of personal balance. Our discipline of musical time awareness prepares us for the expression of our innate talents. We must constantly practice the loving revelation of our Higher Self to the world. Once practiced, we can confidently place our talents on the scales of love in any situation. We are then prepared to improvise confidently over any set of changes. In this way we improve our life and the life force of all.

In this discipline of spirit, music is our great and obvious teacher. Music is in perfect balance at every level, resonating every aspect of our being. Musical elements exemplify the perfect balance of our physical, mental, and spiritual attributes. Music touches our hearts so deeply because it is a system of perfect relationships. Music, like love, only succeeds when voices are clear and strong on their own, and in balance with other voices at the same time. At any minute of the day we have the opportunity to plug into this species-wide grid of musical power and energy.

Exercise 45: Falling in Love All the Time

Connect. What part of your self are you trying to share? Be true to that self. Release the tiger. Bring on the clown. Let your heart lead you. Match your message with the delivery. Move from the place that says the most about you at the moment.

Reflect. Willingly synchronize with your playmates. Choose to follow in the sure knowledge that concerted action generates connection and transcendence. There are a lot of good ideas out there besides your own.

Accept silence. Constant activity stifles the element of surprise and serendipity. It's the deep, silent wave that carries the power behind the crest. Let the silence define the edges.

Ask for what you want. Assume you are loved. Trust you will receive your request. Be ready to give your all in return. The balance of love results from attention to your intention and the intentions of others.

SYMPATHETIC VIBRATIONS

The sitar has many strings that are never plucked. These strings are sympathetically resonated by vibrations originating from the plucked strings. The sympathetic strings are tuned to the overtones of the plucked strings, and those harmonic partials are picked up and resonated in the unplucked strings. A radio tuner works in the same way. The receiving elements are tuned to sympathetically resonate with the frequency of the chosen station.

Our body-mind is played upon by overtones of spirit emanating all around us. We "pick up vibes." We are sensitive instruments of divine consciousness. We are moved on physical and psychic levels by people and situations. What makes one moment a groove and the next a rut? What strikes the perfect balance on the scales of relationship? How can we create the easy flow of resonant time, avoiding the deadly grind of conflict and stagnation?

We do so by tuning our attention to the songs of the heart and proceeding in harmony, listening and adjusting ourselves at every moment, following when it best serves the music, taking the lead as our intentions and the tempo of the times demand. With practice we perform without a thought. Like the great soloist, we can play our way through life, expressing our true identity effortlessly. This is the message of the inner child. Keep playing! An entire workweek becomes as simple and lighthearted as whistling a tune.

The best way to hear our own part in all this is to watch for the reaction of others. Are we met with smiles, open faces, welcoming countenances, and hearty response? Or do our actions return to us in averted eyes, turned shoulders, raised voices, or a laser stare? To live musically we must notice how others are resonated by our music. The more we notice, the more facile we become at change, experimenting here and there with different ways to express our emotions. We choose the tone of voice, facial expressions, body language, and so on. This is not a suggestion to put on an act, it is the challenge the conductor places before the player. Expand your range, improve your facility on your instrument, widen your repertoire. Every one of us is a treasure of emotions, creativity, and empathy. We are musical by nature. As we practice listening skills we will see the sparkling facets of spirit all around us. People are in a dance.

The energy and consciousness we channel into the world assume material shape in the things we make, and temporal form in the things we do and feel over time. Every action, every word, every anguish, philosophy, and joy take form in the world, especially in the hearts and minds of the young. Each event has a unique time envelope, just like the tolling of a bell or the blast of the bomb. Your child's laugh has a niche in time. As does your life.

To demonstrate a musical spirit, one must take responsibility for one's creations and stay with them, listen to them, appreciate them as they resonate in the various resonating chambers of experience: the heart of your lover; the safety deposit box; your living room. Practicing the expression and appreciation of our own loving interpretation of musical qualities puts us in the groove, on top of the beat, in the flow.

A Native American prayer says, "Blessings to my father, mother, and all my relations." I originally thought this referred to one's family and clan. As I think about it now, though, I am beginning to see this as a prayer for balance. We all have innate abilities and limitations. It is our responsibility to use these talents in considered relationship to everything around us. Through attention to the changing harmony within "all our relations" we express the essential resonance of the earth. To the extent that we ignore the dynamics of harmonious relations, dissonance prevails, and the cultures that nurture us cease to grow.

The health of the community and clarity of communication are products of harmonious exchange. You become part of this exchange by bringing the active expressions of your inner spirit to the scales of love. The more we place on the balance, the more we appreciate the value of everything. This culture of exchange is required for the growth of true passion between lovers in the dark, as well as for the culture of true progress between races, nations, and neighbors down the block.

The entire earth hangs in the balance as our collective love affair with life swings the balance up and down. Are we hiding under the Walkman earphones, plowing down the street, imagining the most important thing to be the job, the car, the image? We are all singing in one giant frog-choir of humanity. If we listen and sing at the same time, sooner or later we will sing as one. What a joyful racket!

7 DANCING ON THE EDGE

"A flower, your friend's happiness, your friend, a dog, your nose, a hellish case of resentment, a postage stamp, your 'I,' a love affair, an automobile—all are essentially a changing nexus of causes and conditions. Our experience is a dance of appearances . . ."

—from *Entering the Stream,* by Samuel Bercholz

Living in a constantly changing world, we crave permanence. In his book, Bercholz has collected writings on the message of the Buddha that illuminate this paradox. The world is shown to be an ever changing dance of karma (cause and effect). Everything is evolving, mutating, becoming what it is not, including one's very soul. This ever changing nature is the only constant. The nexuses form in the vortexes that develop here and there in the swirling current of appearances.

A nexus is a bundle of connected threads, a manifestation woven from the intermingling forces of space, matter, and time. Power and materials are balanced at a nexus to articulate a specific physical form. Ideas and intention form nexuses of feelings and spirit. Through the principles of resonance, we can see that a nexus is formed from patterns, rhythm, harmony, and balance.

At the center of the nexus, like in the eye of the storm, all is calm, still, and silent. This is the immovable point of reference where all the threads attach. Our truest knowledge and expression of who we are—our "I" nexus—emerges from this silent place. The Buddha sat in stillness under the bodhi tree and waited for enlightenment. All the threads of his past and future met there in the silence. He cast his thoughts up to heaven and bent over and touched the earth. In that moment he established a harmony that resounds through the ages.

The causes and conditions manifesting any nexus are analogous to the forces and materials we have been talking about in our musical metaphors. The pianist attacks (force) the score (material) and music is made. Sunlight (force) strikes a leaf (material) and life is sustained. A meteor strikes the moon. Love strikes a waiting heart. An idea takes the nation by storm. Each one of these interactions between cause and condition is a manifestation of yet another nexus, a resonant articulation of time qualities.

We have examined the music of the humming atom, the counterpoint of conversation, and our part in the various choirs of the natural world. We have seen resonance at work between mates, within families, over history. This final chapter sets all of this within the frame of silence, the realm that surrounds all sound, motion, and inspiration. Awareness of musical time increases as we acknowledge the silence framing all experience. We get the clearest view of this silent realm from the edge, the borderline between what we know and the infinite potential beyond the known.

The resounding spirit of the Buddha's enlightenment is a clear example of Dane Rudhyar's notion of Sound. We hear vibrations of sound waves moving against our eardrums. We hear music, stories, prophecies, tales of heroism and disaster. The sounds resonate at our chakras, composing meaning, blasts of inspiration, and waves of emotion, all of which exert silent influence on our body-mind. These silent artifacts of musical time are overtones of the Sound animating all creation from just over the edge. These are the echoes of the *aum*.

Our awareness of death is the fundamental tone of the Sound in our consciousness. Our inevitable demise roars at the edge of our life like a tornado. We can try to ignore it, but we know we can't avoid it. It roars in silence. All the resonant beauty of life operates between the silence of the womb and the grave. The Sound sings all songs, but makes no sound. The classic Buddhist paradox states emphatically, "Emptiness is form. Form is emptiness."

AT THE EDGE

Our life happens between the two stillpoints of birth and death. Between these boundaries—deeply appreciated but truly unknown—the fundamental tones of life energy are modulated by genetics, environment, and intention just like a musical composition modulates the contour of musical time from silence to silence. Our ideas framing birth and death modulate all of our choices, shaping everything we honor, cherish, and fear. Death is at the center of the nexus of each personality. It has remained the primary concern of entire cultures from the ancient Egyptians to modern Islam.

Our pervasive concern with mortality reveals that we do indeed perceive the Sound roaring at the edge of our life. Perhaps what we recognize in animals as the survival instinct, what we sense as the fragile grandeur of the old growth forest, and what glints at us from the depths of a crystal are overtones of this same Sound. Our sense of a separate self is a variation on the basic theme of existence, which sings over and over, "To be or not to be."

Astrophysicists hear a constant background noise in every corner of the sky. Analysis of this noise has provided the crucial foundation for the Big Bang theory, which postulates a singular moment of creation bringing all time and space into existence. The background noise is said to be the echo of this primordial release of energy ringing throughout space.

In a similar way, no matter where our human heart and mind venture in the universe of ideas and feelings, there is the unmistakable tone of oblivion. It is the ceaseless ringing of the funeral bell, the neverending realization that the edge is just one step away.

The certainty of death is the fundamental keynote of our experience of time. Even when we are the most "on" there seems to be lurking in the depth of our bony souls the dark dream of the day when we will be "off." Loss of youthful innocence arrives when we recognize death as our constant and silent companion, when we know in the pit of our stomachs we will always be just one missed red light away from the edge.

Like the beat of a drum, an individual lifespan occupies a certain period of elapsed time. The beginning, middle, and end of any life, song, or eon form a unique temporal artifact. Within our time all the beauty and ugliness, success and failure, peace and conflict weave together like voices of a fugue. The first scream of the infant is sung by a choir of cells calling out in unison from the protoplasmic depths, *"I'm alive now!"* The last breath sings the benediction—the amen—to a life that will never sing again.

Different situations, personalities, and events play off each other throughout our lives just like melodies, rhythms, timbres, and forms play off one another in music. The exercises in this book train the body-mind to recognize these elements of musical time. Musicians practice rhythm, melody, and musicianship. The activities in these pages are inspired by the musical model and help develop pacing, self-expression, group dynamics, and so on.

Events create a temporal geometry. Like shapes take up space, events take up time. Each shape has its unique function and character in three dimensions. Each experience is a temporal artifact that has its own effect on the quality of time as it passes. The more we are aware of how our personal instrument (body-mind) creates these artifacts, the better we can harmonize with our surroundings, deepening and enriching the experience for ourselves and all those we encounter.

Our human instrument resonates over the entire range of experience. We are open to spirit at the crown and grounded to the earth at the root, we sense distinct octaves in this music at the chakras. And the music is rich and diverse. Just as the motion picture would dissolve into a blur without the instant of blackness around each frame, all the music of the world would be meaningless without silence.

RETURN TO SILENCE

In the opening phrases to Beethoven's Fifth Symphony, silence takes center stage in the midst of a profoundly active musical soundscape. Imagine a performance of this well-known composition. The conductor lifts the baton. Bows are raised, and lungs are inflated. There is that electric moment when one of the world's greatest time artifacts looms on the other side of silence. The preparatory beat is snapped off, and the baton comes down, and . . .

And for an instant nothing happens. The initial downbeat of the Fifth is a silent rest (figure 1, page 185). The first three notes enter, but they are just pick-up

Figure 1: Opening Measures of Beethoven's Fifth Symphony in C Minor.

notes propelling the orchestra into a long, sustained tone. Time is suspended there for a moment, held in a *fermata*. This first grand tone is cut off. Silence returns. Then the entire motif is repeated a step lower. After the second fermata, a wave of rhythm rises under a simple sequence of the theme, driving us up and over, finally breaking on a real downbeat. This arrival is yet again suspended in a fermata. Ahhhh! We made it. Safe at last. Oh really? Following this "safe landing" are two searing repetitions of the opening salvo, complete with silent downbeat, fanfare trumpets, and thundering kettledrums. Beethoven reminds us that we are dealing with the forces of fate itself, and fate is never easily satisfied.

The opening of the Fifth is all starts and stops. It jumps to life again and again out of moments of deep silence. The players must know the conductor's intentions well. Everyone must leap into the sea of sound from silence, and immediately take off into the swirling current of the music. The first phrase is often played with subtle *accelerando* and *ritardando* (speeding up, slowing down). The members of the orchestra must breathe as one.

The use of silence as the point of reference was an incredible stroke of genius. It speaks to the crux of Beethoven's personality. The black silence that imprisoned him in his deafness sits immutably at the center of the nexus in the opening bars. When the orchestra plays those moments of silence, a sonic image of a great soul calls out through the ages. These silent moments might be Beethoven's truest rendition of the Sound. His message seems clear: *all music is born in silence.* How can we remember, move from, and respect the silence in this way?

Follow Beethoven's example. Honor the silence. Enshrine it. Afford yourself the time on the edge. Schedule the silence. Arrive five minutes early. Bow your head before the meal. Take a breath before you answer a question. Stroke your child's head between sentences. Feel your weight moving into the dark center of the earth as you fall from step to step on the morning jog. Put the project aside for a day. Then be ready to hit the ground running.

Arising from the ocean of silence, every piece of music is a golden geometry of time. Noise just happens, but music—like the single silken thread in intricate embroidery—has a definite beginning and end. Hearing and appreciating our voice in the composition of our environment begins with accepting the fact that we too are but threads in a grand design. Our life reaches from edge to edge, birth to death. And when the spinner of souls cuts us off, we fall from the tree of life like a leaf in the wind. The earth moves away from the sun and the leaf burns with color, a flame in the shortening light. It trembles and falls, a fluttering footstep in the cadence of the seasons.

Cadence is a term with many musical meanings. A drum cadence is the rhythm played by the percussionists in a marching band as the group marches in time down the street. A harmonic cadence is a series of chords that lead to a conventional, expected conclusion to a phrase. There are *deceptive* harmonic cadences where the first part of the chord series makes us expect one thing, and then the composer heads off into unexpected harmonic territory. Poetic cadence refers to the metered flow of words in a poem (iambic pentameter, and so on). All these musical examples of cadence have one thing in common: they lead us somewhere through a time-field in a predictable, compelling way. Break the cadence of the drums and you get a traffic jam of sousaphones and glockenspiels. Toss in an unrelated chord in the final bars of a Mozart composition and the Friends of the Symphony will rise in indignation from their seats. Break the dulcet flow of Wordsworth and the muses turn in their Olympian graves.

The root of "cadence" is the Latin *cadere,* meaning "to fall." From *cadere* we get accident, deciduous, cascade, chance, decay, and cadaver. The music of words links the closing bars of every symphony to the autumn leaves decaying under our feet. The music of language puts the cadaver on the slab next to the cascading waters of the rapids. Notice how the evolution of language reversed the phonemes of *cadere* to generate "deciduous" for trees whose leaves fall in autumn.

Our sense of musical time is most acute near the end of things. We crave a happy ending to every story—or at least an interesting one. If the body of a work of music is clumsy and ill conceived, a good ending will leave a pleasant memory in the mind. This points directly to our underlying awareness of the edge: we want desperately to be brought there in peace. We want the same peace on the approach to the final bars of life. When we are near the end of a life—anyone's life—that huge hum in our ears and the weight in our heart is our time-sense resonating to the final, inevitable beat at the end of the tune. Our own death, the doorway out of time, is the final wave of the baton. At the close of this cadence we fall into silence.

The ending cadences of a piece of music dominate our perception because they carry us thrillingly to the other side of silence. As the music ends, we step into oblivion for just a moment. But life floods back a heartbeat later. The next frame in the movie flashes on. All of our friends are there at the concert, applauding and cheering. We are awake, appreciative, and ready for the next time of our lives.

A piece of music captures a vision of time qualities, a temporal journey through the birth, life, and death of an incredible sweep of energy and emotion. The trip—especially the end—actually feels great! In this way music shows us that at the center of every nexus of experience is an infinite stillness, a silence proclaiming a new beginning in every ending.

Lots of music slows down as it reaches the close. The blues, many symphonic works, popular tunes, and religious music follow this scheme. Pop tunes also repeat the chorus or a melodic "hook" over and over as the tune "fades out." The jazz form usually requires the tune to be repeated in its entirety at the end. All these conventions clearly signal the approaching silence.

Death takes no time at all. It's the dying, the cadence, the release phase of the envelope that occupies our imagination and nightmares. We have no knowledge of death itself because it is but a point in time. All that we know of death are the stories of how we might journey there. It's the rush, crash, and jitterbug to the climax of life's dance that sweeps us away. There may be pain. There may be fear, remorse, anger, denial, vindication, revenge, and hatred. But underlying all this, like the hiss of the Big Bang, is the fundamental Sound chanting melodies of release, acceptance, and atonement.

Many cultures mark the passing of a loved one with a celebration. The street parades at funerals in New Orleans are joyous occasions. The marchers raucously usher the dear departed through the Gates of Paradise into the heavenly realm.

That lucky so-and-so is free of the earthly burdens. The Dixieland band swinging down the street blasting "When the Saints Go Marching In" articulates time quality of ecstatic release, not grief and remorse. The sendoff resonates deeply in the spirits of those left behind. Death rings with a joyous noise. What a wonderful tune to carry in your heart.

Keep that bright version of the Sound at the edge in mind. We all are released into the ocean of silence when we "cross over." The melody celebrating our passing sings the truest tune. Every step we take in life leads us one step closer to the final chorus. We are not really walking to the corner office, or to presidency of the club, or even to nirvana. We are falling out of time. We are headed for the edge of silence where time doesn't matter any more. All we leave behind is the echo of what we did while we were around. During our turn on the dance floor, we can strive to invoke the best expression of our true self, the purest melodies of earth-pounding feet and star-singing spirits. All the way to the end. All the way over the pounding cascade into silence. The leaves turn such beautiful colors before they fall, don't they?

Exercise 46: Can of Holy Worms

Find a large, resonant vessel like a metal trash can. Clean it out, put it over your head, and sing a long, steady tone. Slowly raise and lower the pitch. At a certain pitch, the air around your head will come alive with mellow vibrations, and your voice will actually become louder. Slip and slide ever so slightly around that resonant pitch, listening carefully for the extra hum that comes when your activating energy (cause) aligns with the harmonics of the chamber (condition). The vessel actually amplifies your voice. Zero in on that pitch.

Holding the resonant pitch steady, reduce the force on your voice. As your voice gets softer, notice how the hum *outside* your head begins to dominate the sound. With practice—ten minutes or so—you will be able to sustain the resonance with very little effort. Listen closely to the sound *outside* your head. The rich, silky tone buzzing is the nexus, the harmony *between* your voice (force/cause) and the vessel (condition/material).

In this same manner, and with the smallest amount of action, every chamber of your life can be resonated, including the office, the bedroom, and the walls of your own skull. You know people who are masters at this: the taciturn professor who inspired your career; the inspirational uncle who never said a word; the coworker who just simply gets the job done; the lover who slays you with a look. These small but powerful messages are received when you are listening with a musical intention. Discovering the nexus of any situation requires attentiveness and a sustained, willing affinity for harmony.

Exercise 47: *Undertones of THE Sound*

Return to the toning exercise (exercise 20, page 82). Review the correspondence between sounds, overtones, and chakras (chapter 2, figure 14, page 57, and chapter 3, figure 1, page 85). As you tone, become aware of two levels of sound. There are the vibrations coming from your throat, of course. But with concentration, you will notice a sound moving in the corresponding body cavity with a purer and clearer resonance than that of your voice. Feel a quality inside your body similar to what you felt around your head when you were toning in the vessel. This second sound has a smooth, humming quality to it. The lower tones fill up your belly and chest. The upper tones ring in your head.

Try to sing softer and softer, maintaining the resonance filling up the various cavities. Change the shape of your mouth slightly to focus the vibrations. Eventually you will need very little energy in your voice to sustain the full resonance. You are now sensing the nexus, the dance of causes (energy and will) and conditions (your body-mind) that give rise to who you are.

At one moment music tells us that preparation and staging are all important. The next instant it whispers in our ear, "All that doesn't matter. Just keep playing!" Musical time is an enchanting realm where humming in the shower can get you just as high as attending the opera or the ultimate arena rock concert. Musical magic is waiting for us all the time in many temporal habitats. We release the magic when we offer up part of ourselves by paying attention to the resonant displays going on all around us all the time.

To a great extent, musical forms reveal the overtones of consciousness accentuated in a culture. Each form of music exemplifies the collective dreams of the culture that creates and enjoys it. The music that comes out of a tribal culture will be inherently different from the music of a culture run by the clock. The jazz buff dreams of freedom and self-expression. The country or folk music lover revels in the earthy simplicity of home, friends, and the fertile ground. The thrash rocker gets off on the outlaw edge, powering through the extreme snowboarding weekend with the roar and tumult of distorted guitars and warp-drive drums blasting on the subwoofer. The joyous exuberance of salsa melts people of many cultures into a steamy brew of rhythm, romance, and flash.

The orchestra is the model of the perfect Western society. Obey the rules, practice, and excel. And be justly rewarded with the accolades of those who aspire to your heights. But step out of the mold, move too far or too fast from the score, and . . . bingo . . . you're out. Question authority? Never! If you challenge the dominant rules of harmony, you can just take your attitude problem and look for work elsewhere.

Listen to music that speaks to your dreams of a perfect world. Musical forms create sympathetic vibrations in a culture just like the throb of a drum beat lifts individuals out of their chairs and on to the dance floor. Martial music rallies nations to war. Protest songs inspire the masses for action. Pop songs stress basic emotions and simple solutions. Respect music's power to resonate hearts and minds. Listen through the sound to the elements of consciousness. Every form of music unites a tribe of souls that are nourished by the musical time qualities of that particular style. The laws of resonance assure us that as we express ourselves with word, deed, and the music we play on the way to work, those qualities will increase. In musical time, like not only attracts like, *like creates like.*

A PERFECT NEXUS

What kind of world is to your liking? What sort of nexus befits you? Explore and respect your limits. Everyone has specific things that put him or her "over the edge." We all have our own impressions of the lunatic fringe, those folks who seem to relish living on the extreme edges of society. But the dazzling variety in music tells us that noise and dissonance for one may be the path to the divine for the next. We may shy away from what seems like a deep and dangerous cave only to discover folks happily living there. The vitality of consciousness on the entire planet depends on tolerance and respect for all forms, not just the ones that make us feel good. The loss of a culture down the gullet of consumerism may mean death to some, and simply the price of doing business for another. What kind of music are you making for the world?

The little town of Cotati, California, has created its own little cultural chamber of delight—or horror, depending on how you feel about accordions. The Cotati Accordion Festival celebrates the various styles (mutations?) of this venerable instrument, featuring everything from classical compositions to the edgy, punk sounds of Polkacide, a band complete with tuba and cranial spikes. The climax (apocalypse?) of the yearly event is the Lady-of-Spain-athon.

The tune "Lady of Spain" is to accordion music what "La Cucaracha" is to mariachi or what "When the Saints Go Marching In" is to Dixieland. An accordion festival without it would be like a Beethoven festival without the Fifth Symphony.

The year I attended, perhaps sixty accordionists of all ages gathered at the foot of the stage in Cotati's tree-lined square. The master of ceremonies started to play the tune, encouraging everyone to play along. What key? No matter. What version? No matter. What tempo? No matter. Little kids wishy-washied away on three-button training accordions. Old grandpas cranked it out on their heirloom instruments. Time warped. The harmony of the spheres was strained. The electrons in their probability clouds shuddered. And still they played on.

"You all sound so great! One more time!" crooned the emcee. One more time for what? When? Cacophony is too precise a description for the sound that was squeezed out that afternoon. At some magical moment divined by a mysterious magi, the doors to cages holding scores of doves were thrown open. There was a quick white blur, the threshing of wings frantic for escape, a breath of air, and the birds were gone to anywhere but there. Mercifully, the Lady-of-Spain-athon came to a wheezing conclusion.

"That was the best one ever!" chimed the emcee. Everyone applauded, smiled, and nodded. They had just intoned the time of their lives. Together in utter dissonance they celebrated the sound they love. For the very young in front of that stage, it was their first real gig. The intention was clear, the instruments were totally appropriate, and the audience was completely receptive. For the folks at the festival, what might seem like the screaming pit of dissonance to others was perfect harmony.

Every family, business, garage band, nation, and global network defines the edge in different terms. "Over the edge" for one group may be business as usual for the next. Every political decision, war strategy, marketing scheme, and personal choice helps to create a nexus, a singular vortex influencing the surroundings through resonance. Individuals make the decisions that together create the vortex, weave the nexus. To live musically we must pay attention to how our actions contribute to the composition of life.

THE WHOLE CULTURE

Have you ever wondered how a frog no bigger than a walnut could make such a raucous sound? Many types of frogs have large tympanic membranes situated on their heads. These are their eardrums. Unlike the human eardrum down at the end of the ear canal, the auditory receptors of these frogs are fully exposed to the air.

The vocal chords resonate the exposed eardrums like the magnetic driver resonates the cone of a speaker. Through resonance, the frog's hearing receptors are also vocal amplifiers. The tiny frog has a built-in amplification system. Having ear and voice linked in this way naturally brings a whole pond of frogs into sync. They can't help playing and listening at the same time—it's the same organ!

In our own way we are constantly participating in frog ponds of culture, hoping that our call will be heard, wondering if anybody is listening. Our innate musical time sense is like the frog's eardrum. Music proves it is our nature to play and listen at the same time. As we sing away we align with other voices in families, clubs, bands, companies, neighborhoods, and chat rooms. The resulting noise creates a cultural timbre, a cultural resonance. Rudhyar calls this "the culture whole." What tone does your family broadcast? What about your race, region, political party, nationality, or poker club? Will more beer help the frog pond choir? How about less TV or more prayer? How do you chime in? Are you listening? Can you feel others listening to you?

The world rings with our music. Just as we focus the activating energy of our voice into the chambers of the body-mind, we can send our musical intentions into the various board chambers, judge's chambers, and governmental chambers of our communal body, resonating cultural overtones with our choir-mates. The term "body politic" hints strongly at this dynamic.

The choices are many. The Sound has infinite partials. You choose the keynotes: knee-jerk reactions, mob mentality, peaceful coexistence, apathy, graduated levels of hypocrisy, bemused curiosity, rampant political correctness, logically unimpeachable paranoia. You can be visionary or addict, cynic or student, sage or fool. Your voice joins frog orchestras of like voices, and the croaking gets louder.

Pay attention! What kind of calls come back at you? The echoes create the musical qualities of life going on all around you. Are you in a choir of care or a madrigal of madness? Choose your songs. Listen. What's the dominant time quality at play? Is it ego or love? Sexual compulsion or empathy? When we "get a feeling" about something, that's when we are in the middle of a nexus. What happens when all the voices of a kind go off at once? Is it devastating? Inspiring? Bland? Confusing? Aggressive? Comfortable? Productive? Destructive?

What overtones of consciousness do you amplify with your life? Is it guts? Heart? Inspiration? Machismo? Survival? Every action we take spreads waves of influence through the nexus. Every gesture adds to the music. The slap to the face. The knowing wink. The fist on the table. The $40,000 purchase. The birthday flowers. Road rage. Credit-induced tourist oblivion. What is your message? Remember, just like in the frog pond, it all adds up.

IDEAS LIVE AMONG US

I have a favorite hot springs in the San Gabriel Mountains of Southern California. You must drive over dirt roads for miles to get near the place, then you hike a mile or two down a rough trail to an oasis tucked into the deep folds of a desert canyon. An ice-cold mountain creek slithers by the pools.

I was soaking in bliss when a young man joined me. We began talking. We both reflected on the incredible beauty of the place and the magic of the earth as a whole. Then I asked him what he did for a living. He said he was in the military. There are several army and air force bases nearby in the desert.

He explained that he was a missile officer. He spent five days at a time in a silo under the desert floor. Not bad duty, he reflected. But it was stressful. He never knew if the drills he performed were real or not. When the sirens went off, his commanding officer handed out the keys to the launch controls. On an order he unflinchingly turned the key. He never knew if his actions would send off a nuclear missile or not. "Well, of course they won't tell you," he chuckled. "Some weak-brained soldier might get a sudden rush of independent thinking, refuse to turn his key, and stall the launch destined to save the Free World."

Watching him sink into the soothing waters of the springs, I asked him if the stress was getting to him. Would he sign up for another hitch? "It is good duty," he repeated. "Good pay, lots of time off." Actually, though, he really wanted to pursue his true calling. What's that?

"I want to go back to school, get my degree, and teach geology at a junior college," he said as he looked out contentedly over the steaming springs. "I really love the earth."

This man "blew up" the world every now and then. Simultaneously, he carried in his heart a deep caring for his planet. He wanted to share his love of the earth with eager young minds, presumably before his beloved earth was blown up for real. He was an active member of two cultures in apparent conflict. His military culture-self was willing and ready to seriously harm, perhaps destroy, the very world that his spiritual culture-self revered and honored. I perceived this as puzzling and inconsistent. Years later another friend of mine showed me that such puzzling inconsistency may not be all that rare.

Jared is a Harvard man, and very smart, open, eclectic, and caring. He is also an enthusiastic amateur musician. We were telling each other our life stories on a beach in Mexico. He was a "red diaper baby," the child of active Communist Party members in the '50s. In contrast, my parents were John Birch Society members, active on the exact opposite end of the American political spectrum. We compared notes. We both stared down through the banister at livingroom meetings of idealistic adults exercising their respective political personalities.

"Wait a second," he said. "How could a pair of radical right-wing reactionaries turn out a crazy musician like yourself? It just doesn't seem to make sense! Did your parents actually like music?"

In Jared's perception, right-wing political culture could not have been fertile ground for my kind of person, a free jazz musician with anti-consumer tendencies. There was a culture clash here that did not make sense to him.

Putting the earth-loving missile officer and Jared side by side, I realized that ideas have lives of their own. They grow and flourish in the fertile brain matter of whomever might accept them, but they are rooted in another place, somewhere near the edge. Ideas appear to be easily independent. One idea does not demand or preclude the resonance of others in the same environment. Ideas that seem completely antagonistic can resonate right next to each other in the same brain. Many conflicting harmonies may be intoned simultaneously. Altruistic philanthropy may flow from the corporate magnate who devastates rainforests and busts unions.

Modern music shows us how traditionally isolated elements of expression can wonderfully coexist. Joni Mitchell was one of the first to bring the bata drum of West Africa into contemporary pop music. Some pop music of Indonesia blends Brazilian samba with the gamelan orchestras of the homeland. The rave dance scene exploits everything from samples of newscasts to nature sounds, all embroidered into a dense fabric of computer generated beats and sonic soundscapes. The composers and performers of today are willing and able to "catch" musical ideas and weave them together to create astounding hybrids.

Ideas have their own genesis, life span, vulnerabilities, and death process. They seem to visit us from the next dimension beyond time. The fact that we can hear music in our heads hints at this next dimension. The world of archetypes described by Jung gives us a glimpse of the realm of ideas as well. Our responsibility as cultivators of society lies in how we do our gardening.

THE DOORWAY OF MISTAKES

There was a weekend jazz club right down the street from where I used to live. The hall was small and intimate—the owner's private salon, really. A tiny balcony hovered over the Steinway. A vocalist-pianist from San Francisco was making an afternoon appearance. This was 1980, ten years before Bobby McFerrin's "Don't Worry, Be Happy" would hit it big.

That afternoon Bobby McFerrin was singing standards with a small combo. After a few numbers, he took the stage alone, sat down at the piano, and began improvising. Free improvisation is different from playing a jazz chart. You put yourself on the spot, composing as you play. From the way he leaned into the keyboard it seemed that being on the edge in this way was something he really enjoyed.

Looking down from the balcony barely ten feet above his head, I could see he was playing and listening intently. The concentration and joy were palpable. But then I sensed a tension. He began to work the music a bit too hard. He wanted to take it to a place where it didn't have the resilience to go. He got in a rut, and was forced to "vamp," repeating a simple four-bar figure over and over, waiting for the impetus to go on to the next section.

He was stuck, laughing to himself, shaking his head, and rolling his eyes. Non-musicians could have missed the frustration, but I could see it as clear as a bell, having been in the same time warp many times in my improvisations in the dance studio. I stuck my chin out over the banister, looked down, and our eyes met. "You're in the middle of it now!" I commiserated.

"Tell me about it," he replied looking up, never missing a beat. Putting his head down and digging back into his problem, he pulled out of the holding pattern and continued on to a soulful ending, well appreciated by all.

In every creative field, mistakes and dead-ends have many times been the door-ways to the next great innovation. The classic example is the fateful trip of Christopher Columbus. He set off expecting one thing and stumbled into a world he knew nothing about. Blunder of blunders and, presto, a New World. Improvisation reveals the mechanisms behind screw-up-driven discoveries like this.

The special challenge of the improvising musician is to continually reveal new material unearthed from the mines of the past. Some aspects of this can be practiced in a technical, left-brain mode. Old patterns are reshaped. Variations on familiar riffs are worked out. You practice your material over and over, in different keys and styles, incorporating technical elements and riffs modified from other players. Sometimes during this practice, gems may float and tumble your way, seemingly of their own accord. A deep discipline must be applied to capture the new material working its way into your bag of tricks.

Mistakes are another great source of new material. Every mistake is a completely unique blunder just over the edge into the unknown. A source of new music is found when we creatively deal with all the misplayed notes, jumbled rhythms, and the cold fear of "locking up" that happens when you run out of ideas. When you trip over your own fingers, sometimes your whole body-mind crashes through into new territory. Awash in the unknown, you blindly keep on playing. Your brain, forced out of touch with the known universe, steps back out of the way, and something new emerges into the light from the edge. You make a mistake, but you keep dancing. You ride a wave, a seed from the Sound catches on your shirttail, and you carry it back in step with you from the brink.

The sweet thing about free improvisation is that you really can't do anything wrong. Ruts, blunders, rhythmic stuttering, and locking up may all feel like mistakes. You cannot deny the flutter in the belly, or the mottled cloud of desperation spreading over your mind's eye. But after running on the edge for a while you come to appreciate these feelings as the undeniable shudders of innovation making the quantum leap from the infinite sea of Sound into the nexus of your music.

Musical mistake-management boils down to one prime directive: simply keep playing. Your will power establishes a carrier wave ready to receive all new information. Don't allow a mistake to distract you from the intentions latent in what you are doing. Maintain your ride on the carrier wave of intent. Try to repeat the "mistake" freshly arrived from the other side of your known universe. Repeat it again. Listen to how it fits with what you did before, and work it into the fabric of the ongoing music.

Everybody says, "It's good to learn from your mistakes." But to be useful the learning has to go deeper than simply avoiding the old circumstances. In order to learn from something you need to examine it closely, feel its edges and shapes. Listen to it again and again. See how it fits. A mistake is an indirect result of some sort of intentional action. Mistakes are never malicious. The mind or heart was just looking in another direction. To learn from the mistake, we need to pay attention to the new direction, to recognize the mistake for what it really is—something brand new. We have to accept the unfamiliar path as a direction, a revelation into new territory.

In the recording studio and on the movie set, artists record many "takes." They will put down version after version of the same piece of work, hoping that one out of the many will prove to be the standout of the bunch. Follow this model. If it feels like you can gain something from doing it again, so be it. Many times after making "mistakes" again and again, a new interpretation makes the jump and inspiration is captured on tape or film.

Keep on playing. Keep an eye out for the subtle but revealing patterns in the jumble. The weed may turn out to be the exotic hybrid. The wrong answer might put a new slant on a boring topic. The ridiculous non sequitur could encapsulate the essence of the idea. How many babies are conceived during a "mistake" of passion and then turn out to be the parents' pride and joy? How many wrong turns lead us to the perfect building site? How many shortages have led to innovation and progress? How many cosmic rays smashing through chromosomes lazily floating in the gene pool actually spark the most fitting of life forms?

Mistakes are the doorway to the edge, that place where it's all happening. When the one thing you so dearly expected is lost in a mistake, you are released into the emptiness where everything else under the sun is waiting for you. Stay on top of the beat and keep on playing. Mistakes draw the infinite possibilities of the Sound into your midst directly and undeniably. What could possibly be more enchanting than the swirling, breathless, iridescent, lover's-kiss softness of butterflies in your stomach? Take a chance. Improvise. It is no fluke that "improve" is the heart of that word.

In the world of musical performance, improvisation is the dance at the edge. Without written music, the artist is relying purely on instinct. Many classically trained musicians are terrified of "making stuff up." And it is daunting. Avoiding memorized patterns, letting go of formal melody, the improviser sets off into the very heart of the nexus of each performance, diving into the silent source of inspiration.

PLAYING WITH THE CHANGES

Many musical traditions have an improvisational element. Baroque compositions (1600–1750) were constructed on the foundation of a *continuo,* a structure of chords written out in harmonic shorthand. Members of an ensemble would improvise their parts from this outline. The great concertos of the Romantic Era (mid to late 1800s) contained a *cadenza,* sections where soloists showed pyrotechnic skill while improvising variations on the themes of the piece. Many tribal forms use improvisation to capture the power of the performance moment. Starting with the blues and early jazz, and continuing through all contemporary forms, American pop music has featured the spontaneous expression of soloists.

There is a common thread to all improvisational forms. The rhythmic, melodic, or harmonic foundations of the theme are repeated while soloists "make up" fitting variations over the underlying structure. In traditions emphasizing harmony, this structure is called "the changes." At the end of the improvisation the original theme is usually restated. Faithful to the sonic genetics of the blues and jazz, rock and roll usually features a soloist wailing over the changes of the tune.

No matter how structured, controlled, strategized, or air-conditioned our life may be, we are basically working our way through a grand improvisation played out over the changes of our lives. Our genetics, surroundings, and life-long habits create the framework for our personality, our continuo. No amount of plastic surgery or Scientology can disengage us from genetic themes. Cultural patterns can be just as hard to alter. But like the soloist in front of the band, we do have ultimate freedom to improvise new variations over these established structures. Especially in more affluent cultures, we have freedom to do our own thing. Some cultures will tolerate original variations and some will not. It's the same in families, corporations, and Rotary Clubs. What constitutes healthy tolerance is a group decision, and is always open for debate.

Like humming into the garbage can, it takes very little effort to create a new time quality in your life. Doctors tell us that a half hour of aerobic activity three times a week can extend your life by years. Listen for the harmony between the voices going off in your life right now. Create a new interpretation of the old tune by simply accentuating a new complimentary element. But do it often. Practice makes perfect.

The goal of improvisation is not just to come up with unique material. There is a wonderful trick in many classic jazz solos. Snippets of familiar tunes like

"Mary Had a Little Lamb," or "Yankee Doodle," will slip into the phrasings of a player. The context makes the old cliché brand new again. Every riff is a new branch growing from rootstock played by someone else. Nothing is absolutely new. Like genetic evolution, or the genesis of ideas, new combinations are the essence and reward of honoring and enjoying the past.

Embracing a wide variety of paces, styles, and roles informs us of our wider potential, opening a road to freedom and self-determination. Learn a new step to an old dance just for the sake of diversity and flexibility. By doing many dances we discover the ones that reach down deep, grab on to our identity, and won't let go. We find our bliss. Like sliding your voice around inside the vessel on your head, exploring a variety of niches in the temporal habitat will eventually bring deeper resonance to your life.

THE TIME OF YOUR LIFE

A vacation, a near tragedy, an evening at home with your sweetie, that one perfect sunset, and a night at the opera can all be the time of your life. An entire life-era such as college or retirement can also fill the bill. This phrase does not refer to elapsed time. It refers to a feeling. Musical qualities populate our time habitat like birds in a woodland. Aspects of time call out to us over the hills and dales of experience. Time marches on. Or waltzes on. Or polkas on. Or slumbers on. Every moment sends out its unique overtone of Sound. Music is the Rosetta Stone, the worldwide web of resonance that translates themes from over the edge into our hearts. Through practice we can learn to discern the various qualities of time, orchestrating them into a fuller, more expressive rendition of our best intentions.

Full immersion into the currents of time demands a practiced self-awareness. But we suffer from overbearing self-consciousness. The more we notice and demonstrate the universal principles of resonance at play all around us—the tempo, tone, harmony, melody, and inspiration—the more we live a life full of music. Notice the shoe in the dryer, the bubble in the tire, the gentle waves of breath as your child strolls the shore of dreams, the buzzing of the moth against the window striving for the light. Notice your heart against the heart of your lover.

Music brings us to the swirling nexus of creative force at the edge of silence. When our actions approach harmony with this Sound, all the tasks of life become easier and more productive. The wider the bandwidth of this sense of unity, the more joy, power, and love we feel. Listen for the Sound of the earth against your feet as you run. Hear the Sound of spirit as tears fall on the back of your hands as you pray. Exercising our musicality strengthens the body, deepens the breath, opens the heart, cleans out the ears, and sharpens our wits.

The techniques of timing, personal tone, synchronization, and interpersonal harmony that have been presented in these pages will prepare you for expressive musical relationships with your cocreators of the time habitat. Practicing these lessons of music will establish and sustain a sense of harmony for you, your family, and every choir of frogs you join. This practice provides the opportunity for you to express your true Self every moment. Just listen and keep playing. Everyone has a unique part to play in the family, at work, on the ball-field, in the conference room. The power of resonant Sound is available in every beat of the drum, every wail of the guitar, every shimmer of the choir, every pulse of the heart, and every ride on the escalator.

The system in this book is based on the seven chakras, but this is only one way to access the overtones of Sound. If this system does not resonate for you, move on, try another technique. Find one—or improvise one—that speaks to you. How about a system based on four?

Four-part harmony is a venerable approach evident everywhere as well. The four directions are sacred to many cultures. The four elements (air, earth, water, fire) are central to alchemic and classical philosophy. Four-part musical harmony and counterpoint define Western music to a great degree. Soprano, alto, tenor, and bass voices have filled cathedrals, concert halls, and rock clubs for seven hundred years. Air, water, minerals, and biota are the four elements of living soil, the nexus that sustains terrestrial life. Down one notch, three's are sacred to Celts and Christians. The Christian denominations assign definite attributes to the members of the Holy Trinity.

No matter what system strikes your fancy, remember that sentient beings have always heard that Sound, quested for the source, felt a power. So take a breath and sing out! Listen well. Play on. The Word (Sound) is God. On earth as it is in heaven. The Sound contains everything. That gives us a lot of options. We can emulate a style we enjoy and respect, or we can improvise.

ENSEMBLES OF INTENTION

As we learn to recognize the musical aspects of our life, it becomes apparent that we are not singing alone. No matter how deeply we have fallen into the gap separating us from the rhythms of the earth and the holy chants of heaven, sooner or later we catch a wisp of the Sound in the music we make with the ones we love. Our mates, families, coworkers, and neighborhoods make up various ensembles in which we play. The wider habitats of our town, region, and nation also create temporal artifacts that have profound influence in very broad circles.

The quality of time emanating from the United States is completely different from—and in many ways more powerful than—the temporal message of India or China, nations of vastly greater populations. The drum beat of prosperity and power rings from shore to shore in America. And much of the world seems to be falling into step. A timeless theme from India seems to resonate a deep spirituality, and China intones a profound inscrutability. The tone of every individual in these contrasting cultures contributes to the overall tone of the whole. Some cultures change their tune radically in less than a generation. Japan, South Africa, Germany, Iran, and Chile are examples of such societies.

Revolutions are always an evolution of internal dynamics. Again and again the timbre of cultures all over the world has been shocked by the release of tension built up in the hearts of the people. For centuries themes of racial subjugation reverberated through the American culture whole. In post–World War Two America this tone harmonized with an emerging black middle class and northern white liberalism to create major social upheavals in the South. Subsequent reverberations from these songs of freedom are still being felt in the new millennium. Events in Montgomery, Alabama, in the early '60s will resonate in the composition of American politics and race relations forever.

The rich melting pot of the Mississippi delta—where French, Spanish, American, and African cultures brewed the blues—stands clearly at the epicenter of a cultural revolution in music and the arts that has spread worldwide. Delta music in many forms, especially Dixieland and jazz, had already crossed over into white culture before the civil rights movement erupted in the south. What effect did the musical blending of cultures have on civil rights activism?

The human condition is a harmony between the bounded physical world of survival and the unbounded world of the mind and spirit. These two worlds blend and flow together, creating a fertile medium for growth and change. This harmony defines our culture. All of us together compose our various cultures of family, business, community, nation, and world as surely as the members of an orchestra create the sound of the symphony.

The paths we take, and the ideals and values to which we adhere, contribute to our various cultural spheres of influence. And it all adds up. We build a house. We live in a box. We spoil our kids. We choose not to have kids. We march on a picket line. We spend gobs of money on books, drugs, cars, charities, or lawn care. We harp on the past. We fantasize ourselves into paranoid inaction or visionary action. We work a highly exciting and yet somehow futile job. We goof off. We contribute to environmental causes and buy a new computer every two years to stay in touch. As the member of many choirs, each one of us is challenged to perform with grace and discipline. We have a responsibility to listen to the Sound we are bringing into the world through our words and deeds. Are we creating accidental noise or compositions of intent?

Are we just frogs croaking away in some backwater? Is life just a glorified Grateful Dead show, a loose amalgamation of doers and shakers, merchants, techies, and camp followers? The power of intention says it's not so simple. Music shows us that our choices create culture, and we have the talent to weave our nexus on purpose.

WILLING HARMONY

We have explored many ways in which a musical attitude can create a more resonant life. We have introduced techniques and ideas to enhance the response of your body-mind to the many periodic forces moving through the world. We have introduced an idea-nexus suggesting that the most revealing and transformational things happen *between* things.

The belly is the seat of will power. You take in all the elements of life right there. Your diaphragm pulls the air into your lungs. Your stomach receives food and water. Your solar plexus knits together all four of your limbs in a radiant knot of muscle power. If you have the guts for a task, you are well on the way to success.

One step up on the ladder of the chakras, we arrive at the heart. Love rings from your heart. Our heart registers every relationship we undertake, and sends reverberations throughout the body. We can act with passion *and* compassion when we harmonize gut-level feelings with the balancing, loving nature of the heart. I want to suggest that the music created between your gut and your heart may be the clearest and most powerful harmony humans can generate.

Beethoven caught a fateful echo of the Sound in the first few notes of the Fifth Symphony. The infectious rhythm of the Afro-Cuban clave has insinuated itself into scores of musical genres. The tonal imperatives of the harmonic series are expressed in hymns, pop tunes, commercial jingles, and symphonic masterworks. The chants, mantras, and invocations of traditional cultures around the world bring the words of the gods into our midst. Looking at the music of the human instrument inspires me to suggest one more melody, one more simple song, one more mantra. The words to this song are "willing harmony."

Use these words to invoke the fiery passion of the human will in harmony with the tender compassion of the human heart. Repeat these words on your Walking Meditation, on your drive to work, as you do that chore you were avoiding all day. Willing harmony is at once an offering and a challenge, a gift and a responsibility. Like music in all its forms, willing harmony is draped with garlands of discipline and joy. Feel willing harmony ring in your gut and your heart *at the same time.* Compose your Self.

NOTICE, LISTEN, CULTIVATE

As the farmer saves and selectively breeds his or her seeds, our job is to strengthen our various cultural environments through conscious, heartfelt stewardship, mindfully articulating the ideas that blow into our fields of action from just over the edge.

Just because an idea germinates and flourishes does not make it fair, logical, or culturally sustaining in the long run. In the Nazi era, lots of Germans loved classical music, worshiped the Savior, cared deeply for their families, and revered their homeland. Does the evil of their socio-political activity invalidate their expression of these very human traits that many of us also prize? With all the irony, hypocrisy, apathy, and cruelty going on in today's world, how do we know if our choices really mean anything? How do we train our inner ear to guide us to our highest place in the resonance of our various cultures?

We can start by listening for the Sound swirling and surging around us. Through the invisible, massless, eternal power of resonance, divine consciousness imbues every atom, star, and heartbeat. The interconnected nature of music shows us that qualities of time work together to create a composition with predominant traits and effects. The driving drums and blaring horns of the Sousa march and the rhythm and blues band have much in common. They both resonate the Sound of power and direct action, a clear echo of undeniable will. The tender pop melody and the captivating chant of the Pygmy villager reach us with similar clarity and simplicity of voice. They are telling us something, whispering in our ear. A contra dance with a confident caller, a synchronized basketball team, or a production team on the factory floor can all be ensembles of intention that inspire us to play our hearts out. That urge is the love of rhythm and harmony we all share. That love tugs on our heart, drawing us closer to the edge of time where the Now meets Forever. All of us have been given the gifts of an innate musical nature. Don't be shy. Sit down on the stool and take out the horn. All you have to do is play. You'll have the time of your life.

A PRACTICE GUIDE

This guide will help you construct your own program for developing musical intelligence and personal resonance using the exercises in this book.

The first approach is to simply pick one or two exercises that capture your imagination and practice them on a regular basis. Some exercises lend themselves to daily practice, others to a weekly routine. Establish your own cycle and repeat for at least six repetitions. Most exercises take less than ten minutes. Development of more specific practice can be undertaken by following the steps below.

1. Tune in to your body. Where do you feel active energy? Where do you feel a lack of energy? Focus on the chakras and the associated attributes of consciousness, and consider which element of music touches you the strongest. With these ideas in mind, consult chapter 2, figure 14 (page 57). Choose a chakra for the day's practice.

2. Assess your energy level. Do you want to work in a meditative mode or an energetic, aerobic mode today? Remember, physical exercise can be invigorating when you feel tired.

3. Using the results of steps 1 and 2, refer to the chart on page 208 (figure 1). The chakras, attributes, and musical elements are listed in the left column, and the energy levels are listed along the top. Find the list of exercises in the appropriate square. These are the activities you have chosen for today's practice.

4. Choose a few numbers from the chosen practice area. There is a short description of each exercise in appendix B. Review the descriptions of your chosen numbers. Find an exercise that catches your attention. Go to the text and begin.

	Meditative	Semiactive	Active	Energetic
Crown Chakra Spirit Inspiration	8, 10, 13, 27, 47	8, 27, 28, 46	25	
Third Eye Chakra Insight Form	1, 8, 9, 20, 25, 26, 28, 43, 45	8, 25, 27, 28, 34, 35, 41, 42, 44, 46	34, 36, 41	
Throat Chakra Expression Melody	8, 16	4, 6, 7, 8, 14, 24	2	12, 17, 32, 37
Heart Chakra Love Harmony	1, 3, 7, 38, 47	35, 43, 45, 6, 25, 33, 42, 45	23, 34, 37	
Solar Plexus Chakra Will Tone	16, 18, 19, 21, 42, 49	5, 20, 38, 42, 44	11, 31	15, 32, 39
Genital Chakra Identity Rhythm and Pattern	30	3, 4, 7, 22, 30, 44	4	5, 12, 17, 32, 39
Root Chakra Survival Pulse	1, 13, 26, 27, 29, 42	27, 30, 42	2, 11, 23, 31	15, 37

Figure 1: Practice Area Chart.

SUGGESTIONS

Work with a partner. Many of the exercises work well with one person reading the instructions, the other doing the work. Having a partner allows an active exchange. The harmony of cooperation is palpable when the exercises are done as a team.

Choose *two* exercises for each practice time. The first one should expand and project the vibrations of an area of your body-mind that is feeling strong and expressive at the moment. Then choose another area that needs attention. Consciously direct energy from the strong area into the area in need. You are your own best coach. Play on!

B DESCRIPTIONS OF EXERCISES

Exercise 1: A Walking Tour of the Universe, page 21

Keynotes: pacing, relationship (observer/object), diversity. A very slow walking meditation where one concentrates on the inner qualities of objects one at a time.

Exercise 2: Pacing Yourself, page 28

Keynotes: pacing, self-expression, playful. A semiactive to active walking excursion. You sing a tune and dance to it as you move along.

Exercise 3: The Building Blocks, page 30

Keynotes: pattern, style. A simple movement game tapping into the feeling of duple and triple meters.

Exercise 4: The Power of Patterns, page 31

Keynotes: play, creativity. A playful harmony between vocal patterns and dance-like movement.

Exercise 5: Root Tone, page 38

Keynotes: will power, breath, tone. Using the torso muscles to generate a strong vocal tone.

Exercise 6: Harmony for Two, page 43

Keynotes: harmony of two, singing, confidence. A partner exercise introducing musical intervals and the emotional content they convey.

Exercise 7: Scat Attack, page 48

Keynotes: self-expression through humor, innocence. A romp into gibberish. A private expression of all your variations on "blah-blah-blah."

Exercise 8: Words for the Wise, page 48

Keynotes: attention, expression, *aum* vibrations. Playing with the essence of a snippet of conversation. Real life sound bites in contrast to the *aum.*

Exercise 9: The Listening Half, page 55

Keynotes: insight, attention, perception. Recognizing musical elements in music. Taking note of musical textures and the time qualities they resonant.

Exercise 10: Moving As One, page 59

Keynotes: connection, spirit, smoothness. Moving under your halo.

Exercise 11: Tempo Tour, page 68

Keynotes: gravity awareness, choices, intentions. Playing with the qualities inherent in different paces on a walk.

Exercise 12: Creekside Dance, page 68

Keynotes: focus, direction, balance. An energetic hopping dance.

Exercise 13: Death Watch, page 70

Keynotes: roots, greeting death, view of heaven. A breath exercise where you conduct yourself to the edge of oblivion.

Exercise 14: Content/Context, page 72

Keynotes: speech training, expressing your Self. A movement and vocalization activity showing how one aspect of self-expression automatically influences others.

Exercise 15: Walk on the Wild Side, page 74

Keynotes: pacing, power, timing. A guided power walk linking breath with will power.

Exercise 16: Your Habit Habitat, page 75

Keynotes: will power, self-realization. An exercise program in itself, this exercise gives you the technique to supplant old habits with new ones.

Exercise 17: Dancing Together, page 77

Keynotes: playful, sexy, improvise. A partner dance exploring rhythm, communication, and a mutually willing harmony.

Exercise 18: Conducting Yourself Properly, page 78

Keynotes: will power, inner balance. A breathing meditation.

Exercise 19: Yogananda's Wake-up Call, page 80

Keynotes: links breath to body. Experience the forces of will power in every part of your body. A technique inspired by Paramahansa Yogananda.

Exercise 20: Lines of Force, page 82

Keynotes: attention, balance, warmth. A muscle toning and body awareness activity.

Exercise 21: Your Resonant Tone, page 84

Keynotes: tone, integration, unity. A toning discipline linking musical tone with the chakras. Finding resonance in your body-mind.

Exercise 22: At the Crossroads, page 87

Keynotes: balance, honoring yourself. Stimulating awareness of the second chakra identity center.

Exercise 23: Dance for the Heart, page 93

Keynotes: roots, relationship, spirit. Rhythmic and active. A dance joining earth and sky with a focus on the human heart that stands between the two.

Exercise 24: Vocal Calisthenics, page 98

Keynotes: self-expression, listening, pacing. Techniques for clear and expressive articulation. Expanding the range of your instrument.

Exercise 25: A Harmony of Thoughts, page 109

Keynotes: relationship, attention, awareness. Using your mind to examine the overtones of various daily activities. Practicing insight and atonement.

Exercise 26: Carrier Waves, page 113

Keynotes: connection, ritual, silence. A meditation for tuning into subtle body-mind currents.

Exercise 27: Tin Can Telephone, page 113

Keynotes: fundamental tone, spirit. A semiactive meditative activity setting every chakra humming.

Exercise 28: Crowning Glory, page 113

Keynotes: gateways, integration, clarity. Riding on the halo.

Exercise 29: Your Personal Underworld, page 130

Keynotes: root knowledge, insight. A guided meditation down into the earth to meet your inner guides.

Exercise 30: Pacemaker, page 133

Keynotes: pacing, intention, self-hood. Using small, rhythmic motions to set your body-mind on a different pace. Retuning your tempo for the moment at hand.

Exercise 31: Pumping Up, page 133

Keynotes: pacing, will power, stamina. A dance done in place for increasing energy and groundedness.

Exercise 32: Windjammer, page 135

Keynotes: playfulness, breath, closeness. A partner dance.

Exercise 33: An Empathy Symphony, page 135

Keynotes: empathy, opening, peace. Bringing the essence of familiar surroundings closer to your heart.

Exercise 34: Laughing Out Loud, page 138

Keynotes: perspective, pathos, transformation. Turning a bad humor into a good one. Tragedy plus time equals comedy.

Exercise 35: Score One for You, page 140

Keynotes: self-realization, mindfulness, discipline. A journal exercise involving daily entries and examination. A procedure for orchestrating new and meaningful themes in your life.

Exercise 36: Out There, page 143

Keynotes: connection, will power, direction. Building motivation, personal vision, and expressive habits of forward motion.

Exercise 37: Spot On Again, page 150

Keynotes: concentration, diversity, motivation. A dance for balance, placement, and confidence.

Exercise 38: Personal Intonation, page 151

Keynotes: breath, tone, focus, balance, self-love. Using tone to transfer energy from one area of the body to another.

Exercise 39: Flying on Time, page 159

Keynotes: patience, forgiveness, direction. Dancing with a feather in free-fall.

Exercise 40: Scales Study, page 162

Keynotes: love, balance, courage, talent. A partner meditation in trust, tolerance, and acceptance.

Exercise 41: Some Musical Homework, page 164

Keywords: playful, timely, home. Rituals to bring magic into our midst.

Exercise 42: Earth in the Balance, page 166

Keywords: roots, nourishment, respect. New habits for a planet in distress. Connecting personal actions with global needs.

Exercise 43: Practice Tips for the Flow, page 173

Keywords: focus, integrity, flexibility. A guide for playing your part in group situations.

Exercise 44: Tempo Minder, page 175

Keynotes: tuning in, concentration, intent. Setting your personal metronome to a new beat anytime, anywhere.

Exercise 45: Falling in Love All the Time, page 177

Keynotes: clarity, empathy, willingness, cooperation. Skills for asking and accepting loving attention.

Exercise 46: Can of Holy Worms, page 188

Keynotes: steady tone, attention, and transcendence. Creating and appreciating an experience of harmony. Learning to be quiet enough to perceive the inner voice.

Exercise 47: Undertones of THE Sound, page 189

Keynotes: listening, silence, breath, unity. Experiencing the nexus generated by the relationship between your physical body, your best intentions, and your Higher Self.

C SUGGESTED LISTENING

Following are brief descriptions of many musical styles and traditions. This is by no means a comprehensive list of musical styles. These have been chosen for their distinct use of one or more of the seven elements of music, and the clarity to which this use resonates the overtones of consciousness associated with the chakras.

The numbers after each listing indicate the chakras most highly resonated by the music. Specific artists are given when I feel their music is especially effective in activating overtones of consciousness.

Adult Contemporary (4, 6)

This style of jazz plays on the "soft wave" FM channels. Kenny G, Rick Braun, Michael Franks, and John Tesh are mainstays of the genre. Jazz instrumentation and forms are packaged for the general market. Certain aspects of Muzak production are evident in this mainstreaming effort, but the music does create a free-wheeling ambience that can be great for driving, background, and general sonic furnishing. Live recordings are rare, since the Sound of the style is by definition generic in nature.

African, Pop (1, 3, 5)

Artists include Angelique Kidjo, Baba Maal, the Boukman Experience, Muta Baruka. African pop blends traditional call and response forms and sonorities with Western melodic sensibilities and studio technique. Very danceable.

African, Traditional

Ghana, the *djembe* and *djun djun* (2, 3, 6): Very fast and powerful, these two drums, and their dances, are making their way into world culture. The djembe is a highly expressive drum with booming low tones and piercing high tones. The djun djun holds the lowest bass parts, many times played with a bell.

Mali, the *coro* (4, 5, 7): The native African harp, the coro produces a magical, liquid sound. Accompanying vocals are sweet, passionate, and heavily tinged with the influence of Islam.

Nigeria, the *bata* (1, 2, 4): Drums and vocal chant. Highly energetic and somewhat complex to the Western ear. Vocals are generally sung in unison. A very natural, earthy sound. Source: Bembe Records, *The Rough Guide to World Music.*

Zimbabwe, the *mbira* (4, 5, 7): The mbira is the hand-forged grandfather of the "thumb piano." It produces a bell-like watery sound. Complex interlocking melodies make mbira music the most contrapuntal of African styles. The Xona people use it to accompany their haunting and childlike songs.

Afro-Caribbean (2, 4, 6)

Including the various style of *salsa, meringue, zuok,* and *calypso.* Slaves brought the West African rhythms to the New World. The rhythms blended with European song forms to create a rich tradition where searing horns, vibrant vocal, and improvisation play major roles. There are many traditional and contemporary styles. Source: Bembe Records.

Bluegrass (4, 5)

With roots in Celtic songs and instrumental music, bluegrass is a truly American form. Tender melodies in harmony, and blazingly fast articulations on a wide variety of stringed instruments join to create songs and melodies of home, heart, loss, and the open road. Source: Sugar Hill Records. Artists include Sam Bush, the Stanley Brothers, Flatt and Scruggs, Nickel Creek, Laurie Lewis, and many others.

Blues, Funk (2, 3, 6)

Funk is a rhythmic style of blues-based music. Characterized by highly synco-pated figures and punchy melodic bursts, funk draws its power from a more direct application of the rhythmic elements of African drumming to popular dance music. Funk sensibilities are evident as far back as the "jump" styles of jazz and gospel in the '30s and '40s. They are dominant today in hip-hop, rap, con-temporary R & B, and even heavy metal, post-punk, and acid jazz.

Blues, Rhythm and Blues (1, 5)

When black artists began to gain recognition and acceptance in the white mar-kets, rhythm and blues came into its own. Electric instruments, a full drum set, more complex (and even orchestral) arrangements entered in. Early rock by both black and white artists drew heavily from the gospel traditions of the black churches. The human voice was still the centerpiece of the style, but instrumental stars emerged as well. A steady beat, the simple blues cadences, and the power of personality merged in the music of Elvis, Ike and Tina Turner, Eric Clapton, Chuck Berry, and scores of other artists. Motown music was a commercialized hybrid of gospel, R & B, and the blues. Motown served as the bridge bringing black culture into the mainstream of American cultures.

Blues, Traditional (rural) (1, 3, 5)

The blues is credited as the rootstock of many American styles from rock to jazz, showtunes to hip-hop. The most traditional forms are still sung in the rural areas of the Mississippi Delta. A single guitar and voice, usually male, sings the laments and passions of the lonely man, the spurned lover, the hard-working soul. Source: Alligator Records, Arhoulie Records, Smithsonian releases. Artists include Howl-ing Wolf, John Lee Hooker, Muddy Waters, Robert Johnson, and a vast pantheon of immortal voices.

Blues, Traditional (urban) (1, 3, 5)

The rural blues migrated to the cities starting around the turn of the twentieth century. The raw, animal nature survives this trek. More females became stars in this style. Instrumental accompaniment became more complex. The plight of the black race in America was, and is to this day, a dominant undercurrent to urban blues, and the jazz, rock, and soul music that evolved from it. Artists: Ma Rainy, Bessie Smith, Big Joe Turner, Etta James, Willie Dixon.

Celtic (fusion) (1, 3, 5)

Centered in Ireland and England, this movement, much like reggae in the New World, links traditional musical forms with the techniques of recording and performance of popular American forms. Full drum sets, electric bass, electronic treatment of traditional instruments, and full-throated, aggressive lyrics brings Celtic music fully into the pop mainstream.

Celtic, Traditional (1, 5)

The Celts were a loose group of many nationalities that stretched from northern Spain, across western Europe, and north through the British Isles and beyond. They left a large genre covering a centuries-old tradition: rollicking fiddle tunes, jigs, and reels; haunting ballads and laments; polkas, dance tunes of all types, and tear-wrenching vocals telling stories of lost loves and wandering travelers. Stringed instruments of all types, flutes, and simple drums mark the style today.

Classical, Baroque (4, 6, 7)

Stretching from the mid-sixteenth century to around 1750, the Baroque was the musical culmination of the High Renaissance era (or "Age of Enlightenment") in Europe. Melodic counterpoint, instrumental virtuosity, and strict triadic harmony are the hallmarks of this style. Noted composers: Vivaldi, Gabrielli, J. S. Bach, Handel, Cuperin, Purcell, and many others.

Classical, Beethoven (3, 6, 7)

Beethoven was also unique. He grew deaf early in life. The passion, bitterness, and pain he suffered as a musician and a man is evident in every bar of his music. He stands at the brink between the controlled, convention-clad classical era and the free, almost anarchic, display of the Romantic. In Beethoven's music, especially the string quartets, we see the evolution of a man and a culture. He treated music as Sound, and viewed himself as a divine messenger. For him, each instrument had something to say, adding something unique to his compositions. The Fifth Symphony is perhaps the boldest personal statement in Western culture. The Sixth is the first programmatic work, every note depicting some real aspect or object of nature. This marriage between the personal and the universal, so evident in Beethoven's music, has become the challenge of every individual (and nation) since his time.

Classical, Gregorian Chant (3, 4, 7)

In the late middle ages the Catholic church codified the music to be sung in the Mass. Chanting their prayers to God became a highly evolved form of prayer for many monastic orders. Sung in unison, the tones and melodies of the chants adhere to strict rules of interval and scale (called *modes*). They resonate a deep calm, a swirling spirituality, and a rich fertility of devotion.

Classical, Impressionists (3, 6, 7)

Led by Ravel, Debussy, and Satie, this school stretched harmony beyond the triads and circle of fifths. They truly experimented with new sounds and forms. Painting with tones and combinations of instruments, these innovators opened up musical vistas through which jazz artists would walk twenty years later.

Classical, J. S. Bach (4, 6, 7)

Of special note, of course, is Johann Sebastian Bach. More than any other composer, perhaps, Bach personifies the European ideal of the musical artist. His compositions are rich with melodic expression, always adhering to the ideals of harmony handed down through the liturgical tradition. He celebrates the clarity of the individual voice in his many concertos and other pieces featuring the solo instrument. His approach to harmony is at once very strict and highly adventurous for the time. The sheer volume of work—not to mention his many children that followed in his musical footsteps—exhibit a creative force of refined power and inspired grace.

Classical, Minimalism (6, 7)

Using musical forms to establish environments of sound, composers such as Phillip Glass, Steve Reich, and Brian Eno blended the simplicity of tribal-like repetitive phrases with the cyclic, nearly static sensibilities of the electronic frontier.

Classical, Mozart and other Classicists (4, 5, 6)

It seems Mozart may well have been a truly unique human being. He had the ability to visualize the entire score to a piece of music. He would sit down and transcribe one part at a time from his mind to the paper. His compositions were formed as a whole. In this way his music captures the essence of the divine mind that conceives the composition of nature all at once. When we think of classical music, Mozart comes to the fore as the perfect exponent of the classical culture of the West. His music is solid, playful, celebratory, and passionate. His melody and harmony blend to form a tapestry of sound unrivaled by his contemporaries, and many say unrivaled since.

Classical, Renaissance (5, 7)

A blend of the folk melodies and the sacred music of central and western Europe. A growing aristocracy expressed itself through the compositional freedom rulers extended to the musicians. Instrument building techniques were improving. There was a growth in secular sponsorship of the arts. Music from this period has a rambunctious, rollicking feel, as well as many examples of touching melodies and stories. The grand tradition of the balladeer and minstrel evolved here. Court musicians were celebrities, somewhat immune to persecution from their lords because they carried the histories, praises, and exploits of one realm to the next. Source: Nonsuch Recordings.

Classical, the Romantic Era (5, 6)

A few noted composers: Wagner, List, Chopin, Tchaikovsky, and Johann and Richard Strauss. The Romantic era (1850 to 1900) marks the full maturation of the Western development of musical forms. Composers and performers expressed intensely individualistic visions of musical Sound. The rules of classical harmony were pushed to the limits. Melodies gushed and crashed through a richer and richer orchestral soundscape. Virtuoso instrumentalists claimed the status of rock stars. The waltz took Europe by storm. Wagner captivated the hearts of an entire civilization, galvanizing in sound and spectacle the culture whole of the Germanic race.

Country Western (4, 5)

This style rivals any other form of pop music in sales, popularity, and mass appeal. Simple tunes and forms based on hymns, sweetened blues, and folk melodies, country western demands a clear unadorned timbre from vocalists, and straight forward, heartfelt tunes and lyrics from the songwriter. Vocal harmony is a main feature, drawing a resonance from the church singing that nurtured the predominantly white country western artist.

Disco and Trance (1, 6, 7)

Both are characterized by a jogging tempo, heavy bass, shimmering melodic lines, and electronic instruments. Disco (late '70s to mid '80s) was a popular response to the go-it-alone rock dance styles. The pounding beat and repetitive melodies created a trancelike state. The disco club scene was huge in Europe and extensive in urban centers in the United States. The universal need for trance (and the freedom it inspires) has been embraced widely and exuberantly by the electronic-heavy trance or rave music scene. Today, so-called R & B pop tunes look back to the romance, sexuality, and urban sensibilities of disco. Some disco artists include Gloria Gaynor, KC and the Sunshine Band, and the Bee Gees; trance artists include Lost at Last, Hamsa Lila, and numerous "mix DJs."

Folk, Solo Singer/Songwriter (5)

The American folk music tradition has roots all the way back to the troubadours of medieval Europe. In the late eighteenth and early nineteenth centuries, folks sat around hearth and campfire, singing the "old tunes." Cowboy tunes of the Old West, Appalachian tunes from England, blues by way of the church, and popular songs of the mid-nineteenth century, all fed into the grand tradition of telling stories to a small group of folks with words and song. Arlo Guthrie, Pete Seeger, and Bob Dylan brought this tradition into the American culture in the '40s, '50s, and '60s. The Annie DeFrancos of today, and even, to some extent, the rappers and hip-hop ranters, owe a nod to the folkies who kept alive the great American spirit of speaking your own, personal mind through your own personal music.

Jazz, Be-bop ('40s–mid '60s) (3, 5, 6)

Be-bop mixed the ancestry of the blues, the extended harmonies of the Impressionists, and the new muscular self-confidence of an emerging black middle class, and created a virile hybrid. Incredible speed, range, adventurousness, and daring marked the careers of Charlie Parker, Dizzy Gilespie, Miles Davis, Oscar Peterson, Max Roach, and scores of other innovators of this style. The captivating sauciness of swing is at the core of be-bop, but the personal voice of the players and the urgency of the music foreshadowed the role of the individual black musician in the evolution of the American culture whole. If not for Miles and Charlie, James Brown, Chubby Checker, Chuck Berry, Michael Jackson, and Puff Daddy would have existed in another social universe. A great source is the Jazz Heritage Society record club. Labels: Verve, Blue Note, Atlantic, Columbia Archive.

Jazz, Dixieland (1, 3, 6)

The Mississippi Delta was the crucible for many of the dominant forms of American music. Including Dixieland Jazz. Here in the early 1800s black rhythms met European song forms and instrumentation. The Dixieland music epitomized by "When the Saints Go Marching In" brings into play the firmly American tradition of unabashed improvisation. Simple melodies are simultaneously interpreted by an ensemble of horns, drums, and vocalists. Brass instruments step to the front, and a hip-swinging, celebratory form of musical expression took deep root. Dixieland borrowed the "legitimate" aspects of ragtime such as strict compositional form and instrumental proficiency, and "jazzed it up" with free-wheeling breaks and solos.

Jazz, Swing (1, 3, 5)

For decades black and white popular music ran on different tracks. White popular music was a product of the so-called Tin Pan Alley, a style of song writing that produced thousands of songs for theatres, vaudeville in particular. Black musicians were limited to indigenous blues, gospel, and segregated forms such as Dixieland and roadhouse music. In the early '30s the two worlds met in such artists as Cab Calloway, Louis Armstrong, Red Nichols, and Benny Goodman. Swing music took the beat of the early jazz artists, the song forms and dance sensibilities of vaudeville, and created the first "fusion" style in mass-market American music. Swing became a way of life, much like hip-hop is today. The raw power of the monster swing dance bands was threatening to the "older generation." The wild and directly "hands on" dances that swing inspired swept the nation and the world. While most of the big names in swing were white—Glenn Miller, the Dorsey brothers, Woodie Herman, and Artie Shaw—the essence of the style was definitely black, jumping in from Fats Waller, Count Basie, and, of course, Duke Ellington.

New Age (4, 6, 7)

Steve Halpern commercialized this genre in the early '70s. Electronic pastels, and instrumental tapestries create atmospheres of sound, too diffuse to actually be called compositions. Great attention has been devoted to the psychic and spiritual effect of sound in this style. Much research on the healing aspects of music came out of this genre. Overwhelmingly consonant, with the power of pulse and rhythm diminished in preference to tone and texture, New Age music is evolving to include more acoustic elements. Source: Higher Octave.

Rap (1, 2, 5)

Rap is a contemporary flowering of the same cultural seed stock that generated gospel, jazz, be-bop, soul, and much of rock. "Signifying" to your brothers on the corner, and pointed social banter and verbal jousting has been part of the black experience since the turn of the century. The device of quick instrumental jousting and one-upmanship was a hallmark of every black musical form. When T-bone Walker made the first rock and roll record in the early '50s, this black jive was shoved in the face of white America. And the message has gotten louder all the way to Tupac and Eminem. It says, "Listen. Or suffer the consequences." Rap can be sexual, violent, and self-involved. But rap has spread around the world due to the need for individuals to be heard among the skyscrapers and pulp information.

Reggae (1, 4, 5, 7)

Like any mature style, reggae has many facets and substyles. The basic elements to reggae are rock and roll instrumentation, vocal starts, social struggle and commentary, and tribal rhythmic and melodic influences. The signature figure is a chunky rhythm guitar playing on the second and fourth beat of the bar. The native *niabinge* drumming of Jamaica serves as the basis for the music born on this Caribbean island. The godfather of the style is Bob Marley, who recorded much of his most influential music in New York. Passion, humor, social dedication, and the spirit of love and humanity permeate Marley's music, and his influence is felt in his sons Ziggy and Demian, as well as scores of old time and contemporary groups. Third World, Steel Pulse, Pato Bantan, and many other artists are world-touring megastars. "Dancehall" styles give the reggae rappers their stage, and the reggae beat has made some sort of reggae cover a prerequisite for nearly every pop band in the last twenty years.

Rock and Roll, '50s (oldies) (1, 2, 3)

Leonard Bernstein tapped Elvis as the most influential figure in the twentieth century. His reasoning pictured Elvis as the bridge over which black culture, in the form of the beat of black music, crossed over into American white culture, thereby beginning the social evolution of world cultures. Early rock and roll was black, an extension of "race music" that thrived in black society. Elvis was weaned on tent revivals and blues-based bible-banging hootenannies. Most early rock tunes bounce heavily on the springboard of the itinerant blues men like Leadbelly, Howling Wolf, and Muddy Waters. The element of swing was also central to the dance-oriented early rock. Source: Chess Records.

Rock and Roll, Classic Rock ('60s–'70s) (3, 5, 6)

Dean Martin knocked the Beatles out of the number one slot on the charts with "Everybody Loves Somebody Sometime." Through the '60s and '70s, the true "pop" song continued to rival harder edged musicians like the Rolling Stones in popularity. But through the leveling effect of mass media, and mass marketing, the tuneful traditions of Tin Pan Alley and the ethnic juice of rock and the blues homogenized in these decades. Bob Dylan, originally a disciple of Arlo Guthrie's proletariat folk music, evolved into a major—and lasting—rock icon. Groups like the Eagles, Yes, and Genesis kept elements from the classic pop writers of the '40s. Solo acts like Billy Joel, Elton John, and the folk rocker Jackson Brown continued in the age-old tradition of the balladeer storyteller. Electric instruments, high-tech recording and performance techniques, and the mystique of immense popularity and wealth made a life of "sex, drugs, and rock and roll" the unspoken goal of a generation. True to its black parentage, rock in all its forms emphasizes the beat. But on the other side of the family tree is the folk singer and the troubadour. This lineage infuses the best rock with poetic vision and a personal, intimate appeal.

Rock and Roll, Metal (1, 3)

All music speaks to a culture of some kind, and heavy metal, speed metal, hard core metal, and rap metal do just that. More clearly than almost any other popular genre, the sound of metal rock states very clearly what it's all about: defiance, immutable personal freedom, and (sometimes) big hair. The sustained energy of a great metal band in concert is truly a ritualistic offering. The violence and raw volume of the music leaves no doubt that the overtones of consciousness built into this style is a force to be reckoned with, sooner or later. To resonate third chakra power and intensity, nothing can rival a great metal band. Metallica, Black Sabbath, and Judas Priest are some bands included in this genre.

Soul (1, 4, 5)

Soul music, and soul sensibilities, is an extension of the social and spiritual power of the black religious community in America. Many of the great soul artists, notably Aretha Franklin, Stevie Wonder, Al Green, and Diana Ross began, as so many black artists of all types, in the church. R & B styles and the "testifying" of the gospel singers resonate in every bar of soul music, from Aretha Franklin all the way to the soul-rap hybrids of today. Soul is praise music. And what is called R & B today has moved away from the blues and is swimming luxuriously in the currents of soul. Even the name "Destiny's Child" speaks of forces beyond mortal control, and the wrenching quality of the voices of many soul artists resonates in the tradition of the Blind Boys of Alabama and the Golden Gate Quartet, the vocal groups Elvis heard as a young boy.

Techno and Trance (1, 2, 6, 7)

If the new physics demonstrates a fusion of East and West in the sciences, then techno music plays out this blend in sound. Techno is by definition a product of the technological development of society. Instead of lamenting the rise of electronic instruments and "canned" beats, techno celebrates and informs the trends. The ten-hour improvisations of skilled DJs create the sonic superstructure for ritual-like "raves." Frequency, tone, range, and dynamics are arranged by these "mix masters" to exquisite detail. Snippets of sampled sounds garnered from the mass media of present and past often add political text to the predominantly instrumental sound. The beat is straight from disco music, the textures from the electronic avant garde. The artistic goals are direct from Timothy Leary and your local native shaman. The tribal element is strong in techno music. Personal and group ecstasy is the goal. Creating a new tribe of revelers, ready to celebrate and dance for hours, is the truthful result of the rave scene. The prevalence of drugs and electronic hubris flattens this truth. *See also* Disco and Trance.

World Music, Andean (1, 4)*

Panpipes, stringed instruments, simple drums, and sparse vocals make up the early tradition of music from Peru, Columbia, and other Andean regions. More European song forms came into the newer tradition that started in 1500. The music is rooted in rhythm and repetitive, chantlike melodies. The flutes and high

---

* For all the world styles, *The Rough Guide to World Music* is the touchstone directory.

strings of the *charanga* give it an altitude that speaks directly of the thin, bright air of the mountains.

World Music, Bali (2, 6, 7)

The gamelan is the traditional musical ensemble of Bali. The ensemble is a true orchestra, with many different timbres playing complex parts in extended compositions. Pitched metallic instruments and flutes predominate. The compositions are at once primitive sounding and highly sophisticated. The compositions are held in the memory of living masters who teach the parts by rote to the players. The art of performing gamelan music is a cultural phenomenon in itself. The music is as rich as any orchestral tradition. To the Western ear, much of the music may sound chaotic and dissonant. But the ritual roots, and the centuries-old life of the form give it a regal nature that can easily win you over.

World Music, Balkan Vocal Music (3, 4, 6, 7)

The Women's State Choir of Bulgaria popularized Balkan folk music in the West nearly twenty years ago. Now, folk music camps feature entire Balkan programs. The haunting nature of the vocal style reaches across nations, grabbing the hearts of many people. The wonder of the vocal tradition—a blend of Orthodox chant, Islam prayer, and post-Romantic classical harmony—is how it embraces dissonance. The strongly triadic European harmonic norm is shattered with the velvet hammer of the predominantly female choirs. The compositions, based on simple and ancient folk tunes, use dissonance as a wand, brushing away the stodgy thirds and octaves of classical harmony. Used originally to grind their way through winding valleys, communicating from village to village, these edgy sonorities do not grate on the ears—they wake them up.

World Music, Brazilian (1, 2, 5, 6)

Black slaves, Portuguese masters, émigrés of many nations, and a vast, throbbing rain forest have created perhaps the most culturally diverse, yet instantly recognizable music. The culture whole of Brazil includes the Ife religion from Nigeria (there, called *condomble*), the respect for the regal nature of the composer's art, and an unstoppable celebration of personal beauty, the beauty of nature, and nature's sweetest creation, human love. The samba, bossa nova, Brazilian jazz, and the many popular styles in the country all rely on a well-tempered jungle beat and melodies of innocence and directness.

World Music, East Indian (4, 6, 7)

George Harrison of the Beatles brought Indian classical music into the Western music realm in the mid-'60s. As rich and highly evolved as any form—perhaps beyond any form—Indian music is built on complex melodic and rhythmic formulas called *ragas*. Similar to "the changes" in jazz in that the raga serves as a basis for improvisation, the music is nonetheless strict in technique and discipline. The deep spiritual traditions of the Indian subcontinent infuse the music with significance. The instruments of the tradition—the sitar, tambora, tabla, and santour—make use of delicacies of sound unmatched in the world. Noted artists are Ravi Shankar, Ali Akbar Kahn, Zakir Hussein.

BIBLIOGRAPHY

History and Society

Bronowski, Jules. *The Ascent of Man.* New York: Little, Brown and Company, 1973.

Campbell, Joseph. *The Masks of God: Ancient Mythology.* New York: Penguin Books, 1982.

Fideler, David, and Kenneth Sylvan Guthrie, ed. *The Pythagorean Sourcebook and Library.* New York: Phanes Press, 1988.

King, Ross. *Brunelleschi's Dome.* New York: Walker and Company, 2000.

Putnam, Robert D. *Bowling Alone.* New York: Simon and Schuster, 2000.

Music and Healing

Andrews, Ted. *Sacred Sounds: Transformation Through Music and Word.* St. Paul, Minn.: Llewellyn Publications, 1999.

Beaulieu, John. *Music and Sound in the Healing Arts.* Barrytown, N.Y.: Station Hill Press, 1987.

Campbell, Ron, ed. *Music: Physician for Times to Come.* Wheaton, Ill.: Theosophical Publishing, 1997.

———. *The Roar of Silence: Healing Powers of Breath, Tone, and Music.* Wheaton, Ill.: Theosophical Publishing, 1989.

Garfield, Laeh Maggie. *Sound Medicine.* Berkeley, Calif.: Celestial Arts, 1987.

Steiner, Rudolf. *The Inner Nature of Music and the Experience of Tone.* Spring Valley, N.Y.: Anthroposophic Press, 1983.

Music History and Musicology

Carlin, Richard. *Man's Earliest Music.* New York: Facts on File Publications, 1987.

Chernoff, John Miller. *African Rhythm and African Sensibility.* Chicago: University of Chicago Press, 1981.

Davis, Miles, with Quincy Troupe. *Miles: The Autobiography.* New York: Simon and Schuster, 1989.

Hart, Mickey, with Jay Stevens. *Drumming at the Edge of Magic.* Novato, Calif.: Grateful Dead Books, 1990.

Isacoff, Stuart. *Temperament.* New York: Alfred Knopf, 2002.

Payne, Philip W., ed. *The Swing Era: 1941–42.* New York: Time-Life Books, 1971.

Music Theory

Mathieu, W. A. *The Listening Book: Discovering Your Own Music.* Boston: Shambhala, 1991.

Meyer, Leonard B. *Music, the Arts, and Ideas.* Chicago: University of Chicago Press. 1973.

Physics of Music, The. Excerpts from Scientific American Magazine, 1948–74.

Rudhyar, Dane. *The Magic of Tone and the Art of Music.* Boulder, Colo., and London: Shambhala, 1982.

Zuckerkandl, Victor. *Man the Musician.* Princeton, N.J.: Princton University Press, 1976.

———. *Sound and Symbol: Music and the External World.* Princeton, N.J.: Princton University Press, 1973.

Science and the Natural World

Butterworth, Brian. *What Counts: How Every Brain is Hardwired for Math.* New York: Simon and Schuster, Free Press, 1999.

Cole, K. C. *The Hole in the Universe.* New York: Harcourt Inc., 2001.

Hayward, Jeremy W. *Perceiving Ordinary Magic: Science and Intuitive Wisdom.* Boulder, Colo., and London: Shambhala, New Science Library, 1984.

Lovelock, James. *Gaia: The Practical Science of Planetary Medicine.* Oxford: Oxford University Press, 2000.

Nuland, Sherwin B. *The Wisdom of the Body.* New York: Alfred Knopf, 1997.

Ornstein, Robert. *The Psychology of Consciousness.* New York: Viking Press, 1972.

Sacks, Oliver. *Uncle Tungsten.* New York: Alfred Knopf, 2001.

Thomas, Lewis. *Lives of a Cell: Notes of a Biology Watcher.* Toronto/New York: Bantam Books, 1974.

Thuan, Trinh Xuan. *Chaos and Harmony: Perspectives on Scientific Revolutions of the Twentieth Century.* Oxford: Oxford University Press, 2001.

Spirit

Bercholz, Samuel, ed. *Entering the Stream: An Introduction the the Buddha and His Teachings.* Boston: Shambhala, 1993.

Khan, Sufi Inayat. *Music.* Claremont, Calif.: Sufi Publishing Company/Hunter House, 1988.

Wilhelm, Richard, trans. *The I Ching or Book of Changes.* Princeton, N.J.: Princeton University Press, 1950.

The Music of Words

American Heritage Dictionary of the English Language. New York/Boston: American Heritage Publications and Houghton Mifflin Company, 1969.

BIBLIOGRAPHY

Funk, Wilfred. *Word Origins and Their Romantic Stories.* New York: Random House Value Publishing, Inc., 1979.

Rheingold, Howard. *They Have a Word for It.* Louisville, Ky.: Serabande Books, 2000.

Thomas, Lewis. *Et Cetera Et Cetera: Notes of a Word Watcher.* New York: Penguin Books, 1990.

GLOSSARY

beat

A general term referring to tempo, meter, pulse, and rhythmic impulse of music. "Staying on the beat" means to articulate your instrument in synchrony with the predominant pulse, meter, and style of the music. The beat is the impetus (pulse) of music.

brass

Instruments made of brass or other metals, intoned by the buzzing of the lips in a mouthpiece. This family includes the trumpet, French horn, trombone, tuba, and a number of other bugles, lower brass, and valveless "natural" horns.

cadence

A series of chords that leads to a harmonic conclusion closely related to the pitch center or key of the compositional section.

chord

Two or more tones sounding at the same time, or described on a score as sounding at the same time. In the Western harmonic tradition chords are classed as major, minor, augmented, and diminished. This classification is determined by the intervals between the first three ascending tones in the chord.

clave

A short, dense piece of wood, usually rosewood, played in pairs, articulated by striking one against the other, resulting in a very short, piercing click. Also, the rhythmic patterns traditionally played by the instrument of the same name in African, Latin, and Afro-Caribbean musical styles.

consonance

Any interval or intervals established between tones perceived to be pleasing to the ear. In the Western classical music tradition, consonance usually refers to harmonies limited to the major and minor triads.

counterpoint

A style of music where several melodic lines move simultaneously through the composition. The fugue is the exemplary contrapuntal form. Dixieland jazz, symphonic composition, and free improvisation all use counterpoint to a great extent.

cueing

The practice of giving indications to your fellow players in an ensemble. A conductor cues directly with hand motions or eye contact. Jazz and pop players cue each other with sound cues woven into the texture of the performance, body language, and so forth. Reading cues is all-important to the improvising musician and "pick up" player, who must tune into a new group or unfamiliar tune on the spot.

difference tone

See Undertone.

dissonance

Tones sounding together that are generally perceived as clashing or grating on the ears. Dissonance can resolve through a movement of a melodic line away from the "offending" sonority. Dissonance can also be intentionally sustained to create unique harmonic qualities as in progressive jazz, Balkan folk music, and "avant-garde" classical composition.

down beat

The first beat of a measure of music. Also, in duple meters, the first beat of the duple figures. *See also* Meter.

dynamics (ff to pp)

The general term given to the volume levels of music. Dynamics can grow or diminish very slowly over several measures, or change very abruptly. Handed down from the Italian Renaissance, the terms are still expressed in the Italian language (for example: forte, piano, pianissimo, and so on).

ecology

The science of relationships within the environment. It is a wide discipline, including general ecology of the entire earth, and specialized aspects such as stream ecology, human ecology, microbial ecology, and forest ecology.

ecopsychology

A relatively new discipline relating the effect of the environment on the psychological health and function of the human being.

electron volt

The energy an electron gains or loses as its energy potential changes by one volt. Atomic accelerators ("atom smashers") excite atomic particles with energies in the *billions* of electron volts.

entrainment

The tendency for resonant systems to sympathetically vibrate to other resonating systems.

form

A conceptual framework for an artistic artifact that has been established over time within a culture or subculture. A jazz standard, symphony, polka, gospel tune, and popular song are all composed to fit their respective forms. The idea of a "new form" is a bit of a misnomer because all new artistic forms—just like life forms—are generated from existing ones. "Newly evolved" form might be a better term for artistic innovation.

frequency

The number of cycles of a periodic action (like a sound wave) per unit of time. In music, frequency is defined by vibrations of a fundamental or overtone in cycles per second (Hertz).

fundamental

The pitch generated by an undamped, freely vibrating, resonant sound source. The fundamental is the first harmonic of any musical tone.

genre

A well-established style of music, usually associated with a specific culture, geographic area, or social movement. Genres have distinctive characteristics. In music a certain rhythmic pattern, grouping of instruments, or preference for certain compositional materials all sustain and define genre.

harmonic

 A discreet tone of a single frequency generated by the vibration of a string or other resonant system, being part of the harmonic series of the system. The first harmonic of a string intones the frequency of an entire, freely moving string. The second harmonic (partial, overtone) is generated by the string vibrating in two equal lengths and produces a tone one octave above the fundamental. The third partial is generated by three equal lengths within the fundamental, and so on; the system theoretically generating an infinite number of overtones. *See also* Partial.

harmony

The simultaneous fitting together of resonant tones. Western harmony is traditionally based on the first few acoustic overtones within a single fundamental tone. Other styles of music exploit other attributes of how tones fit together, emphasizing what may be perceived as dissonant to Western ears.

heat death

The notion that a continually expanding universe will eventually be randomized to the point of maximum entropy, and all potential energy will be dissipated throughout the universe, never to be available again.

Hertz, Hz

A measure of frequency. One Hertz (1 Hz) is equal to one cycle per second.

inside parts

In music where several voices are sounding together, usually the bass and melodic line are predominant, but the parts moving between these two voices carry great influence, many times defining the harmonic structure and texture of the composition. In choral music the alto and tenor voices are the inside parts, moving below the soprano voice and above the bass.

interval

In music, the distance between pitches, either in sequence as in a melody, or sounding together as in a chord. In Western musical parlance the intervals are generally named in reference to the intervals inherent in the major scale steps. A "major 2nd," therefore, is an interval defined by one note and another two half tones away. Confusing the issue, a "minor 2nd" is the interval of one half step.

intonation

Playing in tune, in reference to a common pitch.

jam session

A musical event where musicians gather and play with folks they do not regularly play with, or play tunes they are not familiar with. Also free improvisation, where the players all improvise new material simultaneously.

key

The pitch center of a composition in the Western tradition. The keynote is reference point for melodic and harmonic structure.

melody

A sequence of resonant tones that together make a conversational statement in sound.

meter: duple, triple, compound

The regular grouping of beats into twos, threes, and so forth, through an accent, or implied accent, on the initial beat of the grouping (the "down beat"). Duple meter is based on a two beat structure, triple meter on a three beat scheme. Complex meters result from the combination of a regular pattern of simple meters, that is, $2 + 2 + 3, 2 + 2 + 3, 2 + 2 + 3 = $ a compound meter of 7.

monoculture

In agriculture, where only one crop is grown in a wide geographical area.

musical time

The physical, emotional, or spiritual quality of temporal experience.

nonharmonic tone

For instruments: a tone that is not part of the natural harmonic series of an instrument.

octave

An interval between two notes equal to the doubling or halving of vibrations per second of one of the tones. Sounding together the tones sound very close to being one tone. This sonority is called unison.

orchestration

The art of choosing which sound sources will play which parts in a composition.

overtone

Any harmonic of a resonant tone other than the fundamental. *See also* Harmonic; Partial.

partial

A harmonic of a tone. In the case of a string, the first partial is the fundamental, freely vibrating tone. The second partial is the first overtone of the fundamental, the octave, the wave pattern of which is vibrating at twice the frequency of the fundamental. *See also* Harmonic.

phoneme

A one-syllable vocal sound.

phrase

A conversational unit of expression in musical time. Like music, dance composition is constructed in phrases. Typically, popular tunes have four or five phrases that make up the song. Orchestral works, being longer in length, utilize many phrases, many of which are variations on previous material.

pitch

Pitch refers to the relative frequency of musical tones. For any given instrument, a "high" pitch is in the upper register, and a "low" pitch is in the lower register. "Staying on pitch" means to play in tune.

polytonal

A compositional style where melodies or harmonies with different tonal centers or keys are played at the same time. Many compositions of Charles Ives, Tahitian choirs, and forms of Chinese and Indo-Polynesian music employ polytonality.

pulse

In music, the regular division of time by an unaccented beat, that is, the tempo. In general, any regular division of time, such as the drub of tires on the road, the heartbeat, the seasons, and so on.

quantum

An indivisible unit of energy. A photon is the quantum of light.

quantum levels

The energy states within the electron cloud of atoms. An electron makes a "quantum leap" when it moves from one quantum level to the adjacent one. The wonder of quantum mechanics is that the electron moves discreetly between these levels, making the leap based on a probability rather than a physical certainty of arrival. This unpredictable aspect of matter is at the foundation of modern physics.

quasar

Or quasi-stellar object. One of several classes of starlike objects that are moving at exceptional rates of speed relative to the earth; they usually emit high levels of radio frequency radiation.

reggae

A genre of music emerging in Jamaica in the late '60s and early '70s. Reggae linked native drumming and vocal styles from Africa with vocal, instrumental, and recording techniques from American popular music. Reggae was a form of protest music in Jamaica during that country's struggle for independence from Great Britain.

resonance

In physics, where a periodic driving force of a system is at the same or integral frequency as the undamped frequency of the system in question, creating a harmonic relationship between forces and materials within a system. Another term for resonance in music is *sympathetic vibration*.

rhythm

A grouping or subdivision of the beat. Rhythms gain personality based on what pulses are accented or omitted in the pattern.

riff

A signature phrase or motif. There are rhythmic riffs ("shave-and-a-haircut . . . two-bits"), and melodic riffs as well. Each player develops his or her own riffs that define the player's particular style of improvising. The repetitive "hooks" in pop tunes, musical clichés, and standard instrumental flourishes are all considered riffs. Coming up with new ones, or finding original ways to use existing ones, are the signs of a creative improviser.

root

The lowest tone in a triad.

salsa

A diverse genre of music with many styles based on the marriage of Afro-Caribbean rhythms and song forms, Spanish folk tunes, big band instrumentation from the United States, and jazz. Salsa traditions evolved primarily in Cuba, Puerto Rico, and New York City. The clave rhythmic patterns are central to salsa.

scat singing

A style of singing where the vocalist improvises a melodic line and instead of using lyrics, sings with a sort of babbling series of syllables and "vocalese" utterances. Many times these vocalizations are inspired by the vocalist's impression of how an instrument might sound playing the same melody. Jazz artists like Ella Fitzgerald helped popularize the style.

Sound

From Dane Rudhyar. The audible sounds we hear impact us with meaning and emotion. Sound (capital *S*) refers to the vibratory essence of the physical world, and the harmonic nature of relationships on all levels. All the different musical time qualities are variations of Sound.

standard

A song or tune that has been played and recorded by many artists over an extended period of time. Also, the form to which tunes in a given genre usually adhere. One could write a tune based on the jazz standard form as established by the hits of Cole Porter and Louie Armstrong, let's say. But your tune itself may or may not become an actual standard. Time will tell.

sympathetic vibration

The resonance resulting when a physical system is set in motion by the harmonically related vibrations of another.

syncopation

A shift of accent in a musical pattern where a normally weak beat is stressed. Salsa rhythms, New Orleans–style jazz, and hip-hop are highly syncopated.

tango

A style and genre of music and dance from Argentina. Modern tango composers, like the late Astor Piazzola, are very innovative in their composition, releasing great drama, romance, and intensity in the music.

tempo

In music, the speed of the pulse. Generally, the pace of musical time, such as a relaxed afternoon or a rushed meal.

texture

In music, the texture literally refers to how an experience in musical time *feels*. Most often the term refers to how a composition sounds.

timbre

Tone color. The characteristic sound of an instrument or sound source. For example, due to its structure, a tuba playing very high in its register has a different timbre than a trumpet playing the same pitch.

time field

The qualitative contour of a temporal experience, bounded by duration, and modulated by musical time qualities within that duration such as musical tones, personal expression, natural occurrences, and directed intent.

tone

Any sound that carries meaning and emotional impact. A musical tone is generally considered to be a complex wave pattern generated by a musical instrument. When produced and/or perceived with creative intent, any sound can carry tone.

tone color

The characteristic sound of an instrument or sound. Different timbres result from the myriad combinations of overtones within any dominant fundamental tone. For example, a clarinet and a trumpet impart different tone color to the same pitch due to the fact that the physical attributes of the respective instruments produce a different series of overtones generated at the same pitch. Also timbre.

tone poem

A style of composition where a story, mood, or scene is depicted in sound. Debussy's *Prelude to the Afternoon of a Fawn,* and Miles Davis' *Sketches of Spain* are both tone poems.

triad

A three-note chord consisting of a root or fundamental tone, a second tone a major or minor third above the root, and a third tone a major or minor third above the second tone (the fifth).

undertone

A tone generated by the interference pattern between two other tones. The frequency of an undertone is the mathematical difference between the two original frequencies. When two notes are only slightly different in pitch, an undertone of very low frequency results, which pulses annoyingly in our ears. This undertone is the physical manifestation of being out of tune.

unison (octave harmony)

In harmony, unison means two or more instruments playing the same note or in octave relationship. In melodic playing, it means many instruments playing the same melody at the same time.

variation

In music, a passage in which elements of a previous section are clearly incorporated.

walking bass

A technique of playing a series of bass notes directly on the basic pulse of the music. These notes clearly outline the harmonic progressions of the composition. Jazz bassists use this technique extensively.

white noise

The sound produced when a great number of frequencies from the entire audible spectrum are sounded together. Waterfalls, tires on the road, the sound "shhhhh," and the roar of a jet all contain a high proportion of white noise.

woodwinds

The family of instruments including those intoned with a vibrating reed and flutes of all kinds. Sometimes in symphonic works the French horns (a brass instrument) are rehearsed as woodwinds due to their range and timbre.

INDEX